SISTERS AT SINAI

SISTERS AT SINAI

NEW TALES OF BIBLICAL WOMEN

JILL HAMMER

2004 • 5764
The Jewish Publication Society
Philadelphia

The Jewish Publication Society
2100 Arch Street, 2nd floor
Philadelphia, PA 19103

Design and composition by Sandy Freeman

Manufactured in the United States of America
        07 08 09 10 11 12 13   10 9 8 7 6 5 4 3 2

Library of Congress Cataloging-in-Publication Data
Hammer, Jill..
    Sisters @ Sinai : new tales of biblical women / Jill Hammer.
        p. cm.
    Includes bibliographical references and index.
    ISBN 0-8276-0726-1 (hardcover)
    ISBN 0-8276-0806-3 (paperback)
    1. Women in the Bible. 2. Bible stories, English - O.T.
3. Women in rabbinical literature. I. Title.
BS575 .H28 2001
221.8'3054 - dc21

                                    2001050207

TO JEREMY GOLDMAN

*one who lives simply and acts rightly
and speaks the truth in his heart*

—Psalm 15:2

Contents

Acknowledgments

The support I have received throughout the process of creating this book has been abundant. I acknowledge it with gratitude. Wrestling with my stories has been difficult, but my work has been illuminated by the care and concern of friends and colleagues.

I must first thank my editor, Ellen Frankel, who suggested the idea and organizing principle for this book. She encouraged its publication and lent me her consistent interest and support. I also thank Carol Hupping and the rest of the staff at the Jewish Publication Society. I know they put tremendous effort into all that they do.

Next, I must give credit to my teachers, who have fulfilled our tradition's sacred expectation of them by transmitting to me and to others their craft, wisdom, and passion. Alicia Ostriker and Peter Pitzele have been my spirit guides throughout this work. I have sought to emulate their energy and sensitivity. I am particularly grateful for Alicia's careful proofreading of the manuscript and her insightful suggestions. Allan Kensky, dean of the Jewish Theological Seminary, has taught me traditional midrash and has warmly encouraged my forays into the modern variety. I also gratefully acknowledge Enid Dame, teacher and writer of midrash; Alice Shalvi, rector of Machon Schechter in Jerusalem; and Neil Gillman, philosopher of the Jewish Theological Seminary. They have inspired me by example and by giving me a midrashic context within which to write. Avivah Zornberg, my teacher while I lived in Jerusalem, opened my eyes to midrash in a new way through her sparkling insights. Burt Visotzky, midrash scholar of the Jewish Theological Seminary, and Diane Sharon, Bible professor at the same institution, gave me critical tools for analyzing biblical and rabbinic exegesis. May their Torah of loving-kindness endure.

I am pleased to thank my friend and colleague Rivkah Walton, founder of the Institute for Contemporary Midrash. Rivkah hired me as an editor, published my work, and edited some of my stories, even at 1:00 A.M. She also introduced me to many of my teachers. My journey from writer to author was made significantly easier by the enthusiastic interest of writer Naomi Hyman, who edited *Biblical Women in the Midrash*. I thank Marc Bregman and Howard Schwartz, makers of midrash, for their scholarly and creative suggestions, and Arthur Strimling, storyteller and playwright, for his insightful comments.

I am indebted to my friend Justin Lewis, whose sensitive comments kept me from ripping up pages. I am also grateful to Joy Rosenberg, Patricia Fenton, Kelly Washburn, Shoshana Jedwab, Jennifer Stern, Yaffa Pearlman, and Devorah Schoenfeld for their acute insights and their supportive presences. I thank my father and mother, Leonard and Erna Hammer, for their loving interest in my arcane writing, and my brother, Marcus Hammer, for being proud of me. Finally, my deepest gratitude goes to Jeremy Goldman, who was my husband and tireless supporter for many years, and who edited many versions of these tales.

I have received good wishes from countless colleagues, friends, and teachers; and while I cannot thank all of them by name, I hope that they know how much their interest has meant to me. May they reap as abundantly as they have sowed.

Introduction

Why are there two redactions, Jerusalem and Babylon?

*To teach us that there is not one and given two, that
there is room for more....*

  —ALLEN MANDELBAUM, *Chelmaxioms*

A story is a body for God.

  —RACHEL ADLER, *Engendering Judaism*

In the very middle of the Torah are two words: *darosh darash* (he
shall surely seek). The context is a priestly rite, but the context,
as any rabbinic midrash will assert, is unimportant—every verse
of the Torah applies to every other verse, every time and every place.
Midrash, the creative interpretation of the Torah invented by the
Sages and carried on in various forms into the present day, comes
from the same root as these words—*darosh darash*—and means "seeking." I have come to interpret the words that are at the heart of the
Torah to be a positive commandment: Make midrash. Interpret. Tell
the story a different way. Reveal something new.

  Ancient legends relate that the Torah was written in black fire
on white fire (Deuteronomy Rabbah 'Ekev 2; JT Shekalim 6a), and
some say that the midrash is the white fire that forms the spaces
around the black letters. The midrash is defined by the outlines of the
words, but it is as infinite as the white expanse. The vast realm of
interpretation is already hidden in the Torah, and it is up to us to find

it. A midrash on the Revelation at Mount Sinai teaches that every individual heard God's revealed word a different way (Midrash Tanḥuma Shemot 25), and perhaps one of the implications of this is that each individual has a unique interpretation to add to the whole.

What is true of individuals is also true of generations. In the mystical commentary *Kaf Ha-Ketoreth*, we are taught that "according to the words of the Sages the Torah has seventy aspects, and there are seventy aspects to each and every verse; in truth, therefore, the aspects are infinite. In each generation one of these aspects is revealed, and so in our generation the aspect which the Torah reveals to us concerns matters of redemption." How profoundly radical to say that in each generation the Torah means something new. If the generation of the medieval kabbalists revealed the aspect of redemption hidden in the Torah, perhaps our generation reveals the aspect of liberation, by drawing out voices in the text that once were silenced. It is my belief that to reveal what was hidden is sacred work, work of which the Sages say, "It is not yours to finish this work, but you are not free to desist from it" (*Pirke Avot* 2:21). In that spirit this book is written.

The Tree with Roots and Wings: Sources of Midrash

The roots of midrash are ancient, with forms and conventions developed almost two thousand years ago by the same rabbis who wrote the Talmud. Rabbinic collections of midrashim are based on a way of reading the Torah in which every word is important; in which every verse in the Bible can be related to every other verse, in or out of context; in which pure invention can be seamlessly grafted onto existing text. These collections fill in the "white spaces" in the text, creating both new stories and new laws. The Sages speculate about characters, events, and everything else that the text leaves to the imagination. They interpret words, probe the meaning of names and numbers, make linguistic and temporal connections, study characters, create poetic and fantastic imagery, discuss ethical and logical concerns, and extrapolate narratives and conversations. Midrash is sometimes recorded in the form of a conversation or disagreement between two or more speakers.

Rabbinic midrash is an historical and cultural phenomenon, to be studied by scholars and enjoyed by enthusiasts; yet the process of creating midrash did not end with the closure of the rabbinic collections. Jews discovered other ways of prying open a text and adding to it—not the classical ways, but ways influenced by the times, the places, and the needs of the creators. Midrashic activity continued in various forms, such as narratives, sermons, liturgical poems, and folktales, throughout Jewish history. The branches of midrash that have stretched into our own day come in new and surprising forms, reflecting the cultures and concerns of modern wrestlers with the Bible: the novel, play, or film with biblical content; the modern midrashic poem in Hebrew, Yiddish, English, Russian, or another language; the midrashic painting; the midrashic song or opera; the feminist midrash; the dance midrash. This book seeks to stand on the shoulders of giants, to inherit this long chain of midrashic invention.

Why is midrash legitimate? Why is it permissible, even laudable, to tell tales about a canonized text? Perhaps because of the nature of the Torah itself. The Torah is called the "tree of life," and for something to be alive, it has to grow. The Torah grows by reinterpretation. Through midrash, each generation can add its own wisdom and experience to a fixed text and make it dynamic so that it does not reflect a single era but every era in which it is read. A holy text can remain holy only if it stretches into the lives of its readers. The Rabbis knew this long ago, so they told stories of the patriarch Isaac studying in yeshiva, just as they themselves studied in yeshiva (Genesis Rabbah 56:11), and they invented the tale of King David studying the Torah to ward off his own death, for they believed that the Torah sustained their own lives (BT Shabbat 30a–b). They even told a story in which every word a student of the Torah spoke was first given to Moses at Mount Sinai—thus making themselves a part of revelation (BT Menachot 29a). We also know that the tree of life must grow, and so modern midrashists tell stories of biblical characters who love the way we love and feel pain the way we feel pain, of prophets who question God, and of women who struggle to be free. To make midrash, in any age, is to become a character in the action, to wrestle a blessing from the words, to receive a sacred challenge and a powerful gift. We need never fear that we or the Torah will be broken in this mysterious encounter. The text is great enough and strong enough to be profoundly flexible, profoundly generative, even in the modern context where myths are fragile.

The great flowering of midrash by women since the 1970s is a case in point of how midrash helps the Torah grow. The experiences of women have been shut out of the textual and historical consciousness of the Jewish people until very recently, and midrash is one way that women and others who have been excluded from the tradition can reclaim the tradition for themselves, by telling stories that weave their experiences into the communal sense of revelation. Through this activity, they neither reject the text nor accept a position of silence. Rather, they find a way to honor themselves and the tradition through creative action. By writing in the margins, they become no longer marginal. The Bible teaches that "the Children of Israel and the stranger in their midst shall have one Torah" (Numbers 15:29), and we may read this as an invitation to those who have been excluded to include their voices in the Torah. We can become an equal part of a communal enterprise. As Judith Plaskow writes, "if its self-consciousness is modern, the root conviction of feminist midrash is utterly traditional" (*Standing Again at Sinai*, p. 54). Turning to the Torah to reinterpret its words has always been the recourse of Jews who struggle with the tradition; as the Psalmist writes: "If the Torah had not been my plaything, I would have perished in my suffering" (Psalm 119:92). Midrash is liberating, deeply comforting, and life renewing, for by "remembering" ourselves into the Bible, as this book strives to do, we can enrich the past and invent hope for the future.

Not all midrash comes in the form of story, but the midrashic endeavor is partly an expression of a universal need for story. Stories are a way of obtaining justice, of giving voice, of sharing perspective. They can also be a way of expressing gratitude. Stories bring the sacred into our lives. Through stories, Rachel Adler tells us in her book *Engendering Judaism*, we create a shared universe from which we derive a way to live. Humans need stories, and to be meaningful these stories must resonate within us. As humans grow, we need new stories. This is true of the life of a people as well as of an individual. Midrash is a specialized way of creating new stories for a community. The stories in this book about biblical women and their male counterparts are a part of the effort to create new tales that speak of our reality and help us act on it.

Midrash, in its process, is an act of study, of prayer, and of repairing the world. It is an act of study because it begins with textual exegesis, with finding a point of text on which to hang a new idea. Midrash returns repeatedly to the text, examining and exploring it, and it returns to the mind and heart of the midrash maker to absorb what it finds there. For me, this loop is what makes Torah study, and midrash, so engrossing. Midrash is an act of prayer because it is a gift to the sacred: It is a way of offering back to the Torah the fruits of our encounter with it. It is a way, as prayer is, of telling the covenantal story, the story of relationship with each other and with God. Midrash is a way, whether reverent, playful, rebellious, or furious, of speaking from the depths of the religious spirit. And, finally, midrash is an act of repairing the world, because it seeks to uncover the voices that the text does not hold and forces us to listen to what these voices say.

I write midrash to express my belief in the presence of the biblical text and to express my relationship with my mythic biblical ancestors, male and female. I write about biblical women because their lives speak to me, because they have been frequently maligned, and because they struggle so valiantly within the text to break out of the norms that constrict them. I write midrash to give biblical women the honor that is due them as prophets, rulers, and teachers of Israel and to carry on their legacy. I write midrash as a way of speaking to God, of exploring what I believe about the Divine. I also write midrash to sanctify my creative imagination—that is, to allow my art to touch something eternal.

The Mother Bird Method

Occasionally, when I am in the process of inventing midrash, I meditate to conjure up images of biblical characters. Sometimes I imagine a palace through which matriarchs and their companions move, and I follow them and speak to them. Once, almost a decade ago, I imagined myself sitting and studying Torah with the matriarch Leah, who in the Zohar is associated with Divine wisdom. She taught me from Deuteronomy 22:6–7, which reads: "If, along the road, you chance upon a bird's nest, in any tree or on the ground, with fledglings or eggs and the mother sitting over the fledglings or on the eggs, do not take the mother together with her young. Let the mother go, and take only the young, in order that you may fare well and have a long life."

"What does this mean?" I asked.

"The mother bird is Torah," Leah said, "and the nest holds the traditions of the Jewish people. Sometimes it is necessary to climb the tree and take the eggs—to find something in the Torah and use it in a new way. When you do this, be sure to let the essence of the Torah remain. The mother bird must fly free, so that she will continue to give life, to lay new eggs for a new generation of Torah seekers. If you act in this way, the new thing you create will be strengthened."

I did not expect this teaching. Midrash is always surprising, both when it comes from others and when it comes from within. My encounter with Leah taught me an important lesson for my writing and for Jewish life in general. Interpretations change: The Judaism of the Second Temple is not the Judaism of the Rabbis, and the Judaism of the Rabbis and of the medieval world has changed much in its contention with modernity. The presence of women's voices has transformed my own religious community in the last twenty-five years, an astonishing achievement and a great responsibility. What we believe to be revelation also changes over time, although that uncertainty may be disturbing. Yet by weaving what we have known in the past into what we are now, and into what we hope will be, we make our own creations stronger. We root them not only in our own wisdom but also in the wisdom of many generations. As it says in Ecclesiastes (4:12), "a threefold cord is not readily broken." When a new naming ceremony for a baby girl includes verses from the Torah or traditional washing rituals, or when a Rosh Hodesh (celebration of the new moon) draws on medieval women's texts, or when Jews use talmudic texts to help them cope with modern medical and scientific technology, we root our future deeply in our past.

Most of my stories contain, in addition to biblical material and my own ideas, pieces of rabbinic midrashim. When I start to delve into a particular character, I first look closely at the relevant verses of the Bible, which are often terse. Sometimes I look at other parts of the Bible that I think are relevant, even if they are not obviously so; this is an important part of the rabbinic method as well as the modern one. I try to read the verses in different ways to see if there is any way to reinterpret their meaning. Then I look for what the Rabbis say about the character. Sometimes I accept their statement: Miriam was a midwife. Joseph married Dinah's daughter. Very good . . . grist for the mill. And sometimes I reject their interpretation entirely: When the Rabbis blame Dinah for her rape or demonize Vashti for her rebellion, I cannot include their perspective, except as a foil. Sometimes the Rabbis have invented a character out of a mere mention of a name, as with Serach bat Asher, the long-lived harpist who appears in two stories in this book, and I borrow their invention. Sometimes I turn the rabbinic theory completely on its head. Lilith was Adam's first wife? Satan tempted Abraham during the *Akedah*? Well, we'll see about that. . . . I may also look at what modern writers have invented concerning those characters: Dialogue with the Rabbis and with modern midrashists as well as with the Torah text makes midrash multiconversational, rich, and many layered. The commentary to this volume is meant to help readers discern the different sources and layers of a story and begin their own dialogue with midrashic tradition.

In his brilliant book *Chelmaxioms*, Allen Mandelbaum created an epic poem on the rabbinic mind that captures it so wonderfully that I have used his lines of poetry as epigraphs. Mandelbaum reminds us that the rabbinic approach is multivoiced, changing, and never ending. It exists before us, moves through us, and moves beyond us; we cannot keep it in one form. Mandelbaum writes:

The speech of God, the speech of man, are loose;
do not use exegesis as a noose;
no maxim, axiom, maxiom, no law
must stand as if it were a gateless wall.

   —*Chelmaxioms*, p. 37

When I draw on the sources I am about to list and explicate, I keep in mind their contradictions, their questions, their refusal to end the conversation.

I primarily draw on the Talmud, which contains many midrashim, and on ancient collections of rabbinic midrash such as Genesis Rabbah and the other volumes of Midrash Rabbah, Midrash Tanhuma, and *Pirkei de-Rabbi Eliezer*. (A brief introduction to these works can be found in "Sources" at the back of this book.) Genesis Rabbah is wide-ranging and its connections between far-flung verses and characters are exciting and creative. Midrash Tanhuma is particularly full of unusual scenes and conversations. *Pirkei de-Rabbi Eliezer* contains mystical material and has some Muslim influence, which I drew on when writing "Second Blessings." I also use early rabbinic compositions, such as the *Mekhilta de-Rabbi Yishmael*. Traditional midrashic literature ranges in date from around 400 to 1000 C.E., so these midrashim come from a wide span of times and places. Stories like "The Switch," "The Tenth Plague," and "And the Walls Came Tumbling Down" were inspired by my reading rabbinic midrashim.

I also draw, occasionally, on apocryphal or pseudepigraphal books of the Bible. These books—although they are not midrash and are in fact contemporaneous with much of the Bible itself—read like midrash to a student of the Bible; some are fascinating variations of biblical narrative. I have used the Book of Jubilees, for example, to help envision some of the characters in "Shimon's Prison." The Book of Enoch provided me with the names of angels in "Vashti and the Angel Gabriel." This literature was written by Jews in the Second Temple period and reflects the religious consciousness of the Jewish people as much as the rabbinic commentaries did in their day.

Rashi is a great friend of mine. A French commentator who lived in the eleventh century, Rashi is universally accepted as one of the great Bible and Talmud scholars of all time. He summarizes and often clarifies rabbinic midrash in his commentary on the Bible, and occasionally slips in some of his own. I often turn to his exegeses for a look at what he has to say about a particular episode. I also often turn to a modern midrash collector, Louis Ginzberg, who, with the help of Henrietta Szold, wrote the masterful epic work *Legends of the Jews* and its bibliographic notes, for which I am even more grateful, since I use them constantly.

I frequently use mystical midrash as a source, particularly the Zohar. Although the Zohar presents itself as a rabbinic collection, modern scholars date it to the twelfth century. The Zohar has a very different midrashic methodology from that used by the Rabbis. The Zohar narratives, while drawing on rabbinic midrash, interpret characters and plot sequences symbolically, as mystical concepts and heavenly events. They see patriarchs and matriarchs as elements of the Divine personality and the Torah as a repository of hidden meaning. The stories "Mitosis" and "The Least of the Handmaids" were influenced by the Zohar and its concepts.

Both biblical and midrashic sources on women are notorious for being skimpy and/or patronizing, for sexualizing women when they are seeking knowledge, blaming them when they are victims, and chastising them when they act for themselves (in fact, until a few decades ago, most modern literature about midrash wasn't much better). Although there is a large volume of biblical narrative and rabbinic/medieval midrash about female characters that is positive and detailed, the androcentric nature of biblical and midrashic texts makes reclaiming them a difficult and painful task. Not everything we have inherited from the Rabbis is just or beautiful. When I read traditional midrash, my emotions often move from excitement at the creativity of the material I am studying to anger at its dismissal of women, or of non-Jews, or of gay people. I have several strategies for dealing with this problem.

First, I search for texts that may be construed in a positive or at least an interesting way. Second, as I mentioned earlier, I sometimes write midrash that is in direct contradiction to the rabbinic midrash in order to reverse a misogynist rabbinic statement, or I may elevate a marginal character the Rabbis ignore. Although I normally will not write a midrash that directly opposes the biblical text—since I believe midrash should be rooted in a biblical verse or verses—I may use that text in an unusual way.

Third, I read other modern midrashim, which allows me to feel part of a community dedicated to grappling with the issue at hand. I read the poetry of Yehuda Amichai, which speaks of the search of Moses for God's face (*Open Closed Open*, p. 29), and I am reminded of my own search. I read the work of Dan Pagis, which places Cain and Abel in a cattle car (Curzon, ed., *Modern Poems on the Bible: An Anthology*, p. 94), and remember how relevant the Bible is to my own time. Or I read the poetry of Wislawa Szymborska, which speaks of Lot's wife and her thoughts (Curzon, ed., *Modern Poems on the Bible*, p. 127), and I am compelled to delve deeper into the Bible's silences.

Finally, I use the feelings of anger or sadness or ironic humor that the rabbinic midrashim and the biblical text sometimes inspire in me to tell a better story. Norma Rosen writes in her own volume of midrash that "midrash, like prayer at its truest, is an activist response to existential despair" (*Biblical Women Unbound*, p. 27). Sometimes what troubles us can be a source of inspiration.

My tales often come from the questions of my teachers, and this is, of course, a traditional spur to Jewish stories. Poet and midrashist Alicia Ostriker's study sessions and midrash-writing exercises have been a source of great creativity for me and have produced core ideas for some of this work. One story here arose from a similarly thought-provoking session run by another poet and midrashist, Enid Dame. Rabbi Neil Gillman's in-depth course on the *Akedah*, given at the Jewish Theological Seminary, provided the impetus for "The Switch." "Second Blessings" answered the call of Dr. Alice Shalvi, who taught a course on women's midrashrim at Machon Schechter in Jerusalem. The Talmud instructs us to "get a teacher and acquire a study partner" (*Pirke Avot* 1:6). My midrashic study has been enriched by my teachers and colleagues with whom I have studied and written.

Some of my stories have come to me simply by reading a biblical text. I find that I have already fully formed the story even before I check the commentaries. The story may come from a discrepancy I notice in a passage or from a question I ask myself about the meaning of a particular verse. "The Mirrors," "The Song of Devorah and Yael," and "The Scribe" are three such stories. Midrash sometimes happens in a flash of insight, and such flashes are valuable new ways of reading an ancient book. I am grateful when they come and sorry when they go. Fortunately, the nature of the Torah is such that, like a mother bird to her nest, she always comes back.

She Says to the Angel: The Fantastical Quality of Midrash

In the Bible it is customary for people to talk to God, but in rabbinic midrash the biblically recorded conversations between human and Divine are by no means the only ones: Moses, Rachel, and others have countless conversations with God in midrash. In the Bible, it is customary to experience strange things such as angels with swords, plagues of frogs, and ladders between heaven and earth. In the midrash, people receive countless mystical scrolls and angelic visitations and enlist the aid of magical worms and harps that play themselves. Midrash takes the already supernatural atmosphere of the Bible and adds to it a new level of fantasy and imagery.

The purpose of this marvelous midrashic invention, I think, is threefold. First, this style of midrash grabs the attention of the audience by revealing a hidden treasure of images: It gets its messages across by being vivid in its storytelling. Second, it involves the audience in a landscape of belief in which anything is possible, a mythic space where our ancestors' spirits can sustain us and give us hope for the future. Third, I think this kind of story is told for sheer pleasure. It is, like the intricate study of the Talmud, a way to exercise the mind, and it is also a way to open the heart. While the talmudic writers of that time are very far apart from us in their way of thinking, I believe they share some of the desire for wonder we ourselves feel when we face our troubled world.

Much of modern midrash is highly realist in nature, but I prefer to set my characters in a world of myth and mystery. That world fits both the biblical and the rabbinic atmosphere, and it suits my own literary preference for the fantastic. It also allows me to make the spiritual power of my characters visible and tangible. The miracles that Abraham, Isaac, Jacob, Sarah, and Hagar receive set them apart as people on a spiritual quest; I want to put my characters on that path. The landscape I work with is a dream landscape, a place where the symbolic becomes real.

In the biblical narrative, it is mostly men who talk to God, or at least, mostly men who get direct answers. God answers Job out of the whirlwind, but God apparently has nothing to say to Job's wife, who has also lost a home and family. God calls Avram to leave Canaan, but God's words to Sarai are not mentioned, although she also is leaving her home. And so on. The midrash has a similar problem. Often in midrashic literature it is the men who get the mysterious scrolls and the angelic visitations. I was interested in portraying female characters in similar roles.

In Genesis 12:10–20, Sarai, having claimed that Avram is her brother to protect him from men who would kill him to get at her, is taken into Pharaoh's harem because of her beauty. This is a rather prosaic situation. However, Pharaoh mysteriously is unable to "know" her. A rabbinic midrash quoted by Rashi fills in, commenting on the words "because of Sarai." It says an angel is under Sarai's orders. She commands the angel to afflict Pharaoh, then commands the angel to leave him alone, to observe whether he has repented and will cease harassing her. If not, she sets the angel on him again. "She says to the angel 'Strike' and he strikes" (Rashi on Genesis 12:17). Sarai's relationship with this angel made me laugh, then fascinated me. What would the world be like if all women had such angels? What would the world be like if Providence were so person specific? I continue to ask these things as I write my own midrashim. The question of our relationship to the world of the spirit pervades this book, echoing my own questions about the things we know are real but cannot see.

Sisters at Sinai: Women in the Midrashic Landscape

One of the major characteristics of midrash is its connectedness. It seeks, on principle, to connect seemingly disparate events and characters. In midrash, Adam passes wisdom on to Noah. Dinah becomes the mother of Joseph's wife, Asnat. Job is the adviser of Pharaoh. Ruth sits on a throne next to Solomon, her descendant. Joshua marries the harlot Rachav. Miriam becomes the midwife Puah, the wife of Caleb, and the ancestress of David. David appears in a vision of Adam's. It is this connectedness, this complicated and insistent lineage, that exemplifies covenant in the midrashic literature. For covenant to be eternal it must be passed on from hand to hand, and midrash never fails to find an heir for each of its characters. The rabbinic conviction that every verse in the Torah is connected to every other verse, and every time in the Torah is connected to every other time, is part of an understanding that everything and everyone is woven into a single fabric. Midrash imagines that the souls of every generation of the Children of Israel stand together at Sinai, each hearing God speak in a different way, yet each participating in one communal revelation. The connection between any two souls is always present. Midrash doesn't create it, midrash only seeks to uncover it.

One of my goals as I write is to connect women fully to this covenantal structure, to give them genealogies and inheritances that are as full as the ones that begin "Adam begat Seth; Seth begat Enosh; Enosh began Kenan." Marge Piercy writes in her poem on Ruth:

> *Show me a woman who does not hide*
> *in the locket of bone that deep*
> *eye beam of fiercely gentle love*
> *she had once from mother, daughter,*
> *sister; once like a warm moon*
> *that radiance aligned the tides*
> *of her blood into potent order.*

> —"The Book of Ruth and Naomi"
> (Curzon, ed., *Modern Poems on the Bible*, pp. 325–26)

The Bible and the midrash skim over relationships between men and women, and they tell us even less of relations among women— certainly we rarely hear of women who love each other as relatives, friends, partners, or allies. Nevertheless, these connections are a crucial part of the covenantal web. For the sacred texts to speak to us, the biblical relation of mother to child, teacher to disciple, spouse to spouse, sister to sister, friend to friend must feel as resonant and complex as our own experience of those relations. Midrash can help us create that resonance and complexity.

The midrashic line of descent, like the endless interpretation of Torah, is meant to symbolize the growth of the Tree of Life, the way we store up the things we know about loving God and each other and keep that wisdom moving from one generation to the next. I am honored and proud to be a small branch on that lush and fruitful tree. In the name of Sarah, Rebekah, Rachel, and Leah; Bilhah and Zilpah; Dinah, Serach, and Miriam; Devorah and Huldah, I welcome you to this sisterhood at Sinai. Sinai is a mountain of scattered seeds of Torah, some lying on the surface, some deep within the earth. I hope you will take as much pleasure in reaping its harvest as I did in planting it.

—Jill Hammer
Shulamit Yosifah Leah bat Leib veRut
December 2000
Kislev 5761

✎ Notes to the Reader

Commentary upon each of these stories appears in the back of this book. Notes include a list of biblical texts upon which each story was built, information about which rabbinic sources were used, and some commentary on how the story came to be written and why. Translations of biblical verses come from the new Jewish Publication Society (NJPS) translation of the Bible (1985), except where it is noted that the author translated the verse. However, some names are rendered differently than in the NJPS version in order to match the transliterated versions of the names used in the stories themselves. Where possible, translations have been altered from masculine ("Sons of Israel") to gender neutral ("Children of Israel"). In many translations of biblical and rabbinic texts, masculine pronouns for God have been used in order to be faithful to the Hebrew original. This is not meant to reflect the author's own conception of the Divine.

All modern sources can be found in the bibliography. Traditional sources are described in the sources section. Readers who are not familiar with the rabbinic sources cited may refer to Louis Ginsberg's *Legends of the Jews*, Hayim Nachman Bialik and Yehoshua Hanna Ravnitzky's *The Book of Legends*, Naomi Hyman's *Biblical Women in the Midrash*, or some other volume of collected midrash to learn more about the rabbinic commentary on a particular character or text.

Bible passages quoted at the beginning of each story will be more meaningful if they are read in their context. Readers are strongly encouraged to find these quotes in the Bible and read them along with the verses that surround them. Midrash is always intertextual, and it is wise to spend some time with the text on which the midrash comments.

In these stories I have treated biblical names with some idiosyncrasy. Names like Rachel, Benjamin, Jacob, Esau, Isaac, and Moses, which are in common usage in English, have been rendered in their English spellings. Names not in common usage, like Avishag (Abishag), Mahalat (Mahalath), Asnat (Asenath), and Shimon (Simeon) have been rendered in transliteration from the Hebrew. Some names, like Miriam, Leah, Dinah, David, Naamah, and Sarah, are spelled the same in both languages.

PROLOGUE

If only there were light enough to feel,
one's way along the walls of the world, to find
the flaw the builders had not seen, to foil
the unassuageable architects, to fall
into fidelity, if there were light.

   —ALLEN MANDELBAUM, *Chelmaxioms*

The story is for the sake of knowledge.

   —AVIVAH ZORNBERG

1

Havdalah

She conceived and bore Cain, and said,
"I have created a man with God."

—Genesis 4:1*

I am large; I contain multitudes.

—Walt Whitman, *Leaves of Grass*

Eve crouched on the green world-carpet. Her feet were pleasantly nestled in the soft grass. She was watching the goats and peacocks perform their favorite dance. She did not have the heart to call to them and tell them the world was ending. Instead, she watched over them, hoping they wouldn't figure it out themselves. Above her, the golden sky-ball was slowly falling onto the mountains. Scarlet painted itself onto the soft blue bowl of the sky. The wolves and cats gathered on a hill and began to howl. Eve howled with them. If the world were ending there should be a ritual for it. She was sure the Voice would approve. The Voice always seemed to approve of rituals.

Behind her, Adam dropped out of a pear tree. He was shivering. Whether or not the voice liked Eve's howl, Adam did not. He put his long arms around her and hugged her to his furry body. She

* Author's translation

stopped the noise she was making. Nearby, a turtle slipped into the rush of foaming water that wove its way through the clearing. The water of the stream was bright against the dimness of the air. Adam and Eve had argued a few minutes before, when the air was still bright. Adam had thought they should climb into the mountain caves, away from the sky-darkness. Eve had thought they should walk into the sea to meet it. They had not been able to agree. Adam had gone to sulk in the pear tree.

Now they both were silent. It grew blacker and blacker. The elephants trumpeted. The owls hooted. Fingers of sound poked at the darkness. A walrus slipped off the edge of the land into the ocean. Eve saw that the sea looked as thick and formless as the sky. There was a splash. Maybe the land was melting. Eve walked to the place where the stream met the sea, where the water churned up white cattails. She was curious about the end of the world. Adam followed her, tentatively hooting, like the night owl, the *lilit*. An echo, or a reply, came back to him across the deep. His feet sank into the crumbly ginger of the sand. Adam smiled. It seemed to Eve that he was remembering something. She felt vaguely uncomfortable that he had been made before her. What memories did he have of the time before her making? Would the world's end be different for him because of his remembering?

As if in answer to her thoughts, the Voice came winging over the bay: a glass hawk, a mountain's breath. *The world is not ending, only the seventh day.* Eve wondered if the segments of an orange all had names. Were they called first, fourth, seventh? Adam and Eve listened with the sharp ears of bats, looking for direction in the soft holy sounds around them.

They began to hear the booms of frogs and the chirping of insects. Eve suddenly knew to make a circle of smooth heavy stones. Adam placed a pile of twigs in its center. He took up two thin sticks with frayed bark. He drummed them for a while on a stone, then rubbed them together like two hungry bodies, harder and harder. Sweat made his brow slick. Eve crouched at his feet and stared intently. To their amazement, a spark like a tiny golden bird burst from the twigs. Eve caught the spark in a cup of dried moss she had pressed into shape with her fingers. Slowly, slowly, the tiny spark lying on the bottom of the cup burrowed into the moss and put out a tongue of flame. Adam took the moss cup and laid it in the nest of branches within the circle of stones. The furry bowl blazed up, a sky-ball on the ground. Eve and Adam had to back away from its heat. Eve saw the look in Adam's eyes again, the remembering-look. Of what did fire remind him?

The clearing was bathed in light. Mice, tigers, and salamanders rushed from the meadow in a thunder of footfalls. Startled crows cawed away. Eve jumped at the sound. The animals were afraid of the new thing the humans had made. Eve and Adam were left alone.

The fire twinkled and smoked. It was hot when Eve reached out a hand to it, but pleasantly warm at the right distance. With no animals to feed or stroke, Eve and Adam began to watch each other. The pop of a pinecone in the flames was exciting, but there was no aftermath. Then they saw that near the rocks that Eve had placed in a ring there was a square object. It had a supple skin around it on three sides. It made no sound. When Adam picked it up it fell open into many leaves, as if it were a flower. On the leaves were black markings in groups and patterns.

"A book," Adam said.

Eve looked curiously. "Like a butterfly," she guessed.

"In a way. It changes," Adam told her. "The Voice told me about it."

Eve pondered. "It doesn't run away from the fire. Perhaps it is like fire itself."

"Black and white fire," said Adam. Eve looked up at him. He looked away. He was hiding something that he knew. She saw that look when he talked about the two trees at the center of the garden. Eve was sure she was missing something. She took his hand, but he would not look at her.

Insects buzzed around them. Behind the insects came angels. Angels were always in the garden. They sang to grass or picked flowers and stored them in jars. In the morning they would place golden grainy bread on stones for Adam and Eve to find. Until now the angels had avoided the humans. A little winged creature had once frowned at Eve when she found it singing in a leopard's fur. Adam had followed one once, and it had darted into a cedar grove and disappeared. But now angels flitted around the heads of the humans. Some even perched on Adam's shoulders, flapping small storklike wings.

"They want to read the book," said Eve.

"It's mine," Adam replied sharply.

Eve was puzzled by Adam's words. Adam's forehead crinkled with worry. He shielded the book with his arms and began muttering to himself. Eve gently shooed away the angels from the clearing with an ostrich feather she had been wearing in her hair, but they returned in greater numbers. She tried to tempt them with blueberries from a nearby bush, but they wanted only the book. A few of them grabbed a corner of it and began pulling. Adam pulled back. "Go home!" he shouted, pointing at the sky. The angels looked offended. They buzzed around Adam's head, chanting psalms in an irritated way.

Adam pored over the book for hours. The angels loitered on tree branches and dandelion puffs, making an occasional grab when Adam dozed for a minute. Eve waited quietly, wondering why Adam didn't ask for her help. Then there was a noise in the bushes.

The noise drew out into a low drumming sound.

At first Eve thought it was a bird, but the voice did not sound like any creature in the garden as much as it sounded like Eve. Eve was intrigued. She glanced at Adam to see his reaction. Adam looked frightened. He began to hum loudly, as if he did not want her to hear.

Eve pointed to the bushes, but Adam shook his head. "You shouldn't leave the fire," he said.

"Why not?" Eve asked. "The animals are away from the fire." She pointed to a frog on a lily pad. The low drumming sound went on, like a heartbeat.

Adam closed the book with a snap. "Don't go into the woods," he insisted. "There are dangerous things there."

"Like the trees at the center of the garden?" Eve asked angrily. "I listen to you too much. This time I want to find out for myself." With Adam's voice pursuing her, Eve ran off into the woods.

At first Eve ran in blackness, but soon she was able to see dim outlines by the light of the rents in the sky. The woods were strange in the darkness, but they smelled familiar. Eve forged ahead, brushing aside vines and rose briars. A pair of foxes moved out of her way. She passed a panda in its bamboo patch, munching on twigs. From time to time the rhythmic thumping became louder, fuller, luring her forward. It began to echo her footfalls, as if it were her shadow moving ahead of her.

Eve was feeling her way through a fern grove when the feathery plants were suddenly, brilliantly lit. Eve thought day had returned. Then she realized that the light was a strange color. Looking up, Eve saw a huge blue-white disk in the sky. She was afraid of it and put her hands up to her eyes.

"It's the moon," said a voice beside her.

Eve looked next to herself in consternation. Another Eve

stood there. Where Eve had parchment pale skin and dark hair, this new Eve had skin like ink. Her white hair streamed down her black skin like a hundred comet tails, squiggling and curving. She had the same triangle of fur at the place where her legs came together, but it was white as milk. The second woman was smiling at Eve and drumming her fingers on a tree at the center of the grove. It was the sound Eve had heard in the clearing. Eve saw why Adam had smiled at the fire. This woman was like the echo of a flame.

Eve felt strange inside. "I thought I was the only one of what I was," she said. She did not know where else to begin.

"Oh, you are," said the second Eve. "*My* name is Lilith."

And then Eve remembered the word Adam had called at night when he was dreaming. She knew this woman was a memory Adam had from before she had come to be.

"I do not want you here," Eve said.

"Neither does Adam," said Lilith. "I have been banished from the garden because I would not obey him and lie beneath him, because I named myself. I have been given this night only to convince you. Then I must leave again, forever."

"Convince me of what?" Eve asked suspiciously. Only the voice and Adam ever tried to convince her of things. She did not want to listen to Lilith.

"That you too need to leave the garden."

Eve shook her head angrily. "This is my home. Even if it is dark now, it is still my home. I will not leave."

"I also have a home," said Lilith. She looked a little sad, less fiery.

Eve felt curiosity uncurl within her. Where did one live if one was outside of Eden? "Where is your home?" she asked. "What do you do there?"

"I live in the sea," said Lilith, "and give birth to children."

"Children?" Eve did not know the word. She was getting frustrated by her lack of vocabulary. She needed more words.

"Like kittens. Like fawns. The small who will grow larger."

Eve smiled. She had seen young creatures playing in Eden, chicks and lambs.

"But they are all taken from me," Lilith said, and now her voice had an angry tone. "Each one of them is taken, and the angels have told me I will never see them again, unless . . ."

"Unless?" Eve asked.

"Unless you too give birth to children. My children are the souls of yours. Until there are bodies for them, they cannot remain in the world. My sons and daughters need you in order to become free."

Eve remembered the elephant squeezing out her calf by the river. "I do not want children," she insisted.

"There can be nothing new without children," Lilith said. "Without the young, there will be no one to inherit your memories."

Eve thought of the small bear cubs playing in the hills. "Even if I did want children," she said defensively, "I don't know how to have them."

"I know," Lilith said, "and in order to learn, you will have to eat from the tree at the center of the garden. Not the tree of life—which is the tree from which I have eaten—but from the tree of knowledge of good and evil. Then time will begin, and you will know what to do."

"But if I eat from that tree I will die! You are trying to kill me so that you can have Adam back!" Eve started away from the woman beside her. She wanted to break into the woods and find Adam again, keep him away from this other woman who disobeyed the voice.

Lilith grabbed Eve's wrist in her dark fist. "It is true that if you eat from the tree you will someday die," she said, "but it is also true that if you do not eat the fruit, you will never truly live."

"I do not understand," Eve said, trying to break away.

"I know," said Lilith. "That is why I have come."

Lilith walked away from Eve to the center of the glade, crouched, and drew a circle in the soil. Around the circle she placed stones. Then she began to rub two sticks together.

"You are making fire," Eve exclaimed, slowly drawing closer. So Adam had learned to start fires from Lilith.

"Yes," said Lilith. The sparks that flew from Lilith's sticks caught and flamed upward. The fire became a towering pillar, a shape with branches and leaves. The tree burned, but it was not consumed by the fire. Lilith kindled another flame, and a second pillar formed beside the first, a darker column, flickering. Smoke bit at Eve's eyes. She recognized the shapes. Lilith was showing her the trees at the center of the garden, the trees the Voice had told them not to touch.

"Watch," Lilith commanded.

Eve crouched and watched. The fruits of the two fiery trees began to swell, larger and larger, until their taut roundness rivaled the moon. Then they burst like seedpods into the night. Sparks scattered everywhere, glowed in every part of the sky, then disappeared. Eve gasped at their unbearable, momentary beauty. She had never before seen anything that reached so deeply into her heart.

"That is what we are meant to do," said Lilith to Eve. "We are meant to scatter our sparks in the world. Without that task, we are not alive. And so you must begin death, and hope, and children. You must bear bodies for the souls that are waiting. You must begin the story, Eve."

"And disobedience," said Eve quietly after a long moment. "I must begin that as well."

"I have begun that for you," said Lilith.

"When I have picked the fruit, will the Voice be silent?" asked Eve.

Lilith smiled, her dark eyes glowing with the firelight. "You may find that even in rebellion, you are following the sound of the Voice."

There was a rushing of storks' wings. Angels came flying in shimmering bunches toward the fern glade. Gathering around Lilith, they lifted her up into the air. Eve grabbed Lilith's hands and tried to hold her. The angels persisted. Eve was forced to let go as Lilith rose farther and farther from the ground. Lilith waved with an ink-colored hand. Then she spread two immense silver wings and flew away, singing in Eve's voice.

Eve turned and made her way back to the clearing by the sea. Soon there was a reddish glow through a stand of pines. Eve followed it and stepped into a ring of light. Adam was still engaged in a tug-of-war with the angels, who had grown bigger and brighter and more numerous during the struggle. As Eve watched, the angels pried the book from Adam's fingers and leaped off with it into the forest.

Adam breathed heavily and sagged into Eve's arms, where he lay quietly for a minute. "It doesn't matter," he said to Eve. "I read it first."

"What did you learn?" Eve asked. She settled by the circle of stones, folding her legs beneath her.

"The way to the future," Adam answered slowly. His eyes shifted toward her. "Did you find anything in the forest?"

Eve wanted to tell him about Lilith, but somehow she was not ready. She knew it was the first separation between them.

"I saw a night owl hatching her eggs," she said.

Adam handed Eve a roasted apple as a gift. She bit into it hungrily. It was wrinkled and liquid from the fire. Then she arranged a bed of soft leaves and petals. The embers of the fire dimmed as the two humans lay down to sleep. The darkness was no longer frightening. Instead, it rested as a kind of cloak over their dreams.

THE HOUSE OF THE MOTHERS

...for some allege the father
of truth is talk, while some say text;
and—quaere even more perplexed—
who must have been his mother?

　　　—ALLEN MANDELBAUM, *Chelmaxioms*

What would happen if one woman told the
truth about her life?

The world would split open.

　　　—MURIEL RUKEYSER, "Kathe Kollwitz"

NAAMAH AND THE HUMMINGBIRD

*... I will establish My covenant with you, and you
shall enter the ark, with your sons, your wife, and your
sons' wives. And of all that lives, of all flesh, you shall
take two of each into the ark to keep alive with you;
they shall be male and female. From birds of every
kind, cattle of every kind, every kind of creeping thing
on earth, two of each shall come to you to stay alive.*

—GENESIS 6:18–20

In the garden of Solomon's queens, anything seemed possible.
One might say that a walled garden by its nature cannot seem
boundless, but this garden was an exception. Orchids grew by
banana plants. Melons hung by roses. It was a garden of contrast
and contradiction. Solomon added new flowers every day. The gar-
deners said the bees were frequently confused.

On this evening, night was in no great hurry to bring the darkness. From a raised marble pavilion half-hidden by white lilies, two
women robed in silk leaned out into the garden. A blue-throated
hummingbird darted in and out of the bell of a delicate flower. A
moment later, it was visiting another bell. Then, in a motion almost
too quick to be seen, it alighted on the scarlet lip of a trumpet
flower. The bird sat there comfortably, silently dipping its head
toward the nectar inside the bloom.

Naamah, wife of Solomon and mother of his heir, let her wrap fall and stretched out over the railing. Her eyes followed the bird with a keen interest. Her new daughter-in-law, Maacah, wife of the crown prince Rechavam, leaned out next to her. Maacah had been sequestered at home throughout her childhood. Everything was new to her. The previous day she had found an embroidered hat and used it as a chair cushion.

"If we were inside that blossom," Naamah said to Maacah, "we would now see that bird's tiny tongue move faster than a poet's! We call the hummingbird *yonek-dvash*, 'the one who suckles honey.' It drinks only the nectar of flowers."

"I have never seen one," said Maacah shyly.

"If honey is the symbol of the Torah's sweetness," Naamah said, "then the hummingbird is a Torah scholar, sucking all day long."

"Is it a real bird?" asked Maacah. "If I did not know better, I would say that some craftsman had made it."

"Oh no!" Naamah laughed. "The hummingbird was made at Creation with the rest of us. But the ones in this garden are the only ones I have seen; Solomon brought them from far away."

Naamah paused and looked closely at young Maacah. The girl's pale face and white silk drapery made her seem like a stone carver's work herself. Solomon had deemed her pure enough for his eldest son, although she was considered nervous and strange. Naamah leaned over the railing to smell the jasmine, which spread tendrils in a fan along the wall. She could feel an outburst hanging in the air. Maacah was terrified of the court. It was only a matter of time.

Sure enough, after a few minutes of silence, Maacah began to cry, wiping her eyes on her mantle. "I feel like a peculiar bird myself," she explained in an embarrassed tone.

"Do you not feel at home here?" Naamah asked.

Maacah shook her head. "All I have ever known is a few narrow stone rooms in Gibeah. It seems like a joke that I am to be queen someday, when I do not know what it means to order my own life! And—" Maacah stopped and glanced at Naamah timidly.

"Go on," the queen prodded. Maacah had been acting strangely ever since she arrived. The queen wanted to know why.

Maacah swallowed. "I have had frightening dreams ever since I came to court. I dream that there are snakes hissing at me, each with a hundred tongues." She put her face in her hands.

Naamah thought of her son, who was, regrettably, somewhat snakelike. She put her arm around the girl. "You are afraid of the people around you," she said to Maacah, "and you should be, for some of them are dangerous. But you must not be afraid to face the future, no matter what it holds. You have gifts of the heart you are only beginning to discover."

"I'd rather die than be queen," Maacah sobbed. "I want to go home to my narrow room. Jerusalem is too wide for me!"

"You cannot find your life's purpose unless you face what is in front of you," Naamah told her firmly. "Even these exotic birds flitting around our garden have purpose."

"What purpose do they have?" Maacah asked timidly, as her sobs began to subside. "They look as useless as I feel."

"There is a story about the hummingbird," said Naamah, "and it involves my namesake, who was Noah's wife in the time of the Great Flood."

"Oh, please tell me," pleaded Maacah. "There were so few stories told in my house."

So Naamah sat on the smooth lip of the stone pavilion, settled her rich blue and silver robes around her, and began.

"When Noah heard God's word that the humans and beasts of the world had been judged, he accepted God's judgment in his heart. He was not one to rail against the way things were. But his wife, sons, and daughters-in-law were a different matter. They tried to convince their friends and family to prepare for the flood and save themselves; but no one would listen. Everyone thought they were fools. Soon they realized that only their small family would be saved. Noah and his sons began to build a wooden box, an ark, so that life would not be completely destroyed.

"But my tale truly begins with two women talking, just as we are now. You see, the wife of Noah's son Shem was called Liba. She was kind and loving and brave, but she had one oddity: She was afraid of closed spaces. She and Shem lived in an open tent beneath a great cedar. They cooked on an open fire. The cities of Cain were renowned for their houses and splendid towers, but Liba had no curiosity to see them. When Japheth and his wife, Maia, would go off to trade their harvest crops, Liba would make them plum tea and contentedly bid them farewell. Liba was wild as a strawberry. No one knew her parentage, since she had been abandoned as a small child. No one knew why she would not go inside.

"When Noah revealed God's plan to his family, they began to dedicate all their energies to the ark. Ham cut down trees and planed them. Japheth laid out the framework. Ham's small wife, Isis, crept into nooks and crannies and sanded them smooth. Shem designed stalls and cubbies for animals. While the ark was still a maze of ribs and gateways, Liba would bring beams for Japheth to hammer into place. But when the ark's roof began to cast a deep shadow on its floor, Liba fled the building site and would not return. She did not want to go inside the ark.

"Naamah was the wife of Noah. She was a weaver. Her weaving was so magnificent that some called her an evil witch who could cast spells with her colors. Those people did not see Naamah's heart for what it truly was. Naamah had a bright spirit. She never worried for the future. But as she wove and packed and dried and smoked, provisioning the ark, she became more and more concerned about Shem's wife, Liba.

"As Naamah worked on her loom on the roofless porch, in the shade of the rustling birch stand, Liba would sit beside her and make garlands of flowers. Liba loved flowers, and she liked to bring Shem new fragrances and colors. While the two women worked, Naamah would try to soothe Liba's fears about the wooden ark. But Liba would not listen.

" 'If Shem wants to go on the ark in pairs he must take another wife. I would rather drown than live in that coffin,' Liba would say, and refuse to discuss the matter any further.

"At night by the well, Naamah would put down her water vessel near Liba's and speak of children and the future. Liba would smile sadly and nod and go off with her jug of water toward the old cedar tree. Shem became quieter, worked with less energy. Naamah resolved that somehow she would convince her daughter-in-law to enter the ark when the rain began to fall.

"When the animals began to come, Naamah did not know whether to laugh or cry. She would be picking apples in the orchards to dry for the journey and would come face-to-face with a pair of bears or ghostly white tigers. Or she would find frogs tangled in the weaving on her loom. Sometimes she would slip out at night to relieve herself, and meet with a snowy owl or a hook-beaked hawk.

"Eventually Naamah's concern went away. These were the righteous among the animals. They waited near her house, playing with each other or curling up lazily with their mates. Giant turtles and smooth-flippered penguins walked around the fields freely, patient but puzzled. Naamah and her daughters-in-law brought water, seed, leaves, and meat, trying to satisfy the needs of the huge gathering of animals. Liba brushed the horses and fed the zebras with handfuls of grain, but she still refused to enter the ark.

"People began to avoid Noah's land. For weeks the local people had lounged near the meadow where the ark lay, like jackals at a lions' kill, and giggled about Noah's lunacy. Now, as larger and larger animals came to wait for the rain, Naamah's neighbors had stopped laughing. One day Liba came home with a bruise on her cheek where a rock had struck her. People were becoming angry.

"On a particularly stormy day, the day Noah set a window in the roof of the ark, Naamah looked up from her loom beneath the birches and saw a flash of color moving among the wildflowers. At first she thought it was a large exotic insect. Then she realized it was a bird. It had wings that moved too fast for her to see and a jewel-like splash of brilliant blue at its throat.

"Just then, Liba came wading through the yellow blossoms. She stopped suddenly as another bright object whizzed past her, joining the first on its meandering path through the meadow. Liba had never before seen a bird that drank from flowers. She chased the two birds and called to them, singing with joy.

"In the days that followed, Naamah often stopped her work to watch the blue-throated pair as they fed. The hummingbirds took a special liking to Liba, perching on her shoulders and head as she sat by the birches. Sometimes neighbors would drop by to tease or threaten, and the birds would shelter Liba with their wings.

"When the first drizzle began to fall, Liba was calm. She hugged the family good-bye and ran off into the forest before anyone could stop her. Shem sobbed while he herded goats and water buffalo onto the ark. His tears mixed with the raindrops. Noah patted his eldest son on the shoulder, conveying with his touch what he could not say in words. Then he went on prodding the elephants.

"The animals bleated and complained as they were led up the wooden ramps into the boxlike structure. Several stepped on

Naamah's feet, but she barely noticed. She felt the loss of Liba, of other people she cared for, of the world as she knew it. She even missed her neighbors' curses. A pair of albatrosses winged through the open rectangle in the side of the ark. Finches nested in a tuft of straw. But no small hummingbirds flew through the cavernous door.

"The ark filled with specimens of all God's creatures. The rain became heavier. Naamah went to get her final box of precious things: carefully laundered linen, her grandmother's sloppily woven green blanket, a pot of dried fruit. The best of her tapestries. Ham's first tooth. A blue shell Shem had brought her from the ocean. A dried fig leaf from Eden, handed down through the generations from Eve herself. Naamah lingered on the porch, desperately hoping that Liba would change her mind. Nothing moved among the yellow wildflowers or the clean white birches. Finally Naamah hurried away from the neat stone house. She could not hold back her tears.

"Noah shouted at his wife when she appeared at the corner of the field. 'Where were you?' he demanded. 'Hurry, it's almost too late!'

"The animals were all on board. So were Ham and Japheth and their wives. Shem stood at the door, looking out with desperate, despairing eyes. Puddles and even small ponds were gathering, drowning the grasses and the earthworms sleeping in the soil. The whole field had become a marsh. The ark teetered a bit in its resting place. It was time.

"Shem disappeared into the belly of the ark. Naamah lifted up her muddy skirts and climbed through the entranceway. She could smell a hundred varieties of animal sweat. She could also hear angry voices in the woods, coming closer to the ark. Noah and Naamah, with a rhythm born of many years spent together, began to hoist the door panel upward.

"Were it not for the sapphire gorget, Naamah never would have seen the bird on the edge of the marshy expanse of grass. She abruptly stopped raising the door, eliciting a disturbed grunt from Noah.

" 'Look,' she said. 'There are more coming.'

" 'Naamah, we can't wait,' Noah said urgently. 'We have no more room, and the flood is almost upon us.' But then he heard the faint hum, the hum of wings moving too fast to be seen.

"The hummingbirds were flitting toward the ark as fast as their double-jointed wings could carry them. And in their wake, running as if in a trance, was Liba. It was almost as if she were borne on their tiny feathers. Noah and Naamah watched in total silence as the trio raced toward them. Sensing that something was happening, Shem scrambled to a place between his parents. He let out a cry of joy. As Liba and her escorts reached the ark's edge, Shem lifted his wife onto the half-closed door and into the ark. The hummingbirds danced around Liba's head as she embraced her husband. Noah and Naamah closed the door. Naamah had never been so grateful for a splash of color in all her life. Within minutes, the driving rain set the ark adrift. A few fists beat at the walls of the ark, and then there was the sound of rushing water.

"The next weeks were a chaos of adjustment to strange circumstances. Food had to be prepared without fire. Animals had to be fed in near darkness. Tempers were short. The men of Noah's family stayed in one section of the ark, and the women in another. Physical intimacy was too uncomfortable in such close quarters. Even the beasts separated from their mates. Animals bleated to lost kin, whose cries were carried to the ark on the blasting wind. The shrieks of humans were audible even over the pounding rain. When objects bumped against the ark, Naamah would shudder. She kept far from Noah and even from her children. She was sure that all meaningful life on the earth had ended. Yet the two hummingbirds stayed together, perching on the antlers of a stag or on the back of a hippopotamus.

"The family tried to make themselves useful in order to pass the time. Liba did no chores, although she occasionally visited and combed the horses and zebras. Her two sisters-in-law teased and chided her, but to no effect. Liba had chosen a small nook in one corner of the ark as her home, and there she stayed. She was panicky and depressed in the confined space of the ark, but looking at the hummingbirds soothed her. "Like flowers," she would say, and warble to them in her high voice.

"Forty days later, when Naamah had begun to believe they would be in the ark forever, the rain stopped. After the constant maddening patter of rain, the sudden stillness brought cheers, chirps, and elephant trumpets. Shem, leaning against a rhinoceros, fell flat in surprise. Then he rushed to the window, but no earth could be seen, only a huge expanse of water.

"Noah chose a raven as a scout, and released it from the window, which had been their sun and moon for over a month. When the raven returned, it refused to come back inside the crowded ark, and instead sat on the flat roof of the ark, or circled angrily in the sky. The ark's occupants once again sank into a gray depression, punctuated by the raven's harsh squawks.

"A week passed, and Noah brooded. He knew he needed a bird to search out land for them. Japheth suggested a dove. Noah agreed, and went searching among the roosting birds. A dove tamely stepped into Noah's hands, and Noah raised his arms to the window. The dove arrowed away into the pale sky.

"When the dove went on its mission, the air seemed full of portent. Liba huddled. Even Naamah looked anxiously at the hummingbirds, wondering if they would disappear through the open window. But as the dove flapped over the waters toward some unknown destination, the hummingbirds withdrew to Liba's corner, keeping their tiny counsel for each other.

"That night, Naamah had a dream. She dreamed that six goblet-shaped flowers twined down on golden stems from heaven. The hummingbirds came and drank from each one. As the hummingbirds fed, they began to glow with an inner light. Naamah woke up with the inexplicable feeling that life would go on. When she saw Liba smiling for the first time since she entered the ark, she knew Liba had dreamed the same vision.

"Six days later, the dove returned. In its beak was a miracle: a small olive leaf. It was the first green thing the eight humans had seen in many days. They all clustered around it as if it were a fire on a cold winter's night. Frogs boomed. Silkworms uncurled. Wolves howled in harmony. The hummingbirds soared around the ark. The nightingales sang. Later, Naamah stowed the leaf away in her chest of treasures, next to the fig leaf from Eden.

"Very little could be seen through the ark's small window. Ham clamored to open the ark's great door, but Noah counseled patience. Everyone waited with growing anticipation and fear. Would the waters continue to go down, or would their small cradle of life float forever in a misty seascape? Seven days later, at dawn, Noah released the dove again in a flurry of white feathers. The raven, sullenly perched on the salt-bleached roof, ignoring the bird flying off into the distance.

"This time, the gentle creature did not return; and that afternoon, the ark ran aground.

" 'We must be on a mountaintop,' Japheth exclaimed, running to the window. Noah and Shem jumped up and lifted the heavy bar across the door. As soon as the door was open, Naamah burst past them, teetered on the ledge of the opening, and drank in the sun. In front of her was a cedar grove. Down the hill to her right, the sea lapped against the rocky soil, but here in the grove the land was dry. Naamah leaped from the ark as if she were the gazelle she had slept beside for fifty-four nights. Placing her feet on solid ground was like dancing at a wedding.

" 'The sign of the covenant!' Noah whispered to her, and pointed.

"Naamah gasped at the beauty of the multicolored arch in the sky. It was like her weaving, but far more rich and delicate than anything she had made. It was like a hummingbird stretched out across the sky.

"Shem and Ham reached down to touch the new-grown blades of grass. Isis and Maia emerged from the ark, each clutching a wiggly sheep. But Liba did not come out of the ark's algae-covered door.

"Naamah waited. Finally, Liba stepped from the ark.

" 'Look,' she exulted. In her hand she held a tiny nest of floss, eiderdown, and thread from Naamah's weaving. Two eggs, barely visible to the eye, nestled inside the mouth of the nest. The hummingbirds, alone of all the animals on the ark, had produced new life. The other animals, awed, filed past the proud birds and their eggs. Then they wandered off into the forest or slithered off down the slope into the ocean, bellowing or hissing. Liba waded into the yellow flowers of the field beneath the cedars. As if in celebration, the mother and father hummingbird joined her there, throats flashing every color of the rainbow."

Naamah finished her story. Night had come. A crescent moon slashed the indigo sky like a slit in a silk gown. Maacah gave a deep sigh and scratched a jasmine leaf. As she bent near the white blossoms, a hummingbird alighted nearby, displaying its sapphire throat.

Naamah spoke gently: "Maacah, your new house frightens you, as the ark frightened Liba. But you must be willing to learn the truth of the hummingbird. The hummingbird survives on flowers that last only a few days. Its life is uncertain, but it is not afraid."

Maacah nodded. She seemed lost in thought.

"So now, are you ready to live?" asked the queen, affectionately putting a hand on Maacah's shoulder. Her movement startled a moth, which flitted away into the garden's depths.

Maacah grinned. "I am ready to go in to dinner. That will have to be enough, for now." She took the older woman's arm. They rose from their marble seat and turned toward the shining lamps of Solomon's palace.

The hummingbird watched as the two figures made their way down a stepping-stone path lined with pale blue irises. When they were out of sight, the bird slipped under the jasmine leaves. It added to its nest a white silk thread it had plucked from Maacah's gown. Then it nestled down into the little bowl to lay its eggs. The last of the lilies closed into a nighttime bud. A light spring rain began to fall.

THE ARRANGED
MARRIAGE

*Avram took Sarai his wife and Lot his nephew,
and all the things they had collected, and all the
souls that they had acquired, and they set out for
the land of Canaan.*

—GENESIS 12:5*

And Sarah laughed to herself.

—GENESIS 18:12

The house of Terach, minister at the court of Ur of the Chaldees, buzzed with excitement. Guests were due to arrive. The inner chamber was softened by bright tapestries depicting local gods. Nevertheless, the walls echoed with angry voices. Terach was helping his son get dressed.

Avram combed out the strands of his black beard and arranged the golden robe beneath it. "I still can't believe I agreed to this meeting. I don't want an arranged marriage. Certainly not to a product of this decadent city."

"The daughter of Nofet is a beautiful woman." Terach adjusted a deep blue sash. "You'll like her, she's your half-sister."

---

* Author's translation

"She is?" Avram turned around to look at his father. "I've never met her."

"She's the daughter of a moon priestess. Her mother and I were partners at a ritual lunar event. She's no legal relation to you."

Avram sighed. "Do you think a priestess's daughter is going to leave Ur and travel to a wilderness like Aram-Naharaim?" he pointed out. "When she doesn't even believe in my god?"

"I still don't believe *I've* agreed to move to that wasteland."

The two men would have continued to argue, but a small bronze bell rang in the outer chamber, announcing the arrival of Nofet and her daughter. Terach exited through a thick curtain. Avram heard his father's robes swish as he bowed ceremoniously. Other robes swished in return.

Avram hesitated a moment before leaving the safety of the cloth cave. He held in his thoughts the young woman he had met on a hill outside the city. He had come out after an argument with his father, fists clenched, eager to get out of the suffocating city, and there she had been.

She was dressed like an aristocrat, although she was barefoot and had tucked her overskirt into her belt. Her veil had fallen backward onto her shoulders like a cowl. Her face was as bright and smooth as a citron. She was pacing with her hands clasped perfectly behind her back as if they were sculpted in dark marble. Something about her made everything else come into sharp relief. Avram noticed the sharp pebbles beneath her soles, the supple leather of the sandals hanging from her right hand. He asked her her name, and she told him. Then he asked why she was alone out there on the hill.

She snorted. "If parents had wings, they'd be mosquitoes. I wanted to get out while I still had some blood left."

Avram laughed. "My father's gained weight over the years. He's more like a horsefly."

The young woman offered him one of her dangling sandals. "You could swat him with this."

Her voice was gravelly, exciting. "I'd need a soldier's boot, I think," Avram replied. He gestured up the wadi. "Are you walking to the top?"

"Why not?"

They passed pairs and trios of nibbling ibex with spiraling horns. The woman reached out to touch one. It did not move away. How odd, Avram thought. Animals always ran away from him. Particularly sheep. They were very timid. He had a difficult time with sheep.

"They like you," he commented to his companion as a young ibex slowly trotted away.

"Yes," she said. "It's people I can't generally abide."

They walked in silence for a moment. "What was your disagreement with your parents about?" Avram finally asked. "Money? A husband? A piece of land? A new dress?"

"A dress?" she laughed mockingly. "Nothing that important. It was about the gods, if you must know." She looked embarrassed then. She shook her head when he pressed her further. "No, I want to hear," he said to her.

She plucked the tip off a nearby leaf. "My aunt had the good fortune to marry a god," she answered him dryly. "That is, the king desired her and sent for her. He didn't consult her first. My uncle was unhappy about it, needless to say. This kind of thing frequently happens to women in my family. It's regrettable. It might even happen to me someday. I am told that I am beautiful."

It seemed unwise to comment either way. Avram nodded.

The young woman went on. "I suggested to my mother that deities should not be marrying human women when they have perfectly good demons and demigods to summon. King Nimrod does not need my aunt as a concubine! But she is a handsome woman, and apparently he cannot get enough of those. My mother is an influential priestess. She regards my aunt's new position as a political advantage. An honor, she says." Avram's companion snorted. "What a farce." She abruptly turned her face to where the waterfall sprayed a thin mist over the rocks.

"But we fight over money, too," she added after a minute. "I wouldn't want you to think my family was abnormal."

"I do not think King Nimrod is a god," Avram said. As the words left his mouth, he knew he'd spoken rashly, yet his companion did not seem disturbed.

"Certainly not." The woman pointed to the ibexes as they nibbled, and she smiled a little. "Could King Nimrod fit food and feeder so smoothly together? He is not such a fine artist—although I understand he sculpts occasionally."

"My father also sculpts," Avram admitted as the two began to wade through a low pool. "He owns a statue shop. Although business has been poor since I smashed his merchandise."

She laughed from behind a clump of reeds. "Was he competing with *your* statue shop?"

Avram grimaced. "No, he was competing with my invisible god. I smashed all of his statues except one, then put my staff in the hand of the statue that was left. I blamed it on a fight among the gods. My father didn't believe my story, of course. He had to admit I was right about the powers of his statues."

Another laugh. "I did something like that once."

"Oh?"

"My mother is a priestess, as I said. Each month I had to slaughter a lamb before her goddess and leave it with a dish of round cakes and curds. The lamb was always so terrified. . . . One day I was tired of the whole thing. I drove the whole flock into the temple and asked the goddess to choose her own meal, if she insisted on having one. A terrified lamb chose that moment to relieve itself on the hem of her sculpted gown. Strangely, no divine retribution ensued."

"Was your mother angry?"

"Yes. She didn't let me into the temple again for a year. My mother told me she would be my goddess instead."

"Another usurpation of divinity."

"Yes, and in protest I refused to polish my mother's gown. Was your father angry?"

"Mostly, he stopped speaking to me."

"Perhaps you deserved it."

"Perhaps I did."

As the sun sank, they walked on the sandstone hills above the falls where the leopards sometimes roamed. He could not decide whether to tell her about the voices. He knew his father worried about his sanity. Even his mother, Emtelai, turned her face to the pots hanging from their pegs when he told her he had heard the voice of his god. She was afraid of the king's wrath. He knew this because at rare moments he heard souls speaking. It was a kind of prophecy, he supposed.

This woman's soul was not speaking to him. Yet she did seem to be speaking; he could tell by the look on her face. He took a deep breath.

"You're speaking inside your heart," he said.

She looked startled, blushed like a peach. "How did you know?" she asked.

"I sometimes converse with creatures that have no voice to be heard."

"You can talk to them also?" she asked, her eyes gazing blankly at a spot beneath her feet.

"To whom?"

"The grains of sand," she whispered.

"You talk to sand?" He looked at her, astonished.

She turned away from him. "Never mind. I would rather not have you think I'm a lunatic."

He tried to correct his mistake. "Sometimes I hear my god speaking to me. Once in a long while, I hear the soul of another person. But I never hear *things*. Objects have no voices or emotions—at least, the idols in my father's shop had none."

"None you could hear."

Avram was shocked. "Well, how is the sand feeling?" he asked after a moment.

"Crowded."

Avram laughed in spite of himself. "People feel that way more than you might expect."

"I wouldn't know," the woman said. "I don't talk to people."

"Do you talk to animals?" Avram asked.

"Yes, sometimes. The lamb that piddled on my goddess's skirt was quite pleased with herself."

"I wonder if between us we can hear everything that exists," Avram mused.

"I doubt it. Neither of us can talk to our parents."

Avram laughed. It seemed to him that his god was smiling at them. They began to descend a stepped hillside. "What do you like talking to best?" he asked.

She thought a moment. "Roots," she replied. "I like talking to roots. They have a profound divinity."

"So do people," said Avram.

"Hmmm," said his companion, laughing. "I haven't seen much of that." She was picking her way among the spines of rock behind Avram, her skirts bunched in her hand. Her feet were callused and strong. He hadn't asked her if she ever talked to his god. He was a little afraid of what she would say.

"I have convinced my father to leave Ur," Avram told her. "We are going to a land called Canaan."

"How fortunate for you." The young woman stopped to put on her sandals. "You and your gift will be safe from the king's jealousy."

"You could come with us."

The young woman stared. "I am the heir to a priestly house. I am no wanderer. In any case, the disposition of my person is in my mother's hands. I understand I am engaged to be married."

"Doesn't it suggest something to you, that we found each other here?" Avram said. "Perhaps you were meant to come with me."

"I'm glad we met," she said, averting her eyes, "but I do not believe in providence."

They clambered down the mountain. Although it was dusk, he saw that her face was determined. When sunset came, she told him she could not meet him again. She did tell him, though, how much he had amused her.

A month later they saw each other, by accident, on the city walls where boys sold pomegranate juice. They walked for a few minutes along the ramparts. They were unable to stop themselves. But it was shameful to a woman to be alone with a man. In the end, he had given her a regretful, almost angry farewell, and a half geode full of purple crystals to remember him by. She smiled as he gave it to her, listening.

Since then, Avram had poured his energy into trying to appease his father. Yet now his father wanted to marry him off to a stranger. What would his god think of this marriage? Avram stepped through the curtain to meet his new bride. He was half-hoping that he would hate the woman. He bowed, looking at first only out of the corners of his eyes.

At one side of the room was his mother, Emtelai, frowning slightly, in a green gown. Beside his mother stood his two brothers: Haran, much older than he, and Nahor, much younger. Haran's wife, Levanah, and their children, Milcah, Iscah, and Lot, had crowded into the arched doorway. Milcah was already buxom, giggling and commanding at once. Lot was unfailingly polite, at least in public. Iscah was secretive and stubborn and wise. Avram suppressed a sigh, wondering how long it would be before his two nieces and his nephew faced the ordeal of marriage.

On the other side of the room, closer to the middle of the tiled floor, was a tall woman with milky eyes. Terach had said her name was Nofet. The priestess had a still face and wore a pale blue robe. It seemed that she was blind. Her hand rested on the shoulder of her guide, a young woman in novice's garb. Was this woman his bride? The priestess turned her head to face Avram, her posture eerily perfect. Around her neck was a moon pendant. Nofet fingered it and smiled slightly.

Terach took Avram's arm. Avram finally looked up at the young woman directly in front of him. The loose sleeves of the deep purple robe gave her a regal air. From her jeweled belt hung a half geode brimming with purple crystals, sparkling in the candlelight. Avram looked up into a face veiled with gold.

"Sarai," he said in a breath. And Sarai threw back her head and laughed.

THE REVENGE OF
LOT'S WIFE

*All the sacred gifts that the Israelites set aside for the
Lord I give to you. . . as a due for all time. . . . It shall
be an everlasting covenant of salt before the Lord, for
you and for your offspring as well.*

—NUMBERS 18:19

S top scratching! Believe me, you don't want this stuff under
your fingernails. Sulfur and brimstone are bad for the circu-
lation. Trust me.

Wait a minute. Maybe I appreciate your scratching my nose,
considering that it's been four thousand years since I scratched it
myself. I just want you to listen. Don't call everyone else on the bus!
Especially not that balding guy with the camera! And not that
woman with the bottles of face cream! This is just between us. I
have a sacred task for you to fulfill. I promise you'll be rewarded
with a place in heaven.

What do you mean, you want the story? Are you a reporter? A
novelist? Hasn't your tour guide told you enough stories? I'm not a
mosaic floor, you know. Some things are personal. Wait, don't leave!
I have something I need you to do! Your bus will be here for at least
another twenty minutes! I'll tell you the story!

Yes, I'm Lot's wife. I used to be his accountant, too, when he
had all those sheep. I had four beautiful daughters and a nice house,

but terrible neighbors. *Idit*, my mother used to say to me, *never mind how many rooms you have, the important thing is whether you can trust your neighbors*. But did Lot listen to me? No. He listened to that real estate agent from Zoar. After that fight with Abraham and Sarah, Lot was looking for a big place to show off his success. Ten minutes from the marketplace, the guy said. Temples with the idol of your choice, conveniently located.

When I heard we had to leave Sodom, I was thrilled. I hated the place. No good yogurt to be found, no one ever invited you for *Shabbat*, plus they stoned travelers all the time. You'd have been in hot water if you'd been here four thousand years ago. But I wanted to take all four of my daughters with me. I was getting the two younger ones packed. They were howling over their designer tunics, and I simply couldn't leave the house. In any case, it was clear I couldn't leave Milcah and Iscah with their father—he'd tried to throw them out of the house into a raging mob just to spare the feelings of our guests. I sent Lot out to find our married daughters, Avra and Ayala, and bring them and their good-for-nothing husbands with us. I didn't want to lose any of them. My husband, may he rest in peace on a bed of burning thorns, neglected to inform my two older daughters that we were leaving. He told only his sons-in-law, and they, naturally, refused to accompany us. No one ever takes advice from his father-in-law.

I should have sent one of the angels. Needless to say, when Lot told me our two eldest weren't coming, I was devastated. I was infinitely more devastated on the road to Zoar when I found out he hadn't even asked them. In my agony, I spun around and around, first looking at my poor Milcah and Iscah, in exile, with pathetic small sacks on their backs, then looking at the city, wondering if I could still get Avra and Ayala out of there before the big bang. I looked at the mountains where Lot wanted to resettle my girls in some damp, deserted cave. I looked at the beautiful stone buildings of Sodom, where my daughters were burning. I didn't know where to fix my eyes. I kept whirling until I became completely exhausted, but I couldn't stop. Then something stopped me, like a great hand squeezing my flesh. My skin began to harden, and I became a pillar of salt.

Could God punish a mother for loving her daughters? No, I think it was a kind of mercy. I couldn't bear to leave my older daughters by staying in this world, and I couldn't bear to leave my younger daughters by dying. This was God's compromise. God has made many of those, let me tell you. As I watched my husband and my crying girls disappearing down the road, I knew it wouldn't turn out well.

The first few years I spent consoling Milcah and Iscah. They'd come out to the pillar and weep into their aprons and ask me what to do about their miserable children. Later, their sons went off and founded kingdoms, and my daughters didn't need me so much. I got involved with the landscape, enjoyed the view. Everyone I knew grew old and died. My great-great-granddaughters Ruth and Orpah used to come out and see me. But Ruth went off with Naomi, and Orpah went off with some other woman. After that, I was on my own. By the time of the Talmud, I was thoroughly bored, even though a few rabbis would travel here to recite blessings over me. That was fun, in a way. It gave me an idea.

You see, after the passersby were done reciting their blessings, they'd go over to that pool of bad-smelling groundwater over there and have a drink. For a few hundred years I stared at that pool of water. Now I have a plan. I want to dissolve. That's right. Melt into the water supply. Spend time in the spray of Ein Gedi or in the tangerine grove of a kibbutz. End up in the Volga, or better yet, the East River. I want to infiltrate the whole world.

Why? Because I want revenge. My husband Lot is dead, but there are still men like him. Men who are asked to go to the store and pick up milk, and come home with broccoli and a videotape just to spite you. Men who buy stock in steel mills when you told them to buy high tech. Men who make jokes instead of listening. Men who tell you what you think instead of asking you. Men who give their daughters to mobs out of politeness to their guests! Sons of Lot!

On every husband who doesn't listen to the voice of his wife, I will bring high blood pressure. Heart disease! Watch out, you lummoxes! I'll be in your bowls of salt water on Pesach and in your margaritas by the beach! I'll be in your kosher beef and in your *treif* Chinese food! On *Shabbat*, I'll sprinkle your challah! When you're in the *shvitz*, I'll course through your veins! They'll put you on bland diets! They'll give you bypasses! You'll be sorry you ever heard of Lot's wife!

Excuse me for losing my temper. I certainly won't afflict *your* husband. Unless you think I should.

No husband? A nice girl like you? Don't want one? Well, to each her own. My youngest didn't want one either. No big loss, if you ask me.

Just break me off at the base. You're a big, strapping woman. You've been eating fettucine Alfredo all your life, I can tell. You can do it. No one will know I'm gone. Tourists think every salt pillar in the area is me. Even the tour guides don't know the difference. The Israeli police won't arrest you. Tell them you're exercising your religious freedom. Tell them you've filed a petition with the Israeli Supreme Court asking them to grant equal rights to salt worshipers. They'll leave you alone, I promise. I heard about your generation of women from a passing synagogue director. I'm so impressed with all of you—in my day, when we demonstrated, we couldn't even get a religious divorce for Hagar. But you, you could get ten women together and call yourselves Women of the Salt. Before long, someone would make a documentary about you.

So you're not political. Fine. You don't want fame and fortune. Take pity on my poor daughters, then. They're waiting for me in the other world. I know it. They've probably formed an incest survivors' group, after that terrible business with their father in the cave. Post-traumatic stress disorder, every one of them. I need to see them again, and I will. But I have a mission to accomplish first.

I'm an ancestor of the Messiah, you know. Through my great-granddaughter Ruth, and her great-grandson King David. Who's to say whether I'm not the Messiah's agent? Salt is a sacred substance. Jews use it when they make a blessing over bread on *Shabbat*. Humans need salt to live. Maybe I'll be blessing people while I'm roaming the world. Maybe when I get them to watch their diet, they'll start watching how they treat people, too. Who knows? Maybe this is what God intended all along.

God bless you for this. That feels wonderful! Thank you so much. In four thousand years I haven't soaked my feet. Be well, my dear. I'll see you at your seder. You're having a seder, aren't you? A girl like you should celebrate her freedom. I know how I'm going to celebrate mine.

THE SWITCH

The angel of the Lord called to Abraham a second time from heaven.

—GENESIS 22:15

It was somewhere between the time that the words "burnt offering" left the Divine Throne and the time that it arrived in Abraham's mind that I began to cry. God told me that he would not actually demand Isaac's life, that he would substitute a ram, but that did not console me. If Abraham was going to lift a knife to his son's throat, it meant the end of all my dreams, for him, for Isaac, for the whole people of Israel, whom God had assigned me to protect. My only hope of saving Israel from this soul-killing act was that Abraham might object to God's cruel demand, as he had when God announced the plan to destroy Sodom and Gomorrah. Then I remembered that Sodom and Gomorrah now lay in ruins. Would Abraham believe that his protest had meant anything at all? It was the end of everything I had hoped for.

My name, Michael, means "Who is like God?" and at that moment I thought: Indeed, who is like God? Even Samael, the Satan, the Accuser, would not do this terrible thing to the soul of a whole nation. Then I thought: What if I encouraged Abraham to defy God a second time? What if I tempted Abraham to have compassion? Would my people then be saved? From my place beside the

Divine Throne, I did not really believe that I would succeed in such a rebellion. No, I needed to be someone else. I needed, for a time, to be Samael.

Angels can be anywhere, even in two places at once. Instantly, I arrived at the lowest point of heaven, among the confused and swirling mists. Approaching Samael, I said to the Accuser: "I want to make you an offer."

"The beloved of God wants to make me an offer?" Samael's voice was bitter. It clearly bothered him more than he admitted not to be the beloved of God or humankind. And me, made to give love, he hates most of all.

"Surely you plan to tempt Abraham into disobeying God's request," I said to Samael. "Let me help you. Let me be the one to tempt him. Let me be Samael for a day, and you can be Michael, the beloved."

Samael laughed at me. "Is the angel of Israel planning to thwart God's designs? The Holy One will be furious! How wonderful. This is all most amusing, but I don't think it will work. God may choose to be blind, but I don't think God will mistake me for you, O prince of the Presence. After all, God knows the heart."

"God," I replied with an odd certainty, "will be silent when you arrive at the foot of the Divine Throne. After the command God has given, which obviously plays into your hands, the Holy One will be too embarrassed to confront you. You will be the angel of the Presence, and I will be the Accuser."

"And what will you give me for my trouble?" asked the Satan. "It's no great pleasure for me to sing God's praises for hours while you're off disobeying sacred wishes. What exactly is your offer, guardian of Israel?"

I had thought a long time about what possession of mine Samael would want. "I will reveal to you a secret name of God," I offered hesitantly. "A name that will allow you to invoke God's mercy upon yourself."

"That is a priceless gift," Samael said, "but I have all the names of God I need. I learned them from the pious women I seduced when fallen angels were roaming the earth. In any case, I have no desire for God's mercy. Think again."

I had not expected this. I thought quickly. "I will build for you a palace in the heavens," I said. "You will no longer have to be a wanderer on the earth. You will have a home."

"Ah, but my home is in the heart of humankind, and that suits me. Come now, Michael. Give me something worth my while."

Frustrated, I clenched my fists. "What do you require, Accuser?"

"Sarah, whom you have protected since her birth, whom you defended in the house of Pharaoh, and to whom you announced the birth of Isaac, is a great trouble to me. She is the stalwart root of this new people of yours, and throughout her one hundred twenty-seven years she has thwarted my designs. Cease your protection of her for three days, and I will give you what you ask."

I knew it was not fair to trade Sarah's life for Isaac's, but I thought I saw a flaw in Samael's plan. Abraham's trip would last three days; the Satan would serve as my replacement throughout that time. Surely the Accuser could not harm Sarah while he stood before the Divine Throne. After those three days, I could once again become Sarah's protector, and Samael would be unable to harm her. Hoping I was right, I agreed to Samael's terms and flew away in fear and trembling. Now I was the Tempter, toward the good, I hoped.

I accosted Abraham, Isaac, and their two servants on a rocky hillside at noon on the first day of their journey. I knew Abraham would offer hospitality to an old man leaning on a staff. Isaac went to rest in the shade while Abraham sat with me on a stone. The two servants loitered under an old olive tree, incurious. Abraham offered me some figs. "Where are you going?" I asked.

"To pray," Abraham replied.

"Then why do you need a fire and a knife?"

"We will need to slaughter an animal and bake bread."

Although angels do not usually become angry, I became furious. Abraham was so ashamed of himself that he was lying about the purpose of his journey, but here he was, ready to do this evil thing.

"Friend of God," I cried, determined to shame him into contrition, "don't you know that I was there when God said to you: 'Take your son, your only one, whom you love, and offer him up as a burnt offering?' You may be fooling everyone else, but you're not fooling me."

Abraham sat quietly, a half-smile on his face that only provoked me more. "Have you lost your mind? How can you be planning to kill a son God gave you at the age of a hundred? The most precious thing in your life? Is it fair for God to ask this of you?"

"Even this, I will do," Abraham replied.

"Do you think that faith is all about testing?" I asked. "What if God puts you to an even greater test? Will you be able to pass that one? What about the one after that? When will you finally break?"

"Even more than this, I can withstand," answered Abraham.

I shook my head in sorrow. "Your fate is even worse than you realize. Don't you know that tomorrow God will call you a murderer?"

"I am content with that," Abraham replied, unruffled. He looked over at the cord of wood Isaac had stacked on the ground, and said no more.

I gave up, and peered down at Isaac, resting beneath a bush.

His deep black eyes were shining. Although he was a grown man, he seemed to me like a youth.

"Where are you going?" I asked him.

"To study the law."

"Indeed? Will you be studying it alive or dead?" My sarcasm shocked me. My gentle angelic nature was eroding, and my patience as well. Would these two persist in their deadly conspiracy with God?

"One learns only while living," Isaac said.

"Don't you know he's going to kill you up there on that mountain?" I asked. "Don't you know how unhappy your mother, Sarah, will be, who has loved you and cherished you, who prayed so hard for your birth? Your father has gone mad! Will you obey him and have no compassion on your mother?" Tears rolled down my face as I thought of Sarah, my protégé, holding her dead son in her arms.

"I accept my fate, whatever it may be," answered Isaac boldly, though his young eyes were frightened. "I do not trust you, Accuser, or anything you say to me."

I saw that my new role was working against me, but I could not be silent. "Isaac, if you persist on this path, your brother, Ishmael, will take everything that is now yours, right down to the coats your mother sews for you."

At this, Isaac's face clouded over. "Father!" he exclaimed.

"Here I am, my son," Abraham answered from his place on the rock.

"Here are the firestone and the wood, but where is the ram for the burnt offering?"

"God will provide the ram for the burnt offering, my son."

Then Abraham and Isaac walked on together, without me. The servants followed. On the rocky hillside, a bitterly disappointed angel remained.

Then, desperate, l ran ahead of the four men. In an instant, my fluid angelic body melted into a wide stream. Perhaps if Abraham has more time to consider, I thought, he will change his mind. And indeed, when Abraham, Isaac, and the servants arrived at my banks, they halted. The water was obviously too deep to cross. For a long moment they seemed confused about what to do. Believing I had stopped them, I breathed a sigh of relief. Then Abraham, the man of faith, began to walk into the water, encouraging the three other men to follow him. When the water reached his neck, he began to pray. Against my will, my watery self began to dry up and disappear. God was working against me, just as God always works against the Accuser. I had lost my divine protection, and Isaac had lost his. Had I ruined everything by surrendering my place in heaven?

The four forms receding into the distance, one much smaller than the others, made me want to weep. My heart went out to the loving father and son. They must be in agony by now, imagining what was to come. Surely part of Isaac had believed my words about his fate. Now he had lost his innocence and knew he was going to die. Maybe I had taken away his last comfort, and Abraham's as well.

"Wait!" I called after them, breaching God's silence, hoping to make them turn back. "It is only a mock trial! Behind the heavenly curtain, I heard that there is a ram for the offering—Isaac will not be harmed!"

Abraham and Isaac continued on. Neither one believed me.

I leaped ahead with heavenly speed. Isaac and Abraham separated from their companions and began to climb Mount Moriah. It was really happening. I could think of only one thing to do. My angelic senses had dimmed from my three-day stay on earth, but I reached out nevertheless, and found the ram God had prepared as a substitute for Isaac.

I found the soft and radiant creature tangled in a bush and took it in my arms. Spotting a small cave in the side of the mountain, I placed the ram there, out of harm's way. Then I changed form again, becoming a ram as woolly, as cleanly soft as this one. I knew I had to hurry. I had conceived another plan. I would come to Abraham in the form of an innocent ram; and he, seeing the love in my eyes, would hold back his knife.

Yet as I gathered myself to leap up the mountainside, I felt a wind beneath me lift me from the ground and bear me through the air. At first I thought God was speeding me on my way, but then I found myself caught in a thornbush, my horns tangled in prickly vines. The more I struggled, the more entangled I became. I could not reach the altar Abraham had built. Even more horrible—I was unable to change form. I was trapped in the ram's body.

Horrified, I saw Abraham lift the slaughtering knife over his bound son. The eyes of both men were dry. In heaven, the angels wept bitterly.

"It is unnatural," one angel cried to God, "for a man to kill his son."

"Does Abraham the generous find no generosity before you?" sobbed another.

"Surely," cried Gabriel, the most daring of all, "you are a liar! You promised Abraham that he would produce seed through Isaac. What has become of your oath now?"

Even from my place in the thornbush, I felt the clouds of glory shake and rumble. "Michael," thundered the voice of God, "stop Abraham. Call out to him and tell him not to harm the boy."

Was God speaking to me? Caught in the thorns, I could do nothing. No, it was to Samael that God now spoke. Samael stood in my place, pretending to be me. Was God humoring—or testing—our switched roles? To fulfill the task I had given over to him, Samael would have to execute God's command as if he were truly the guardian of Israel. Although the Satan had been created to inflame the evil urge of humankind, although he would hate the thought of saving a life, he would have no choice. To disobey a direct order from God, that was forbidden even to the Accuser.

He did not need to disobey, I thought sadly, to achieve his evil designs. Abraham had done all the damage already, by raising the blade over his son. It made no difference whether Isaac lived or died. I pricked up my ram's ears to listen for Samael's voice.

"Abraham, Abraham," called Samael.

Abraham answered, "Here I am."

"Lay not your hand upon the boy, neither do anything to him."

Samael fell silent. Then, astonishingly, God added: "For I know you are a righteous man, yet you did not withhold your son, your only one, from Me."

I was stunned. Had Abraham in fact failed the test? Did God count it a sin that Abraham lifted the knife, that he showed no compassion toward his own son? This was exactly what I had feared. I had believed from the beginning that Abraham was never meant to comply with God's terrible command, but Abraham had followed it unthinkingly. Now, because of Abraham's failure, his seed would surely be rejected, and I would never have a nation to protect. The Accuser had won.

Then, all of a sudden, I managed to struggle free from the thicket. Frantically, I caught at Abraham's robe with my ram's mouth. Startled, the patriarch turned around quickly. As I gazed into Abraham's face, I saw in the old man's eyes a sense of awakening. Abraham knew that he had failed the test.

The angel's voice should have been my own voice. By raising my hand to Isaac, I betrayed God's trust, for I failed to honor what God has taught me.

Staring into his eyes, I saw that Abraham repented of the evil he had been about to do, knowing that he had been ready to kill the innocent in God's name.

Then the Satan called to Abraham a second time from heaven: "By myself I swear, God declares, because you have done this and have not withheld your son, your only one, I will bless you and multiply you like the stars of heaven and the sands on the seashore, and your descendants shall seize the gates of their foes. All the nations of the earth shall bless themselves by your descendants, because you have obeyed my command."

Even I had to admit it was a brilliant move. The Accuser had cleverly negated God's stern admonition by promising Abraham a reward for his compliance rather than a punishment. Yet God said nothing to contradict what Samael had said. As Abraham listened to Samael's words, he forgot God's sadness and he forgot what he had seen when he had stared into my eyes. Couldn't he tell the difference between God's voice and Samael's? Did he purposely overlook the difference between the voices because he wanted to believe that he had not made a mistake, that he had not sinned? On fire with his innocence, Abraham caught me by the folds in my white neck, hauled me up onto the altar and slit my throat. He did not see my soul rising to heaven. He did not notice his son, crouched shivering on a nearby stone. Instead, Abraham turned his thoughts to his enemies.

Because of my faith, my foes will be as the slaughtered ram.

Freed from my earthly body, I flew back up to heaven, but my wings had no strength. How could I ever forget the look of joyous faith in Abraham's eyes as he had shed my blood? I arrived before the Divine Throne, ready to repent and be destroyed. By giving the Accuser room to speak, I had failed Israel. Like a bereaved bird, I put my head under my wing and mourned.

When I looked up, I saw that Samael no longer occupied my place at God's right hand. In the empty space was a single ram's horn, hollowed out as if by lightning. "Where is the ram?" I whispered, but heard only silence.

I felt undeserving of the horn, so I picked it up, trudged across the sapphire pavement of heaven, and handed it to Gabriel, the angel of courage. "Here, old friend," I said, drawing back my hand.

Gabriel looked at me sadly. "Oh, Michael," he said. "Samael blessed Abraham with triumph over his enemies, but if Abraham had held back the knife, God surely would have rewarded him with eternal peace, and he would never have had any enemies. How much we all have lost!"

My heart was broken. Beneath us, Abraham trudged down the path toward Hebron, his severe faith untempered. Isaac wandered alone over the mountains, and angels showered him with their tears. Though Samael was gone, I could not step back to my place by the Throne of God. In my heart, I was still the ram, not the angel of God's Presence.

My eyes fell once again on the path to Hebron, and there was Samael. So that was where he had gone after twisting God's message. Horrified, I remembered Sarah, as I saw Samael descending on her tent.

Then God spoke from heaven, saying to the Accuser: "Beware, for you still stand in Michael's place. I forbid you to act with deceit."

"Such warning is unnecessary," Samael replied, with a dignity I hated. "Today I am your messenger, your right hand. I go to announce the truth to Sarah, just as Michael did when Isaac was born."

And so, at the final moment of the third day of Abraham's journey, Samael appeared to Sarah in the form of a beautiful angel. He told her how Abraham had lifted the knife to cut her son's throat. As I cried out from heaven in shock and protest, Sarah doubled over and let out a wailing sound, the sound of a ram's horn. Felled by her grief, she died, whispering words only God heard.

So it came to pass that Abraham, father of Israel, returned to an empty tent. When his servants told him what had happened to Sarah, he mourned for her, mother of his people, who had waited so long to give birth to a single child. He mourned for the wife who had shared his vision with him. As he grieved, his compassion returned; for a moment, he blamed himself for Sarah's death and was sorry he had driven away her son. Had he been right, that moment when he looked into the eyes of the ram? Had he truly failed the test? Should he have refused to slaughter Isaac, maybe even refused to slaughter the ram? Would Sarah be alive now if he had stood up to God as he had on the hills above Sodom and Gomorrah?

From my crouch on the floor of heaven, I timidly gave thanks. Where I had failed, Samael had succeeded, despite his wicked intentions. It was funny, in a dark sort of way. Although Sarah's death had been meant to destroy the people of Israel, instead it had saved them. It had reawakened Abraham's compassion. In his mourning, he would come to understand what Samael had tried to keep from him: that he had failed God on Moriah, by closing his heart to his son. Sarah's death, at least, would teach him that.

I heard God's voice speak a second time to Samael: "You have done Michael's work, as he has done yours. You have no right to be angry. Return to your place."

Samael returned to the lowest place in heaven. I understood with a grateful heart that God was also speaking to me, accepting my repentance and offering me a task. This time, I could perform it as myself. I flew to Abraham's tent as I had once before, in a robe that hid my folded wings, and whispered to him: "Milcah has borne children to your brother Nahor: Uz his firstborn; Buz his brother; and Kemuel the father of Aram, Keshed, Chazo, Pildash, Yidlaf, and Betuel; and Betuel begat Rebekah . . ."

Abraham, remembering the announcement of Isaac's birth, smiled at my words. When he thought of Sarah's joy back then, tears flowed down his cheeks. I placed the ram's horn, which I had taken back from Gabriel, in the old man's hand. Abraham tested its strong, clear sound, which had the ring of Sarah in it. Then he set out toward the mountain to find his wandering son and bring him home.

THE HOUSE OF
THE MATRIARCHS

...the fire that enters every secret seam
of stone or leaf or flesh, a deity
beneath whose blows the hide of things is torn
and all that is at last is read as one
or ashes.

> —ALLEN MANDELBAUM, *Chelmaxioms*

Don't I know you from somewhere?
Didn't I used to be you?

> —ALICIA OSTRIKER, "Neoplatonic Riff"

SECOND BLESSINGS

I

Esau realized that the Canaanite women displeased his father Isaac. So Esau went to Ishmael and took to wife, in addition to the wives he had, Mahalat the daughter of Ishmael, sister of Nevayot.

—GENESIS 28:8–9

As I rode into camp, I saw how the peaks of the tents echoed the peaks of the mountains. This is a mountain family, steep and sheer. Esau stopped our caravan at the center of a circle of blue cloth slopes. I felt a wave of homesickness and wished for my mother, Aisha. The wind blew, and I could feel her fingers in my hair, braiding precious stones into it in preparation for this day. I reached up to touch my jeweled braids, and thought of my father, Ishmael, who had lost his only daughter when I nodded my head *yes, I will go.*

I dismounted from my she-camel slowly, carefully. Her harness bells tinkled softly in the silence. Looking up, I saw a whole host of stately men and women in brightly colored robes. They stared at me with great interest. I am shy by nature, and it was too much for me. After all, these were the people who had cast my father and grandmother into the desert. Might they do the same to me? I felt sick to my stomach as I delivered my grandmother's formal message to her first husband, Abraham. When I finally collapsed during Isaac's speech of welcome, Esau put his arm around me and brought me into his tent. It was a grand one, wide and brown, which used to belong to his mother, Rebekah. My last thought as I dropped off into a feverish sleep was of the red hairs on the back of Esau's hand. Fortunately, I was better when it was time for the wedding feast. We were married outside, since Esau loves the outdoors. He takes a special pleasure in the wilderness.

Esau seems to desire me and resent me at the same time. I am his concession, his proper wife, to offset the two wives his parents do not like. I wear modest garments; I pray to one God, as my grandmother Hagar did before me. Being a descendant of Abraham, I come from the right family. Sarah might have objected to me, of course, but Sarah is long dead. My marriage to Esau has sealed the peace between Sarah's children and the Ishmaelites. Therefore, I am valuable. I fit into the camp routine, am already known as a good worker with a gentle voice. To Esau's family I am normal, but to him I am strange. Sometimes he does not even speak to me before taking me, as if he thinks that women do not understand his language.

Yet I am drawn to him, to his strength and honesty and the curls of red hair on his chest. I remember my grandmother musing about Abraham's deep silences. Esau has the same silences, though not the same quietude. I am sympathetic to his feeling that he is never good enough. It is a feeling I share. In return, he comforts me when I feel like a stranger, awkwardly putting his arm around my shoulders. Esau and I are beginning to learn about each other. He shares my tent often. Nevertheless, it is not only him I have married. There is a whole family of women here, not one of them as I expected.

Rebekah, the tribal matriarch, is like a wraith beneath her regal purple robes, though Esau told me she was strong and proud.

I whisper with her women, who have been with her since she left her home long ago. They tell me that she misses her son Jacob. Jacob was sent away many months ago to marry another proper wife, a kinswoman of Rebekah's, in faraway Haran. He was her favorite son, her brilliant heir. She is lonely without him.

Yehudit is Esau's fierce and talkative second wife. Her bronze earrings have sharp edges. There is something violent about her. When she gets a chance, she darkly whispers to me that Jacob left only because Esau might have killed him. Jacob stole Esau's blessing, she says. He tricked his blind father into giving him, the younger son, a promise of greatness. It was Rebekah's idea, Yehudit tells me, with a hard edge of anger in her voice. I know that Yehudit hates Rebekah. She knows that Rebekah does not approve of her, because she is a Canaanite who keeps her household gods. When Yehudit pours out wine to the sun, Rebekah glares from her tent. Sometimes Yehudit says that Rebekah tricked Esau out of his blessing because the old woman despised Esau's wives. Yehudit never misses an opportunity to remind me that I am merely Esau's concession to his mother.

Esau's chief wife, Bosmat, is a frost-cold woman, with eyes like stones at midnight. Her father was a warrior, and she has always wanted to be like him. She is proud and unflinching. Her breasts are heavy and soft, but her hands are hard and disciplined. Her feelings lie deep within her, like jewelry in a burial cairn. Yet sometimes she smiles when she mixes a new perfume, and wrinkles her nose. Because of this, Keturah likes her. Keturah is the wife of the old patriarch Abraham, and she is popular throughout the camp because she is generous and laughs easily. Also, she is a good cook. Keturah takes the honored place at mealtime. Yet Rebekah is the real mistress here, and she is more intimidating than all the other women. I cannot be angry at her for helping to steal Esau's blessing. She seems too ancient and strong for my anger, more like an old olive tree than a woman.

By the fire at night, I listen to Yehudit whisper of blessings. I feel a sense of loss. I too want to be blessed, to share in Abraham's mysterious connection to God. I remember an old story of my family, which is told in Esau's camp as well. My grandmother, Hagar, wife of Abraham, once spoke to El Ro'i, God who sees. This is what God said: "I will greatly increase your offspring, and they shall be too many to count." While Esau sleeps, I whisper to him that he will inherit this blessing from me. I do not want to tell him while he is awake. He has a terrible temper. I am afraid he will be angry with me if I so much as say the word "blessing."

The old patriarch Abraham takes a great interest in me. I am his sole connection to his cast-out son, Ishmael. Abraham leads me on long walks through the mountains, pointing out the altars he has built. Sometimes he speaks to me of his mother. His wife, Keturah, is kind to me and offers me delicacies from her good-smelling pots. Even blind Isaac, who is almost a recluse, smiles at me and tells me how much he loved my father, Ishmael. It is a good thing that I have some allies here. Bosmat and Yehudit resent me. I am the new one. Sometimes I wonder if they would like me better if I were not so popular with Esau's family. The truth is that Bosmat and Yehudit would have resented me anyway. That is how it is with elder wives. Hagar told me, long ago.

II

*As I stand by the spring of water, let the
young woman who comes out to draw and to
whom I say, "Please, let me drink a little*

water from your jar," and who answers, "You
may drink, and I will also draw for your
camels," let her be the wife whom the Lord has
decreed for my master's son.

—GENESIS 24:43–44

I have found a friend in an unexpected place. I was leaning over a heavy water bucket, exhausted and unable to lift it. A sinewy hand grabbed the handle and hauled it up for me. The hand held the bucket for me to drink, and I did so eagerly, for the sun was hot and I had been working in its rays for many hours. Looking at the face above the hand, I realized it was Rebekah. Her indigo cowl had fallen down around her shoulders. Her silver hair lay uncovered, long and beautiful.

"I used to draw water for my family," she said in explanation.

"I, too," I replied. "It was my time to think."

"Yes," agreed Rebekah. She was quiet a minute. "Mahalat, would you come to card wool with me? The flocks have increased this year. I could use your help."

Her wise, sun-wrinkled face reminded me of my mother, Aisha. I held the bucket so that Rebekah could drink as well. Then I walked with her to her tent. We talked for hours as we carded, finding more and more things in common. We both had grown up in households run by strong women. My grandmother was Hagar the Egyptian, who ruled a tribe of archers. Her grandmother Milcah, Abraham's niece, was the head of a large herding family in Haran. We both remembered hurriedly packing for a marriage in a strange place, having agreed to a destiny without certainty. By evening, I felt courageous. I admitted that I was unsure around my temperamental husband. Rebekah nodded in recognition. After a while, we forgot to card wool. We spoke of our prayers for children, then of our sly brothers Lavan and Nevayot, and the riches they had gained by marrying us off. We compared our pearl earrings. Darkness fell. Always the timid one, I was afraid to go back to my tent. I lay down on one of Rebekah's rich purple rugs, and she sang to me. The sadness in her voice told me that I reminded her of Jacob. Isaac tripped over me when he came back from his evening walk with Esau, and was startled. Rebekah asked him to let me stay.

Now Rebekah and I spend many of our evenings together, giggling and telling stories. Rebekah says I am like the daughter she never had. Once I passed her while she was praying at sunset, and I heard her say that God had given her comfort for the loss of Jacob. I am glad to have made Rebekah smile again, although Esau grumbles that his mother doesn't need another favorite. I try to explain to him her pain, her choices. I am bolder with him now, and also more tender.

The other wives still resent me, but it bothers me less. I smile at them when they gossip. When Esau falls asleep on my belly at night, I think of my father and my grandmother. Ishmael and Hagar, their names fast becoming legend. I wonder if it would heal their anger to know that Abraham's household is warm around me, as it once was around them.

III

When Esau was forty years old, he took to wife Yehudit daughter of Beeri the Hittite, and Bosmat daughter of Elon the Hittite, and they were a source of bitterness to Isaac and Rebekah.

—GENESIS 26:34–35

Yehudit's body was discovered this morning. She had been dancing on the edge of the well, showing gratitude for the gift of water. During such dances she always closed her eyes. She fell in, crushing her skull and orphaning her young daughter. It is unclear whether it was an accident, a suicide, or a human sacrifice so that Esau would regain his blessing. Yehudit could never accept his loss.

Esau is deeply shaken. Of his three wives, Yehudit was most like him, impulsive and brooding. He weeps passionately and has paid a large sum for an elaborate burial. It will be a Hittite burial as she would have wished. Bosmat comforts him with her abundant body, but he is suspicious of her grief. He knows Yehudit was her rival. Also, she is not entirely convincing. Bosmat is hard in her ways; the work of consolation is not easy for her.

When Yehudit fell, I went to Rebekah and begged her to go to her son. She refused. She knows she made Yehudit's life difficult. "He doesn't want me," she said. That was partly true, but I insisted. I know his heart, how much he loves her even now. Finally, she pushed out through the tent flap. A few minutes later, I was afraid that I had done the wrong thing. I ran after her. I found Rebekah in Esau's tent, holding him while he sobbed on her shoulder. Tears from Rebekah's eyes fell into Esau's copper-colored hair. She gave him her blessing, again and again.

I am glad to be the instrument of forgiveness. I am even more glad that two people I love can love each other. The camp is still in mourning, yet somehow a burden has been lifted. Esau's silences are not as bitter now. Yehudit's death has broken Esau's grip on his resentment at what he is not. He is starting to find out what he is. Maybe that was her gift to him.

I do wonder about her death. It is unusual for a mountain dweller to slip so carelessly. Did Yehudit strike a bargain for Esau's happiness? Did she miss her own people too bitterly? Was there someone else she loved, some lithe handmaid or stable boy? Or did she just forget her own mortality one morning?

When the latest tragedy blows over, Rebekah and I will go on pilgrimage. Keturah will leave Abraham's side to join us. Our excuse is that we wish to pray, since I am not yet pregnant. There are other, truer, reasons. Keturah needs to get away from her many children. Rebekah, as usual, needs time to think. I would be glad to have a child, but mostly I want my life to be uncomplicated for a while. I need time to find blessings for myself.

IV

And she called the Lord who spoke to her
"You are El-Ro'i," by which she meant: "Have
I not gone on seeing after he saw me!" There-
fore the well was called Beer-lahai-ro'i. It is
between Kadesh and Bered.

—Genesis 16:13–14

It was near the wilderness of Kadesh that I found my grand-mother's God. Rebekah, Keturah, and I had made camp. Rebekah lit two fires in our tent and invoked Sarah's presence. Keturah built an altar nearby and burned sweet-smelling incense. I took a jug of water and some bread, and set off on a journey. It is still unclear to me how I became lost. It must have been God's doing. Two hours after I had run out of water, I became genuinely frightened and called out for help many times, with a dry tongue.

I sat down beneath a bush for shade and became almost uncon-scious, but then a small black bird appeared out of nowhere. It alighted near me on the sand. Hopping up and down, it chirped at me in words I thought I recognized. Mahalat, granddaughter of Hagar, where have you come from? Where are you going?

Rising from my resting place, I followed the slowly hopping bird over the next hill. There was the well, my grandmother's well. God had shown it to her in the desert while Ishmael lay nearly dying of thirst. I approached it in awe. Near the well lay a waterskin, a worn one. I had seen it often, in a place of honor in my grandmother's tent. I picked it up and held it to my belly, then filled it and drank from it. I knew that Hagar had died. I also knew that I was pregnant.

With the small dark bird perched on my shoulder, I took an oath to call my first child Reuel. The name would serve as a monument to Hagar's God, El-Ro'i. It would remind Esau that his children shared in a blessing. I closed my eyes and felt the presence of a seeing God. After many minutes I opened them, watching the desert. The bird took wing, leading me toward camp.

When I returned to the little tent beneath the desert sky, Rebekah and Keturah were waiting for me. Neither of them seemed anxious that I had been gone so long. "What did God say?" Rebekah inquired.

"I will greatly increase your offspring, and they shall be too many to count," I replied. That made Rebekah laugh loudly. Keturah told me that God had said much the same thing to both of them.

V

Esau took his wives from among the Canaanite women—Adah daughter of Elon the Hittite, and Oholivamah daughter of Anah daughter of Tzivon the Hivite—and also Bosmat daughter of Ishmael and sister of Nevayot. Adah

*bore to Esau Elifaz, Bosmat bore Reuel, and
Oholivamah bore Ye'ush, Yalam, and Korach.
. . .Timna was a concubine of Esau's son Elifaz, she bore Amalek to Elifaz. . . . The children of Tzivon were these: Ayah and Anah—
that was the Anah who discovered the hot
springs in the wilderness. . . . The children of
Anah were these: Dishon and Anah's daughter, Oholivamah.*

—GENESIS 36:2–5,12,24–25

When the camp got word that Jacob was returning from
Haran, Esau disappeared for days. My son, Reuel, did not ask me
where his father had gone, as he might have when he was younger.
He simply became silent. It was up to me to tell him the old story
of Jacob's deception.

There are larger implications to that story, but they were lost
on my son. Reuel seemed excited that he had twelve cousins he had
never seen. He dashed outside my tent to discuss the matter with his
siblings. As Reuel pushed out of our high-peaked tent that summer
day, my rival came in, carrying her grandson Amalek on her back.

Her name is Adah now, though it was Bosmat once. Bosmat
was the name Esau gave her when they were wed: the spice of his
life. It was the custom among her people to give the chief wife a special name. Years later, after the birth of Reuel, Esau made me chief
wife. He gave me the name Bosmat as a kind of trophy. Adah was
forced to go back to her childhood name. It made her old. As for
me, I did not want the name Bosmat: I was happy with my name
Mahalat, which means forgiveness. Yet it is hard for Esau to give,
and when he looked at me with his amber eyes and curling, silver-
ing red hair, I was forced to accept his gift.

"You've heard about Jacob," Adah stated in her voice like an iron chariot. "There will be war between our tribes."

"Perhaps not," I said quietly, lifting Amalek from his grandmother's back and taking him into my lap. "Forgiveness is always possible."

"Is it?" Adah asked coldly. "Perhaps for one who has enough of everything."

Amalek began to squall loudly. I tried to soothe him, Adah snatched him from my arms. Amalek's mother is Timna, a concubine of Adah's son. Timna's claim to fame is that she was a precocious child at Isaac's weaning party. The girl asked Sarah to accept her as a worshiper of Sarah's God. Sarah refused. It hurt Timna deeply. Now that the woman is part of Esau's family, her bitterness has seeped into Adah, who also feels rejected. If Adah has her way, Jacob will be destroyed.

"Amalek has many brothers," Adah said to me, slapping the crying baby soundly. "If he is to make a place for himself, he will need to defeat them, not forgive them."

Adah is very lonely. She does not like her daughters-in-law. Sometimes she breaks down and asks Esau to let her come to flush out birds for him in the brush. She used to do that for her father, and she is good at it. My sense is that she does not like her own neediness. Maybe one day I will take her out into the desert with me to search for my grandmother's well. It may not work, but it is worth the attempt.

We sat quietly in the tent. My daughter, Elah, came running toward us through pools of hot sun. "Father has a woman with him," she cried. I pulled up my black embroidered skirts and stepped outside. Adah followed me. I squinted in the bright light. When I could see, my eyes found the face of my husband. Next to him was standing a woman with jet black hair, a white robe hanging loosely on her thin frame. Esau seemed embarrassed to see his two wives.

"This is Oholivamah the prophetess," he told us. He was blushing. "She dwells by the hot springs of Anah. My father, Isaac, told me of her once. I journeyed to her to ask how I might destroy Jacob."

The prophetess gave a sudden, brilliant smile. "Destroying Jacob was not his destiny," she said.

Esau nodded and went on. "The first night I sat in the hot springs, I dreamed confused, bloody dreams. All my fantasies of vengeance over the years visited me. I wanted to leave then and carry out my fantasies, but Oholivamah stopped me. On the second night, I dreamed only of running away. In the morning I wanted to go, but something kept me by the water. On the third night, Oholivamah sat by me, and I dreamed a dream, such a dream, my wives. I dreamed that I was an angel of God. I shone like the sun. I flew to Jacob and wrestled with him. All night we wrestled, but neither of us could win. In the end, I wounded him, and I blessed him. *I* gave *him* a blessing, can you imagine that? I gave him a new name, Israel, because I see that his work is to wrestle with God. I can value that in him. I am free now."

Esau paused. Oholivamah bowed to us. "Your husband also has a new name," she said. "He has given his strength to the land. He has sacrificed much. He has honored and cared for his parents, who gave him life. He is to be called Edom, red earth, for the place from which life comes."

Esau smiled at the prophetess. "I am ready to face my brother," he said. "I am finally ready."

"There is more." Adah spoke coldly from behind me.

Esau looked down, hiding his amber gaze. "Yes, there is more. I have asked Oholivamah to be my wife. This is part of my destiny."

"How kind destiny is to us." Adah stalked off into the cluster of tents. Her grandson wailed. I remembered how I felt, riding into camp a decade before. There was nothing for me to do except welcome Oholivamah with kind words. Esau left to gather the six hundred men he would take to escort his brother home to Hebron. His sons followed him, begging to hear the story of his nighttime wrestling.

When the men had gone, Oholivamah took my arm and drew me aside, smiling. Her white robe shone in the sunlight like the feathers of a bird.

"Don't fear me," she whispered. "I am not the next Bosmat. I will only stay three years, long enough to give birth to three sons. Then I must return to my springs."

I clapped her on the shoulder, recognizing another woman who drew prophecy from wells. I knew I would learn much in the coming years. "I suppose Esau had to marry four wives," I chuckled. "He is Jacob's twin, after all."

I looked forward to the moment when Jacob and Esau would embrace. I also looked forward to the night after that, when he would come to me and touch me with healed hands. Whatever miracle had entered him, I hoped it would one day enter Adah, Timna, and Amalek as well.

At the end of three years, after Esau's father, Isaac, died, Oholivamah guided us to the land of Seir. Seir was the land God gave to Esau as his inheritance, full of birds and crags and sweet water. Esau loved it on sight. Over and over again, he shouted in his great voice to hear the echoes bounce off the rounded mountains. As I walked its borders, I sometimes heard the gentle noises of my grandmother's well.

Oholivamah has returned to the hot springs. Rebekah and Keturah have passed from this world. I miss them, but my daughter, Elah, is old enough to work at my side, and Reuel has become a fine archer and a good father. Esau is still the fiercest delight of my heart. He has grown into his new name, Edom, as the roots of a tree grow to fit the rocks beneath them. It is hard and rewarding to build a life in a new place, in this mountain of Seir. It troubles me that Adah still refuses to come to the well with me, but I must give it time.

MITOSIS

So Rachel died and was buried on the road to Efrat,
which is Bethlehem. Over her grave Jacob set up a pil-
lar . . . and Israel journeyed on.

    —GENESIS 35:19–21*

There are four faces of Israel:
Jacob, Israel, Rachel, Leah;
Israel with Leah, Jacob with Rachel.

    —ZOHAR 3:281B

L eah's hands were cramped from holding her reed pen. It was one of the many she had taught herself to shave and use. She stretched her arms out above her, feeling tired. She was always tired now. It took an effort to be content. It was hard work to pour herself onto words on parchment, when she would rather sleep and lose her awareness in dreams. It was difficult to strain her eyes by candlelight, looking for holy knowledge among her parents' old scrolls. It was a trouble to seek her mother's God, when now her whole household worshiped other household deities. She was so far from any instruction. But what was difficult was also what she loved, and so she stayed awake.

* Author's translation

Somewhere in the late afternoon, Rachel was walking with Jacob, trading easy, bantering words with her betrothed. Only yesterday, Rachel had come back to the women's house with wide, bright eyes, telling of how her lover had saved her from a marauding wolf. It made a good story, Leah thought wryly, but Rachel and Jacob did not write stories, only lived them.

Of course, Leah too loved Jacob. How not? He was intelligent and energetic, capable and kind. None of Lavan's cousins, servants, or hirelings met Jacob's measure. Her sister, Rachel, knew of her love, and the fact made the two uncomfortable with each other. Trying to cure what could not be cured, Rachel had once suggested that Leah journey to their aunt Rebekah's new home. There, she could marry Esau, Jacob's rough, ungentle brother. Leah had wept at the thought. After that, Rachel had kept her advice to herself.

Because she was his favorite child and because of her usefulness, Lavan did not press Leah to marry. Leah was the recorder for the camp. She often sat by her father's side, recording the number of sheep, of goats, of dates. Countless things. Leah loved to study things, watching their colors and angles. The soft wool of a lamb pleased her much as Jacob's hair did. Almost, almost.

The crunch of pebbles outside her small shed raised her from her reverie. It was Jacob. Leah rubbed her eyes and stood to welcome her cousin. "I brought you the food you asked for," Jacob said without ceremony, placing a large sack at Leah's feet. He smiled engagingly. In the early evening, Leah made rounds to the local poor and elderly, to feed them and to offer her services as a recorder of names and contracts. Few of the neighbors could write or read.

"You seem excited," Leah commented quietly, in an easy tone of voice. She had been Jacob's confidante for years. She listened to him rave when Lavan had cheated him, counseled him when he had quarreled with Rachel. Leah was Jacob's friend, a fellow intellect and sympathetic ear. She did not think he had ever realized that she loved him.

Jacob grinned. "It's been seven years to the day since I came to your family," he said.

"I know," replied Leah. She put aside her reed with a sharp, efficient motion, and closed her eyes slightly, resting them.

Jacob went on, exultant. "Tonight, I'll ask Laban to plan my wedding to Rachel. He'll have to agree. My term of service is up, and I've waited so long to have Rachel as my bride! Finally, I'll be able to go back to my mother and father. My parents have waited a long time for another generation. Now I can continue their tradition."

Leah nodded and smiled. "Don't worry," she said. "You have served my father well, and he cannot deny you what he has promised."

"You're right," Jacob said, and turned to go. "Zilpah asked to accompany you on your rounds," he commented over his shoulder. "She's waiting for you in the house."

"I'll be glad to have her," Leah said. Bilhah's little sister, Zilpah, was devoted to Leah, and Leah was grateful for the friendship. Rachel had been her anchor once, but no more. Perhaps, Leah thought, her lost mother could see her from the milky starstream they had watched together long ago. Surely God could see her. She wondered what God saw. Something, she imagined, like the diffuse, aching mist that settled on the camp in winter. Something like that.

It was late when Leah and Zilpah returned from their charitable errands. Leah took deep gulps of the night air, staying in starlight as long as she could. Zilpah hurried ahead, chilled and a little nervous of the dark. In the chambers of Lavan's womenfolk, candles were still burning.

"Good news! Lavan finally permitted the wedding," Zilpah's mother, Anan, told the two women as they entered. "Rachel will be married tomorrow night." Rachel was enthroned on a pillow at the center of the room. She looked shyly at her elder sister.

"That's wonderful, Rachel. Many blessings on your marriage," Leah enthused with only a slight strain in her voice. Rachel was wise enough not to press her sister. She embraced Leah warmly before turning back to Bilhah. Bilhah, always efficient, was suggesting ideas for Rachel's wedding garments. Leah retreated to her small room in the corner of the house.

Zilpah ran after her, brown braids flying. She came upon Leah silently hunched on her bed, tears spotting her blue robe. Zilpah stroked Leah's head and cooed, mourning wordlessly like a dove. Zilpah could feel Leah's pain as if it were a tangible creature, as if it would raid the sheepfolds and devour everything there.

"I need air," Leah whispered, squeezing Zilpah's hand. Zilpah held on, trembling. Then she let go, and Leah ran outside, cloaking herself in darkness.

Past the herds, past her shed, Leah raced, stopping at the crest of a small hill. Her eyes had dried and now burned, like a kettle left boiling too long. Leah threw her arms up to the sky, which seemed to wheel above her in circles. The hill's edges dissolved in fog. Leah began to fear she had run too far in her grief. Things looked wrong somehow, out of phase. Time seemed to stand still. There were no stars.

By the olive tree at the foot of the hill, there was a sudden movement. Leah peered into the mist, hunching into the tall grass. She discerned a vague, flickering outline. A blurred man-shape was walking toward her. It was blue as if with cold, silver as if scorched by the moon. The figure came closer and closer. Leah waited, wondering why she did not run away. A deep shiver caught her body and shook it.

After a few minutes, the man stood before her. He was tall and strong. His hair was like a thundercloud, black wool lined with light. Crouching, he reached for Leah's hand. She could not feel his fingers.

Leah jerked away, thinking a ghost had come to devour her soul. Then she peered at the figure more closely, and saw something she recognized. "Jacob?" she ventured timidly.

The man smiled. "Almost. I am what Jacob will be in another time of his life. Like Esau, I am his mirror, his second self. I split from Jacob on the night God gave him his second name, and God has brought me out of that future to speak to you. My name is Israel."

Were it not for her mother's, Dinah's, many legends, Leah would have been sure she had gone insane. But her mother had told her that there are worlds beyond this world. So Leah waited, trembling, to hear what the future had to say to her.

Israel paced for a minute before speaking. His feet made no sound on the green hillside. "Leah, I have come to ask you to marry me."

"But Jacob," Leah stammered, "I mean, Israel, it is Rachel you love. Don't you know? You will be wed to her tomorrow."

"The part of me that is Jacob loves Rachel," he answered, "but the part of me that is Israel loves you. Jacob doesn't know it now, but he needs your depths as much as Rachel's heights. He needs your wisdom and compassion as much as her beauty and boldness. I need you in order to be the patriarch I must become. Please, Leah, be my wife."

The thought of being with Jacob fulfilled Leah's wildest

dreams. She had denied herself even thinking such a thing were possible. Her sister's lover could never be hers. She shook her head, trying to blot out the vision, but the man who called himself Israel placed his hands on her shoulders. She could feel them now, firm and warm. His skin became peach colored before her eyes, as if spring had come.

"Listen to me," he said. "You must find a way to marry Jacob." Leah tried to interrupt, but he went on. "Go to your father. Tell him that you will never marry anyone else, that you will go mad if you cannot wed Jacob. Tell him that you are too plain to be sold to another. Tell him he can get twice Rachel's bride-price if he tricks me into marrying you first by veiling you and pretending that you are Rachel. Then he can offer Rachel to me in return for another seven years. You are Lavan's favorite child. He will listen to you."

Leah leaped to her feet, distressed beyond words. "Israel, it's wrong, and it will never work. How can you think Jacob would mistake me for Rachel? He will throw me out of his chambers and curse me."

Israel rose, smiling. "Cautious one, you and I are so much alike. You need not fear discovery. Remember that the part of Jacob that is Israel is inside him even now. That corner of his soul will know you and protect you. It will keep you hidden long enough."

"But," Leah said after a minute, "they will be hurt. And they will hate me."

"For a while," Israel agreed sadly. "But they both need to wrestle with you, far more than they know. We must put them and ourselves through this torment, for I can be with you only through Jacob. We will have our moments, love." He caught Leah's deep, soft eyes with his own. He embraced her and kissed her. "Please do it," he whispered softly into her long dark hair. "I want you as my wife."

The pair separated. Israel's flesh took on a silver, insubstantial tone. "When will I see you again?" Leah pleaded, reaching for him. She was only beginning to realize the enormity of what Israel was saying.

"When Devorah dies and is buried under Alon Bakhut, you will see me again. Many years, but I will wait for you. Go quickly, your father is almost asleep. I must return to my own time."

Not feeling anything beneath her fingers, Leah looked at her lover a long moment. Then she turned and ran down the hill. Israel stood and looked after her with tenderness, thinking of their seven children. He knew Leah would raise them well. She would be thoughtful as he was thoughtful, plan ahead as he did. She would regally bear all that befell her. In Israel's ears rang the prophecy that Jacob would hear at Alon Bakhut, years in the future. It was meant for this moment.

> *I am El Shaddai: be fertile and increase*
> *A nation, a community of nations shall come*
> >*from you*
> *and kings shall come from your body.*

*   *   *   *   *

In an upstairs loft, Rachel slept on a pile of rosy cushions. Jacob had climbed into her window as he so often did. He watched her drowse with profound contentment. As a fugitive from Canaan, sent to marry a distant cousin, he had never expected to find a woman he loved. Rachel had the same ambitious spirit as he did. Her frank, loving nature never failed to move him. He knew from the bottom of his passionate soul that she was the right woman.

Suddenly, Rachel started from her sleep with a sharp, unfinished cry: "The birthright!" The curtains of the oval window blew outward in a sudden gust. Jacob was startled and stared at his betrothed, every muscle tense. Yet he did not say anything, but waited for Rachel to speak. He could sense a fluttering of the holy Presence in the room. He held his breath, hoping for a sign that his hopes would be realized.

Slowly, Rachel's eyes focused and took in the room. "I had a dream," she stammered after a moment.

"There is power in dreams," Jacob replied tenderly. "What did you dream?"

"I dreamed I wrestled with an angel," Rachel said. "An angel with a huge belly, as if she were pregnant many times over. As we wrestled, it grew colder and warmer. It seemed that seasons were passing. Then a strange thing happened. My belly too began to swell. I grew faint. The wrestle became an embrace, as if the angel and I were leaning on each other while on a journey. After a long time, a finger came out of the sky. It touched my forehead, and I began to give birth. Stars rushed out of my womb like silver blood. I do not know what it meant."

Jacob thought for a moment, remembering his own birthright, which had been Esau's. "How did the angel seem?" he asked.

"Like Leah," Rachel answered after a moment. "The angel seemed like Leah. I remember that while we wrestled she sang these words:

> *The land given to Abraham and Isaac*
> *I will give to you*
> *and to your children I will give the land.*

*   *   *   *   *

As the tribe traveled toward Hebron, Jacob's worst fears were realized. Rachel died in hard childbirth, pushing out her son with the last of her strength. After the hurried burial by the road in Efrat, Jacob and Leah mourned separately. Jacob was weak with the guilt of having forced Rachel to travel. The cries of tiny Benjamin haunted his dreams. Leah's children gathered around her. They were afraid Jacob would divorce their mother out of bitterness and grief, force her to wander like Hagar. But when Leah's husband came into her tent on the seventh night after Rachel's death, he was not angry. Rather, it seemed that he was struggling.

"Jacob," Leah whispered tenderly.

"I am Israel now," came the reply. Leah nodded and reached out her hand to him. Leah's husband lay down beside her and, after a week of sleeplessness, slept.

In the morning, the two of them steered the trailing caravan to Hebron. Rebekah arose from her sickbed to greet her favorite son. When Rebekah saw Israel's troubled face, he seemed like another man to her. "Who are you, my son?" she asked him. He cried at her words, remembering the day that drove them apart. She rushed into his embrace. Then both of them went to Isaac, whose mind wandered far beyond the bounds of Canaan. Israel sat with his father and asked forgiveness. Both of them began to heal.

For the months that they lived, the proud grandparents would play with Joseph and Benjamin, Rachel's children. They would laugh with the older children, teaching them the family traditions. Leah would tell tales of her mother, Dinah, and of her sister, Rachel, making legends out of lives well lived. Rebekah mourned her nurse, Devorah, by singing the funny songs she had heard as a girl. Esau and his family were there too, at first awkward, but then giggling and slapping their thighs. Israel would sit with his head against Leah's knees, as Leah whispered with Rebekah of divine mysteries. It was as if Leah had always been Israel's wife. But whenever Joseph or Benjamin was near, their father would gaze into their beautiful, lively faces, and Leah would know that Israel was Jacob again. She tried not to let it sadden her. She loved all her husband's faces, and one of them would always be turned toward her.

> —A tale from the pen of Leah, daughter of Lavan and Dinah, in the forty-fifth year since her birth, her twentieth year as a woman of Israel

PENITENCE

Judah was told, "Your daughter-in-law Tamar has played the harlot; in fact, she is with child by harlotry." "Bring her out, said Judah, "and let her be burned." As she was being brought out, she sent this message to her father-in-law, "I am with child by the man to whom these belong." And she added, "Examine these: Whose seal and cord and staff are these?" Judah recognized them, and said, "She is more in the right than I, inasmuch as I did not give her to my son Shelah." And he was not intimate with her again.

— GENESIS 38:24–26

While Israel stayed in the land, Reuven went and lay with Bilhah, his father's concubine, and Israel found out.

— GENESIS 35:22

They were sitting just on the border of the shade, the sharp line between blinding brightness and succulent gray. Tamar sat in the sun, her coppery skin like a battalion of soldiers with shields. Bilhah sat in the shadows. Her hennaed hair had been doused in well water moments before. Strands were dripping onto the rust-colored cushion beneath her. Tamar poured a cup of black liquid from a stone pitcher.

The two women had been silent for some time. Previously, they had been discussing the famine in Canaan, the men's upcoming trip to Egypt, the respective prospects of Jacob's marriageable granddaughters. Now Tamar dropped her eyes toward the coffee. She did not pick up the conversation where it had left off.

Bilhah picked up an orange from a bowl and began to peel it. She looked at Tamar through the corner of her eye. "I heard something about you from Naftali's wife."

"What was that?" Tamar sipped her cardamom-laced coffee.

Juice squirted between Bilhah's fingers. "She said . . . well, she said that Judah doesn't know you."

Tamar smiled wryly. "So the idiom goes."

Bilhah turned her carob-colored face toward Tamar, squinting as her glance entered the sunlight. "You spend all that time together, exchange all those warm looks, and he never touches you? Doesn't Judah like women?"

"You're thinking of a different son of Jacob. Judah solicits female prostitutes, remember?" Tamar craned her neck to where the twins, Peretz and Zerach, were playing. There were no unusual sounds. She turned away.

Bilhah tore a ragged piece of skin off of her orange. "Then why is he holding back from you? Is he punishing you? Is he in love with someone else?"

"It isn't a matter of romance, it's a matter of ethics. I married two of his sons—I'm practically his daughter, even though I'm also the mother of his children. That afternoon at the gate of Enaim a sin was committed as far as he's concerned. A lesson from God. He doesn't want to make the same mistake twice." Tamar flicked away a fly that had landed on her toenail.

Bilhah snorted. "Reuven and I have made the same mistake a hundred times—and that's a good thing, as far as I'm concerned."

"Even though you're likely to get into trouble?" Tamar asked.

Bilhah laughed aloud. "I'm Jacob's concubine. How much more trouble could I get into?"

Tamar had thin lips like dried rose petals. She moved them slightly, moistened them. "You could be burned at the stake. I nearly was."

Bilhah snorted. "Judah wanted to get rid of you because you were inconvenient. I'm not inconvenient to anyone."

Tamar shook her head. "You could be an embarrassment to Jacob. I was one to Judah."

Bilhah laughed. "You're even more of an embarrassment now that people say Judah must be too old to perform! You can't tell me he stays away from you because you used to be his daughter-in-law!"

Tamar grinned maliciously. "Perhaps he's afraid of dying. My lovemaking had a negative effect on my first two husbands."

"Judah's first wife, Bat-Shua, used to rock the tent when she was with him," Bilhah argued. "Reuven used to say Judah moved to another camp so that his brothers would stop making fun of him for his constant lovemaking. He's not that old, Tamar. You can't convince me it's because he's afraid."

Tamar looked down. "Perhaps I didn't please him at the gate of Enaim," she said.

"Tamar," Bilhah said, "you are the most beautiful woman I have ever seen, and you could hardly be described as cold. Of course you pleased him. Tell me the truth."

Tamar sighed. Her eyes flashed quickly from side to side. The area around the pile of pillows was deserted. "Do you really want to know?"

Bilhah grew very quiet. "Well?" she asked finally.

"He's punishing himself," Tamar whispered, leaning toward Bilhah on one elbow. "For selling Joseph."

"Be still!" Bilhah hissed. "What if Jacob heard you?"

"It wouldn't surprise me at all if Jacob knows." Tamar looked sad.

Bilhah recovered herself. "And that's why Judah won't make love with you?"

"Judah thinks his first two sons died because of his sin against his brother. He's afraid for these two new ones." Tamar gestured to the children. "He's doing penance. I heard him praying one night, and it was clear how he felt. Judah has told God that if Joseph is ever found, he will know he is forgiven and he will treat me as his wife."

"And that's what you would want?"

"Oh, yes," said Tamar, "that's what I would want."

Bilhah giggled. "So this upcoming trip to Egypt—"

"Could be a stroke of good luck for me," Tamar finished. "If Judah finds Joseph there. Actually, I sold the last of the grain to a passing Ishmaelite so Judah would have to go down to Egypt." She looked downward, squinting. "I always thought I'd comfort Judah for the death of his sons by sharing his life. Judah is a good man, but he has some strange ideas about how to achieve spiritual purity."

"Many men do," said Bilhah. "Reuven's tried Judah's way too—but so far he hasn't succeeded for long."

Tamar arched an eyebrow. "And when are you and Reuven planning to run away together?"

"Reuven doesn't want to leave his father," Bilhah admitted. "He feels guilty that he did not save Joseph. He fasts every Monday and Thursday. He goes to visit Jacob every day and comfort him. He can't think about himself." She began chewing her lip. "Jacob hasn't wanted me since Rachel's death. These days he's only interested in Zilpah. She's soothing, like a fleece. Jacob sees me as a governess for his grandchildren. And Reuven sees me as proof of his continuing need to repent. It's maddening."

"It's a pity our men never notice the negative effect their virtue has on us," Tamar mused. "Maybe if they did they'd choose other virtues."

Bilhah lifted a corner of her brilliant orange shawl, which was lying on the ground, and draped it in her lap. "What if Joseph is never found?" she asked. "How will you survive all that frustration?"

"There's always you." Tamar smiled winningly.

"Indeed?" Bilhah poured Tamar another cup of coffee. She shaded her eyes and looked to the west along the row of black tents.

"Here comes that prude Puah, Issachar's daughter! Quick, spill something so she won't sit down!"

The passing woman ignored them. Tamar scooped up Bilhah's orange rinds and tossed them into the field behind the tents. The border between shade and sun had moved. Tamar and Bilhah rose to rearrange the cushions.

SHIMON'S PRISON

He took Shimon from among them and had him bound before their eyes.

—GENESIS 42:24

The guards of Pharaoh's vizier were garbed in impeccable white. Their jewelry glistened as they took hold of his arms. Shimon's brothers stared, horrified. Levi grabbed his wrist, but was brushed away by the stone-faced Egyptians. Shimon was so awestruck that he did not fight the guards as they led him away from the throne room. But when he was thrust into the dust-choked prison cell, he realized the truth.

His brothers were leaving him as a hostage here in Egypt, a prisoner of the harsh and suspicious vizier. There would be no rescue. As the bronze gate clanged shut behind him, he threw himself violently against it. The guards only laughed and spoke to him in their strangely accented language. Shimon, enraged, continued to hurl his thick body against the walls of his cage.

When he came to himself in the dark, there was no one with him. He could not tell whether it was day or night, or how much time had passed since he had beaten himself insensate. Trying to piece himself into a human soul again, he shoved his face into the stinking water that had been left for him, wetting his rust-colored beard.

What had Reuven said? "Now comes the reckoning for Joseph's blood." As he lay on the dirty pile of straw in the corner of his cell, Shimon was too exhausted to prevent Joseph's girl-like cries from rising up in the dark. The sounds in his mind accused him of crimes half a lifetime away.

Joseph's upturned face stared out of the cell's rough-cornered shadows. Shimon could taste his rage again, his anger at his slim, delicate, tale-telling half brother. The inspired dreamer, dreaming up new ways to torment him! Joseph had mocked Shimon's surly temper, teased the angry redhead to chase him. The boy had gotten him in trouble with their father countless times. *I was like a giant dog with a small brain*, Shimon thought bitterly. *I was too stupid to stop playing the game. Even when I went off into the fields to find peace, Joseph would follow me there and interrupt my thoughts. He made fun of me because I could never find the right words to tell what was in my heart.*

Shimon came to loathe Joseph. The bright coat had brought his anger to a rolling boil. As Shimon lay on the prison straw, guilt rose up in the roil of his rage like huge bubbles. Was a coat too small a thing to kill for?

A thump on the door of the cell roused Shimon. Another prisoner, cursing quietly in the city's florid argot, was being led down the black passageway. Hairs rose on the back of Shimon's neck. How long would he be here?

Days passed, marked by the bowls of food and water thrust into his cell and the refuse removed. No one spoke to him. Crouching in the stillness like a jackal on the edge of a camp, Shimon tried to pray. Prayer had always been difficult for him, repentance even more so. Jacob had chastised him for his stubbornness. When he did wrong, it was Leah, his mother, who sat with him for hours. Her patience helped him toward speech, toward regret. Now there was no one here to guide him.

Why was he alone being punished? Why not his brothers, who also had stripped Joseph of his coat? It was they who had taken the Midianite money in their palms!

Another ghost formed from the dark. Shimon was forced to admit that his hatred for Joseph went deeper than his brothers'. The others perhaps had not known it, but for Shimon, the arrival of the many-colored coat had been an excuse. The real offense had come weeks before, when Joseph turned his attention from his older brothers to their sister, Dinah.

Dinah was the light of Shimon's youth, a merry barefooted child crowned with black curls. She was always eager to run after Shimon wherever he went. She did not mind his hulking body or his hours of silence. As she grew, she became a fellow chewer of sweet grasses. She stalked small creatures with him. Dinah and Shimon shared a burning spirit, a desire to find and conquer. Sometimes Shimon's younger brother, Levi, would join them on their wilderness adventures. Levi added a layer of intense concentration to these quests. Dinah's high voice regaled the two brothers with song and bird whistles. When they came home, hungry and tired, their mother, Leah, would gather them all into her arms. It was the best part of the day.

When Dinah had grown older and sadder, Shimon and Levi often dropped by her tent. The three would reminisce and share news of the rapidly growing clan. Dinah would laugh at how the brothers smelled of oily wool and sheep dung. She was a little jealous. She had to stay in her tent like other women. Still, in the night hours when the camp was asleep, she would walk under the stars and smell the fragrance of night. She loved those ambles over sand and stone, alone with the moist chirp of insects and the whispers of wind.

It was Joseph who had told Jacob of Dinah's "unseemly" behavior. The somber patriarch then forbade Dinah to ever again walk alone at night and assigned a maid to her to make sure his command was followed. Joseph had taken Dinah's last freedom.

Shimon felt rage welling up in him again, an urge to smash fists, feet, shoulders into the stone walls of his prison. He knew he must calm himself or lose his mind. He knelt on the floor. He pleaded with God to help him conquer his fury, but his anger only grew, and seemed to swallow his scant air and light.

Breathing deeply, Shimon fought down the harsh memories inside him. He imagined himself as a camel, plodding ahead with no thought of past or future. When a small animal scurried past him, he did not chase it. He fell asleep, exhausted, on the straw that served him as a bed.

As he dozed, he was startled by a tinkling sound at his door. It was not the tinkling of a prisoner's chains but the sound of jewelry on a moving body. Shimon looked up to find the source of the sound.

A shining figure in cloth-of-gold stood at the door of his cell. At first, Shimon thought a vision of God had appeared to him. He stared wildly. Then, he saw that the apparition was an Egyptian noblewoman. He lowered his eyes.

The woman stood quietly for a minute, shining her candle into his cell. A veil was drawn over the lower part of her face and her slender shoulders. Shimon waited, his expression hidden beneath his heavy-skinned eyelids.

"I have heard," said a finely cultured voice from behind the golden veil, "that you are a Hebrew. I have been searching for an exotic diversion, and your arrival is fortunate. I would like to hear some stories of your homeland. You would be rewarded for such tales."

"I am obliged for your attention, lady," Shimon told the noble-woman brusquely, "but I am no storyteller." Shimon did not want to come to the attention of the Egyptian court. The first time had not been successful.

"I only desire something simple," the woman wheedled. "Something rustic. Tell me of your family, your festivals. I am curi-ous to learn."

Something in the woman's eyes reminded him of Dinah. That softened him.

"I might tell you a tale," he said, "but there is no place for a gentlewoman to sit in this filthy cell."

The lady opened the basket she carried. She had brought cush-ions, food, and drink for them both. The food made Shimon half faint with desire. He awkwardly made himself comfortable, thinking that he must stink. He wondered why this lady of rank would take such a bizarre risk for a simple story. She must be quite bored with her privilege. Shimon imagined, suddenly, that she must be very beautiful.

At first, he did not know what to say. He was not a good sto-ryteller or a poet. Where would he find soft stories to please a curi-ous lady? He tried to think of what Dinah would wish to hear, what might make her smile.

Shimon hesitantly told of his childhood in his wealthy and domineering uncle's house, how his uncle and father had cheated each other. The lady laughed, so Shimon went on. He told of Zil-pah, who would tell the children funny tales when Leah was too tired to teach them. Then he spoke of Bilhah, who was the camp's midwife. He recalled how she terrorized the camp with her biting wit. Encouraged by the lady's delicate giggles, he told of how the family had finally crept out of Lavan's camp and made for Canaan. Shimon carefully avoided the story of Rachel's tragic death, searching to remember the good times. The woman seemed delighted, clapping her hands at the amusing antics of thirteen children. Finally, Shimon told his father's favorite story, the tale of wrestling with an angel. Both he and the lady were tired after that.

"I will come again, although I cannot say when," the lady said. As she left, she left a package of food and drink inside Shimon's cell.

Shimon watched her go, his numb mind awakened by the mystery of the strange woman. Her light bobbed down the long corridor, farther and farther away from him. The pains of his youth returned.

Asnat, wife of the vizier Zaphenath-paneah, paused in the corridor, her breath taken away by her daring in coming here. Having spent her entire life in royal courts, she was thrilled by her own courage at entering a prison. Somehow, she would manage to keep stealing out of her opulent house. Her change in religion was not yet known to the household. She would say she was going to the chapel of On to pray. She could not believe her good fortune that the man would speak to her. She was finally learning about her true people.

Her husband's real name was Joseph. He had been a slave in her father's house before he came to Pharaoh's attention. She had taught him the Egyptian language, and he had taught her music. When her mother, Zuleika, had callously scolded her, Joseph was ready with tales of sea monsters and angels. The years of his imprisonment had been dark ones for her. She had refused to marry. When Joseph became a lord over Egypt, he had asked for her hand. Yet he told her little of his family. A great anger came over him when she spoke of it, so she remained silent.

Asnat had heard from the cup bearer that the men Joseph was questioning were Hebrews. She had crept behind a screen in Joseph's throne room to hear what they said. She did not understand why Joseph refused to acknowledge his brothers. When she saw the guards leading Shimon away to prison, she knew what to do. Joseph too had been in prison; and though she had not had the courage to see him there, she had often planned it in her mind.

Asnat did not often act forcefully. She preferred the gentle world of her father Potifar. This secret meeting was the first real action she had ever taken. She still could not believe she had carried it off.

Should she tell Shimon that she was married to his brother?

Shimon could no longer hold back the flood of remembering. From the bare stone beneath his hands, a flash of memory came to him like lightning from a gray sky. His hands sliced through the rich material of a curtain. He was holding a knife stained with blood. Dinah, curled on a tapestried rug, looked at him sideways, gratefully—or bitterly? Imprisoned in his rage, Shimon could not touch her. It was their brother Levi who came to carry Dinah back home.

What an irony. Jacob worried about danger in the night, but Dinah was attacked in broad daylight, on a trip to visit nearby womenfolk. In an isolated field, Dinah had been raped by a local prince. This chieftain's son became infatuated with her and took her to his village to be his wife. Shimon had not known what had happened to Dinah. He looked for her frantically. Then Shechem and his father, Hamor, came to the camp with a marriage proposal. Jacob listened to the proposal and then walked out, presumably to think it over.

This was blunt Shimon's most subtle moment. He told the messenger yes, Shechem could marry his sister. But in order for Dinah to wed Shechem, the bridegroom and his tribe must all be circumcised.

When Shechem and Hamor balked at the painful procedure,

Shimon pointed out that this action would allow their two clans to be related, making them each stronger. Shimon was very convincing, and Shechem and Hamor agreed that the males among them would be circumcised that very day. They rode home, discussing the wealth they would receive from their new neighbors. Shimon went to tell his father of the agreement. He was chastised for insubordination, but that did not matter. The crucial act was yet to come.

The next three days were a blur. Shimon stole swords from Jacob's supply tent. Levi ran on his nimble feet to scout out the village and the surrounding area. When Shimon and Levi attacked the town, there was almost no resistance. Dinah was brought home safe, but scarred.

Nine months later, Shimon watched Dinah and Leah go off into the wilderness carrying blankets and jars. Jacob had ordered that no unfathered child was to grow up in their camp. Shimon wondered whether that violent act of will was worse than Shechem's. Shimon crouched on a nearby hill. He heard Dinah's cries as she birthed her daughter. Then he heard Dinah's cries as her newborn was sent away with a stranger. When Dinah returned, Shimon knew that his sister had changed forever.

Shimon understood then that his anger at Joseph was partly his anger at his own inability to protect Dinah. The helplessness Shimon was feeling now, locked in this stone box, was the same helplessness he had felt on the day Dinah gave birth. A desire to see his wife, Adiva, and his sons made Shimon's throat ache. He had killed families like that in the town of Shechem, families who loved each other. Lovers would never see each other again, because of him. It was a terrible sin, even worse than selling Joseph. He deserved to stay in Pharaoh's prison for the rest of his life.

Over the days that passed, Shimon waited for his brothers to return, but they did not come. During the long weeks that followed,

Shimon cursed himself for a fool. Jacob would never let his beloved Rachel's son Benjamin leave his side. Shimon would be abandoned here. Shimon's eyes grew accustomed to the dim light and the stink of the prison. He watched the passing forms of the jailers, who avoided him. The son of Jacob began to worry that he would lose his memories of life as a free man.

When the lady finally returned, Shimon was grateful for the interruption of his dark, humorless brooding. The young woman, after inquiring about Shimon's health, gracefully settled herself on a cushion. Her pale green veil fell and revealed black lamb's wool hair and a charming face. She gestured encouragingly.

This time, Shimon told a tale of his wedding. He described Adiva's glowing face and beautiful crimson gown as she arrived in the camp. Shimon imitated the expressions of his bride's Edomite escort as they looked disdainfully and a little nervously around them. He spoke of whirls of women and storms of men, howling around the tents in the wilderness. Then he told how Adiva and Dinah had become the best of friends, and how his sister was no longer lonely.

The lady asked for stories of other matches. Cautiously, Shimon told her of his mother Leah's strange wedding and how Jacob married Rachel only a week afterward. He probed the story as one probes a splinter, waiting for the irritating, inevitable pain.

The woman listened, fascinated. Tears appeared in her eyes like stars in an evening sky, one after the other. Shimon did not know how he stumbled onto the story of the rape and its aftermath. Perhaps it was his desire to confess. Asnat's eyes grew wide in shock as he blurted out the end of the tale, already regretting his impulsive words. He was sure the noblewoman would never come again. Why would she want to listen to his grief?

But as the lady left, she promised that she would return. Before she went, she gave him her name: Asnat. It was an act of trust. Shimon was grateful. Prayer still came awkwardly to him, so he made a blessing before he bit into one of Asnat's tasty offerings. It was a way of showing gratitude.

Asnat entered her own peaceful garden. Its painted walls and columns, its sandstone statues by a leaping fountain, its palms and citrus trees soothed her. A nurse looked in and asked if she wanted the children, but she shook her head. She began to weep. She remembered back to the first days of her marriage. Joseph had told her that his God had planned their wedding.

"You see this amulet?" he had said, tenderly fingering the coin-shaped pendant around Asnat's neck. She had worn it since her infancy, always inside her clothes, as her parents requested. "This belonged to my sister, Dinah. You must be her daughter who was given away. Somehow, you, a granddaughter of Jacob, came to be raised here in Pharaoh's court. Even as Pharaoh's vizier, far from my own land, I was able to marry my own kin. I know now that God oversaw all the things that have befallen me, so that they might turn out for the good for me and my family."

Asnat had believed Joseph's words. He had known without being told that her parents were barren. Potifar and his wife, Zuleika, had adopted an infant from a strange man who came to their inner chambers in the middle of the night. Asnat had overheard the story as a young girl. Her parents did not know she knew.

Sometimes, when Joseph was half-asleep, he told her how his family had made a covenant with God to be a holy people, dedicated to God alone; and he spoke to her the many strange names of the generations of Abraham. Yet he would never tell her real stories of their family, stories about growing up, about playing and laughing, stories of brothers and sisters. She wanted so desperately to learn about the mother who had birthed her, and about her grandfather and grandmother. Now, through Shimon, she had learned. It saddened her, frightened her, to know she had come from a place of violence and pain. Shimon had told her, though, that her mother loved her. That gave her some peace of mind.

She had no doubt of her place in Potifar's family, by her father's side. Yet this new family was beginning to touch her heart and stir her loyalty. At dinner she would have to force herself not to ask her husband: "How long do you plan to keep my uncle in prison?"

Lying on a pallet in his cell, Shimon stared at the low stone ceiling and thought about the stories he had told Asnat. Shimon also thought of the thing he had not told Asnat: Jacob's cruelty to Leah for many years after their marriage. The truth was that Shimon's crime against Joseph was revenge taken against his father. A boy like all boys, Shimon had adored his father, chasing at his heels in the sheepfold. Yet when Shimon grew into manhood, Jacob had ignored him, condemned him with silence and with short bursts of sharp words. Shimon, with his muscled body and red hair, reminded Jacob of Esau. Jacob could not forgive his second son for that.

Nor could Shimon forgive Jacob for Leah's loneliness. During the years Rachel was alive, Jacob paid little attention to Leah, aside from a calm respect and a businesslike lust. Inch by inch, Leah had fought her way into Jacob's affections, while her older sons watched and cringed. Jacob had, in time, found love for Leah. The two became friends, even lovers, much to the relief of Leah's children. Nevertheless, in the deepest part of his heart, Jacob belonged to Rachel. Somehow, Leah always seemed happy, mysteriously content with her God in spite of her sadness over Jacob.

Shimon's attack on Shechem's village to rescue Dinah had infuriated Jacob. The patriarch worried that Shimon had upset the desert's fragile peace. Shimon, triumphant in his victory, had insolently answered his father: "Should our sister be treated like a whore?" He realized now that he had been speaking of his mother as much as of Dinah. Leah had been used and discarded many times. In the village of Shechem, Shimon had avenged Leah's honor with his knife.

Shimon remembered Leah's death, his denying cries when Dinah told him his mother was gone. He had run into the desert, pounding his fists into the sand. The pain of his loss had left him numb for years. Now he could remember how he had loved her. Somehow, this dark, confined place had given him room and light to see himself. His memories were bringing some deep part of him to the surface. He could only wait and see what happened next.

As the months went by, Shimon waited with eagerness for Asnat's visits. He spoke to her more and more freely. She began to speak to him as well, telling him of her own life as an Egyptian wife and mother. She had two sons. Shimon confided to her how much he missed his own rambunctious boys.

Asnat's sons were bright, but she worried about them. Last week, she had come home from the perfumers' to find Ephraim striking a slave who had spilled the family's dinner. She confided in Shimon that Ephraim was angry at his father, who favored the elder son, Menashe. Menashe's spoiled demands and tantrums made things worse. The brothers fought constantly, playing tricks on each other with vengeful delight. Her husband, full of his own private anger, would not interfere.

"They're brothers," Asnat said, shaking her head. "They

should love each other. I don't understand what's going through their minds."

"I do," said Shimon. He told Asnat what he and his brothers had done to his younger brother Joseph. He had been too ashamed to tell her before. Yet it seemed necessary. He wanted to warn her somehow.

"Your sons may be Egyptian princes," he concluded, "but they are following a pattern I know well. It is a terrible web. I wish I could untangle it."

Asnat walked off her anger at Shimon in the city streets, pacing for hours. When she finally returned home, she went to her husband's private office. She knew he would be busy, but she wanted to touch him. It was so much easier to understand him now.

The pale shadow cast by her white sheath alerted him to her presence. Joseph carefully removed the gold circlet from his aching temples. Asnat rubbed them.

"This is a change," Joseph remarked.

"I know," said Asnat. "We've been fighting lately."

Joseph nodded. "If I may be frank, Asnat, you seem extremely preoccupied. You haven't been civil to me in weeks."

"I'm worried about the boys," Asnat ventured. She did not dare tell her husband about the visits with Shimon. She had no idea what he would do.

"The boys are fine," Joseph said firmly. Asnat said nothing.

"You're a good mother." Joseph's voice was reassuring.

You lost your own mother so early, Asnat thought. *Perhaps you make an ideal of me. It is not justified. I do not know what I should do next. I do not know how to help you carry the burden of your past. I do not know how to make you see, when you will not even look.*

"Joseph," she said, "you never speak to me about your family."

"We were shepherds, Asnat. There is nothing to tell."

Asnat had to leave before she began to laugh.

It was late afternoon. Shimon was thinking of his mother, Leah. Now that he could feel his love for her, he was ready to face his anger.

In ways unknown to her, Leah had practiced her family tradition of preference. There was no doubt in Shimon's mind that Leah had loved him. Still, he could never penetrate the mystery between Leah and her tenderhearted eldest son, Reuven. The two had been bonded from Reuven's birth. In some ways, perhaps Reuven had made up for Jacob's failures of love. Perhaps Leah had sought to compensate for Jacob's preference of Joseph. Whatever it was, it had been hard for Shimon.

Shimon thought further as the walls of his cell pressed closer. Perhaps it was to punish Leah that Shimon had taken a Canaanite concubine. Certainly his own wife, Adiva, had done nothing to deserve the moment of shock when Shimon brought Cozbi home and installed her in his tent. Shimon could remember Leah's stunned eyes as if it were yesterday. Shimon had never truly meant to hurt his mother or his wife. He told himself that he was only increasing his prestige: After all, his father had four wives!

Maybe he had been afraid of what Leah had suffered. Maybe he had chosen to cut himself off from Adiva before she rejected him. Adiva's coldness to him had shown him that there were consequences to what he had done.

Shimon's guilt had driven him to blame Cozbi. He shouted at her whenever he got the chance. He even struck her, something he would never have dared do to Adiva. Leah's furious reprimands would cool him for a while, and then he would lose his temper again.

Cozbi might have been delicate, but she had a strong survival streak, and she was no fool. The night after a visit from a traveling Midianite prince, she had disappeared. She had left her infant son, Shaul, behind her. It was a permanent reminder of Shimon's failure. Naturally, Adiva did not want the child. Shimon did not know what to do. Miraculously, Dinah adopted Shaul. The boy filled the void in Dinah's life, and Shimon was grateful that his son had a mother.

Leah died not long after Cozbi left. Shimon never had a chance to tell her he was sorry for what he had done. Instead, he had stifled his anger, his love, all of his deepest feelings. He had stopped feeling at all. Only here, in Pharaoh's prison, was he beginning to feel again.

Shimon had reached the last gate of himself. He was able to mourn his mother and let her go. He began, once again, to see through his own blinded rage to the people he had hurt. At least something good came out of it, he pleaded with God. Now Dinah has her own family, a child she can keep.

But he knew, thinking of Adiva's loud, bitter laugh, that something bad had come out of it, too. Cozbi, like Dinah, had lost her child.

His sins were more numerous than he had ever realized. He had lashed out at everyone. The people of Shechem's village. Joseph. Cozbi. Adiva. Leah. Even his own son Shaul. Surely there was some way back from what he had done. There must be some penance he could do to be clean of his many wrongs. Shimon buried his head in his hands and tried to think.

"I would like to meet your sons," Shimon said to Asnat the next time she came.

"Shimon, that's impossible," Asnat replied. "I can't bring them to the prison. They would tell their father."

"Maybe you could disguise me as someone else, bring me to your home for a few hours."

Shimon was longing for daylight, and helping Asnat's sons seemed like a path to redemption.

"They can learn from me," he argued. "I know what it is like to feel uncontrollable rage. I have seen what it is to be spoiled by a doting father. I can teach them." Shimon thought of his mother sitting with him, a screaming child. *Is that what my mother was doing?* he thought. *Trying to teach me how to return? I did not learn enough from her, but I did learn.*

"Let me think about it," Asnat told him.

Shimon had to be content with that.

Asnat, scurrying home along squalid alleyways that had become familiar, thought about Shimon's proposal. She had rarely been brave. If it were discovered that she had taken a man out of prison, might she not be imprisoned herself? She was afraid to risk angering Joseph. She knew that in his heart of hearts Joseph wanted to hurt Shimon the way he had been hurt years before. If Joseph knew his wife had helped her uncle, what would he do to her?

At first, Shimon had simply been a means to an end, but now he was something more. Shimon was her only link with her mother, Dinah, whom she felt as if she were coming to know. Asnat knew she could never tell Shimon that Joseph was alive. Yet perhaps, somehow, Shimon could become part of her family.

Entering the gate of her lush private garden, Asnat looked around her. She realized how hard it must be for Shimon to live in filth and darkness, with nothing to look forward to but her visits.

She had been selfish. Perhaps she was only just growing up.

Asnat chose to take a risk. She would bribe the jailer to release Shimon for several hours every week, in the afternoon when most guards were sleeping in the heat. He would be willing. He could always turn her in if she stopped paying. Her maid would act as a go-between. She could do it.

Within a few weeks, dressed as a cowled Egyptian priest, Shimon saw the sun for the first time in months. Squinting, he felt his eyes fill with tears, and let them come. Asnat gently led him through the busy streets. He tasted the world slowly.

Shimon waited for Asnat's sons in a walled garden. The boys had been told Shimon was a cousin of Potifar's, a pilgrim from the provinces. Looking around at the strange carven images and statues, Shimon felt pain for his lost brother, Joseph, sold into a foreign place. Still, it was wonderful to see the green of the well-tended plants and the whitish blue of the noontime sky.

The two ruddy, thick-haired boys Asnat was leading toward him were so similar to the children that ran about Jacob's camp that Shimon was startled. He swept them up into his arms, surprised at his own rush of emotion. He was even more surprised at theirs.

As he spoke to them, the two boys warmed to him. At first they fought for his attention. He was evenhanded with them, treated them as a team. They reminded Shimon of Levi and himself, taking on the world together. This is who they could be, Shimon thought. The three played for hours, and Shimon learned the individual traits of each restlessly growing boy. Too soon, Asnat indicated that it was time for Shimon to go back to his cell.

Returned to his prison, Shimon felt panic and rage again, but also excitement. The boys had taken to him so quickly. Shimon thought and planned, feeling for the first time in months that he had a future.

The next time Asnat came, she looked grim and in a hurry. Shimon was surprised. "What is it?" he asked her, thinking that their excursion from the prison had been discovered.

"Your sister has written me a letter," she told him.

"My sister!" Shimon was shocked. Life in Canaan seemed so distant that Asnat's declaration took his breath away. "But how did Dinah know of you?"

Asnat also seemed to be having trouble with her breath. There were tears in her eyes. "Shimon, I am sorry to have deceived you all this time," she said. She knelt down on the floor of the prison and took a small pendant from beneath her dress.

"That is Dinah's," Shimon said.

"I was afraid to tell you who I really am," said Asnat. "I was adopted by Potifar, but I am Dinah's natural daughter."

Shimon staggered over to the nearest wall and leaned against it. "I thought you must be dead," he stammered.

"That was what everyone was meant to think, but Dinah knew that I had been given to Potifar. She had vowed never to contact me. But her concern for you led her to break that promise. She sent a messenger to my childhood home."

"Are you sure it was really Dinah?" Shimon cried out.

Asnat nodded. "In her letter, she described this amulet, which I have worn since my birth. She also said that since you were thrown into the prison, Jacob has done nothing. Your wife is desperate. Dinah agreed to find me in the hope that I would be able to do something for you."

Shimon was speechless. His throat burned. His wife still loved him. Even more astonishing, it was his niece who had been caring for him all this time. The two boys he had met in the garden were Dinah's grandchildren. Could he be so old? Shimon grabbed a lock of his hair as if to see whether it had turned gray.

Asnat continued. "Your wife and sons are ready to come here and rescue you, if need be. I told them I might be able to engineer your escape without their help. I have discovered that the jailer is very greedy. If paid well, he might be willing to help us. I would give you provisions and travel gear."

Shimon found his voice. "But Asnat, you also are my family. You are Dinah's daughter. I can't leave you here!"

"Shimon, I can't go with you. I have a husband and two sons."

Two sons. The hatred of brothers and its consequences.

The other important decisions of his life had been made in the heat of passion. This choice, though on a moment's notice, was made with painful consideration.

Shimon's voice, though thick, was steady. "Tell Adiva and Dinah I need to stay here for a few more months."

Asnat drew back in shock. "Why? Shimon, it's terrible for you here. Don't you want to go home?"

"I do. God knows I do. But I have a task here I need to fulfill." My brother Joseph is lost, the dead of Shechem are dead. Let me perform my penance before God by saving two brothers. If I can lighten their burden, perhaps I can redeem myself as well.

In the walled garden with his young nephews, Shimon wrestled and tackled and laughed, and sat quietly, listening. He did his best to treat the two boys equally, each as they needed.

Asnat was reading another letter from Dinah. Asnat seemed older to Shimon, more complex, but also happier. The last days had brought her a new confidence. Now she provided Shimon longer and longer respites from his prison cell. It often seemed to Shimon that she had something else to tell him. He was curious. Fortunately, the prison had taught him patience. He could wait.

The boys raced off to cool themselves in a shallow pool. Asnat took a slow, deep, breath and smiled at Shimon. "Do you think I'll ever meet the rest of our family?" she asked quietly.

Shimon laughed his rich laugh. "I have a feeling," he said, "that God has more surprises in store for us."

THE HOUSE OF
THE MIDWIVES

Alone, the perfect woman steps across
the ford of air.

—ALLEN MANDELBAUM, *Chelmaxioms*

"Mother, I'm pregnant with a baby girl."
"What is she doing?"
"She is singing."
"Why is she singing?"
"Because she's unafraid."

—E. M. BRONER, *Her Mothers*

THE TENTH PLAGUE

*Aaron took to wife Elisheva, daughter of Aminadav
and sister of Nachshon, and she bore him Nadav
and Avihu, Elazar and Itamar. . . . And Aaron's son
Elazar took to wife one of Putiel's daughters, and she
bore him Pinchas.*

—EXODUS 6:23,25

*Shifrah and Puah the Hebrew midwives were
Yocheved and Miriam, and some say Yocheved
and Elisheva.*

—ADAPTED FROM SOTAH 11B

*Elisheva had five joys more than all the daughters
of Israel.*

—BT ZEVAḤIM 102A

Even during the hail, Yocheved had gone to deliver babies. Life does not stop even for acts of God. Egyptian women had special need for midwives who would not be waylaid by hailstones or hungry locusts. The plagues, Yocheved had said, were no excuse for failure to do one's job. But tonight Yocheved's biting voice was absent. She had run to the communal ovens to bake for

107

the journey. Miriam had gone to dispense her wisdom in the huts of the slave-chieftains. Neither would attend a birth tonight. Tonight the Angel of Death had descended. Tonight Elisheva was alone, a midwife sitting quietly by the hearth.

Elisheva dried her hands on her apron. She hummed a small song to her youngest. Family was her comfort in this time of wonders and dangers. Elisheva's father and mother had died years before of overwork and disease. Her younger brother had a friend, Aaron, whom she had loved. So it had been her fate to marry Yocheved's son, older brother to the mysterious Moses. Aaron was kind. She had needed kindness. Her pain at losing her own family prompted her to learn from Yocheved and Miriam their family trade. With that trade had come skill, patience, and enough courage to disobey Pharaoh's decrees. But now that blood had filled the Nile, she was as frightened as everyone else. That morning, she had seen how the firstborn of Egypt were shunned in the streets and even in their homes. Moses said the plagues came from God, but Elisheva found herself questioning why a merciful God would allow such suffering.

There was a knock at the door.

The girl was spotted with the remnants of boils and insect bites. Her dress was Egyptian, her face was a wrinkled dot of fear. Elisheva drew away sharply from the child's outstretched hand.

"Please," the child said, "it's my sister's time."

Elisheva turned slightly away, toward the fire. The boys were asleep in the house's inner reaches. "You'll have to wait," she said. "The midwives have gone out."

Having told the lie, she wished to comfort the child. "Shall I bring you some herb tea?" she said.

The girl did not move. "Please," she said, "I've seen you at birthings before. My sister's bleeding. The baby's wedged inside her somehow. Please come."

Elisheva had never been afraid of death before. Tonight she thought of the plague feeling its way along Egypt's rough-edged alleyways. She could not bear the thought of leaving her four sons alone, without their mother.

"Why haven't you gone to an Egyptian midwife?" Elisheva asked.

"My sister's a firstborn, and so is the baby," the girl admitted softly. "I've been all over. Everyone else is afraid."

Elisheva was silent for a long moment. Anger welled up within her that because of an Egyptian child, she should be in fear of her life the night before freedom.

"I won't come," she said harshly. She turned away and roughly poked the embers with a stick.

The girl was silent then. She slunk toward the low door, brushing against the dead reeds poking from the shabby wall. Elisheva made a small noise, watching her go.

The girl turned back suddenly, her face like ash with a single cinder left.

"My sister is in pain," she said with a clenched face. "She can't even speak. She can barely sit up. She has no strength left. She could die, and you're going to sit here by your warm fire and stir your ashes because she's an Egyptian and because you're scared. What kind of midwife are you? Aren't you supposed to care about all babies?"

The girl's voice was like Yocheved's, toothed and copper plated. The bruised face of the Egyptian girl seemed to mirror every desperate pregnant woman Elisheva had ever attended. The risk seemed great, the reward small.

"I will come," Elisheva conceded, and reached for her warm robe.

The alleys of the Hebrews soon led to Egyptian streets. There was no sound, except the weeping of the bereaved, which was quickly silenced by fearful households. There were no cattle or insects to fill the streets with noise. The firstborns who were still alive huddled in the byres and ruins where others had driven them. Elisheva became grateful that because of the clouds over the city the night was completely dark. There were no moving shadows to remind her of the angel who walked over Egypt. Her gratitude ceased when her foot landed on a corpse. Then she merely walked forward, and thought of nothing.

When they arrived at the house, hunch walled and topped with reed bundles, it smelled of blood. Elisheva felt herself begin to retch from fear. She swallowed and straightened her back. Then she stooped to enter the low opening into the house. The girl scurried ahead of her, breathing hard.

The scene before her—disarranged bedclothes and pots of hot water steaming—was like any other lying-in. Yet a pall hung over the room. There were no anxious voices. An Egyptian god lay useless on a table. The husband had long since run from the house.

The woman in the bed looked up at her with bloodshot eyes. Elisheva was afraid to touch her, for fear she might be slain herself. Like the woman in labor, Elisheva was a firstborn. Yet the white clothes lent some sense of normalcy, and she could not believe the Angel of Death lurked outside. The smoky brown walls of the hut seemed sturdy and safe. Elisheva went briskly to work.

Hours began to pass, punctuated by cries from other houses. The mother had lost much blood, but had enough energy to squeeze out a small body with Elisheva's help. The wet man-child was born backward. An omen of the times, Elisheva thought. She pulled him from the depths of his mother in one clean, practiced motion. His wisp of hair was the color of grated ginger, his skin a shade of horseradish. He was beautiful.

The midwife wrapped up the child and spoke words of comfort to the mother. The mother nursed and smiled at her son. Elisheva thanked God for the instant bond between mother and child. She had seen it so often, but it was always a miracle. The new mother's young sister, eyes fastened on her nephew, finally fell asleep on a reed mat. Elisheva packed her things and got ready to leave. She put on her robe and belted it, but she lingered and kept lingering. She wanted to get home to her own children, but somehow she couldn't seem to set her foot on the doorsill. Four hours passed, then five. A lightening of the sky came, and then it was almost dawn. Elisheva began to hope that, although there was no blood on the lintel, death had passed over this house.

When the gray shadow entered the room, Elisheva saw it first. She felt her old anger return, toward Egyptians, toward this mother and her child. She turned her back to the shadow and held her breath. She thought of Aaron, of his kind mouth pressed against hers.

A minute later, Elisheva could feel the mother's pulse slipping away. The child's lips were turning blue. She herself felt healthy. She breathed a sigh of relief that the plague had not touched her. She began to think of returning home.

Home made her think of all that this home was about to lose. Elisheva whipped around and faced the angel, her anger suddenly focused on the unfair decree that took away innocent life.

"Why are you here?" she screamed into the mist. "Being firstborn isn't a crime! What have this mother and child done worthy of death? They don't deserve to perish for being born!"

Then Elisheva became aware of something within the grayness, something small and shining and still, like a beacon in a storm. From the shining came a Voice.

"Why are you here, Elisheva?" it asked.

"I belong here," she said, weeping. She hugged the mother and child to her with a strength she had known in herself only when she was near her own family.

The soft Voice was audible only to her. Mother and infant had slipped into unconsciousness. The Egyptian girl stood open-mouthed near her bed, staring at the smoky light.

"Your vigil this night has not been in vain," the Voice told her. "This mother and child will live because of you, and there will be an end to the plague on the firstborn: No one else will die on this night. Because you were not afraid to follow a stranger into her suffering, I will bless you and build you a great posterity. I will give to your hands the power of saving life. I will give to your house the priesthood. Your children will offer sacrifices for the nation. They shall be holy to Me. And because you loved this family as your own, your grandchildren will descend from it. With them I will make My covenant of peace."

Through a daze of wonder, Elisheva imagined her sons growing into men. The light faded suddenly, like the end of a dream. On the doorpost was a smear of red like the ones on Israelite doorposts. She felt the new mother pull at her hand.

"We're still alive." The woman spoke with great awe.

"Yes, and you have a beautiful healthy baby," Elisheva told her. She began packing up herbs and cloths. Her family was no doubt waiting for her.

"Wait," the mother said, and held her gaze. "I want you to take us with you. I know you are going to a place where the stranger will be protected. Please give us a chance to live in such a place."

Elisheva was startled. She wanted to refuse. Surely the Israelites would not accept these Egyptians as comrades. Then she considered the vision she had seen.

"We need to leave right away," she said.

"I understand," the mother answered. "We have nothing to pack."

"What is your name?" Elisheva asked her.

"Putiel," the woman said. She squeezed the hand of her young sister, who for the first time shyly smiled.

A generation later in the Sinai wilderness, on a golden dawn, Putiel's second daughter gave birth to Elisheva's grandson. Elisheva and her apprentices, Putiel's sister and daughters, delivered the child. They gave him the name Pinchas, meaning "dark one." His name was in memory of the night of the tenth plague, and in honor of the night sky above Sinai, which Putiel had lived to see.

THE BONES OF JOSEPH

So Joseph made the Children of Israel swear, saying:
"When God has taken notice of you, you shall carry
up my bones from here." Joseph died at the age of one
hundred and ten years, and he was embalmed and
placed in a coffin in Egypt.

    —GENESIS 50:25–26

How did Moses know where Joseph's grave was to be
found? They say that only Serach daughter of Asher
had survived from that generation, and that she
revealed to Moses where Joseph's grave was located.
The Egyptians had made a metal coffin for him and
then sunk it into the Nile. Moses went to the bank of
the Nile . . . and called out "Joseph, Joseph, the time
has come for the Holy One, blessed be He, to redeem
his children. The Shekhinah and Israel and the clouds
of glory await you. If you will reveal yourself, good,
but if not, we shall be free of your vow." Whereupon
Joseph's coffin floated to the surface.

    —MIDRASH TANḤUMA YELAMMEDENU EXODUS 4:2

The lead coffin rested on the bank. It seemed to Moses that the noise it had made as he set it down still echoed beneath the voices of the night insects. It was a wet noise, the noise of tearing earth, of burial. Beside him, Serach panted in the darkness. Her lined and sweating face glinted in the splendor of the full moon. It was the night of the final plague. Slavery was dying. The sleepy buzzing of the night insects was its eulogy.

Serach tapped on the coffin gently with a long fingernail. She touched the gold skin of the bull that decorated its lid. She turned to Moses. Her hair, still black after many years of life, danced gently in the breeze.

"We can't carry this," she stated flatly. "It's too heavy for a tired prophet and an old harpist. We'll have to take him out."

Moses, who after ten plagues had thought that nothing could shock him anymore, was aghast. "He's a sacred ancestor, a prince. We can't just prop him between us like an old board."

"Plenty of Hebrew slaves have been carried that way to their final rest," Serach told him. "He'll be glad to be free of that box after all this time. Leave it to me."

Serach began to hoist the heavy lid with her spidery fingers. Moses leaped to help her, honoring the will of Asher's daughter, but his heart grieved. He did not want to see his ancestor, his hero, as an embalmed Egyptian nobleman. It reminded him of what he might have been. He turned away his face as the lid slid off and thudded into the reeds.

A tender sound from Serach startled him. He glanced at her face, then into the coffin, his breath caught in his throat. The embalming work had been undone. Inside the lead box lay a pile of bones. It was a small pile, for Joseph had been a small man. The wrappings had dried and faded, and lay in small fragments on the floor of the coffin.

"God brings us back to ourselves at the last," Serach said.

Moses felt the hand that had clamped his heart for such a long time suddenly release. "Sometimes before that," he added.

Then his face fell again. "But how will we carry him now?" he asked, his voice full of frustration. The people would already be gathering to leave, and he was needed among them. Yet he knew the promise to Joseph must be fulfilled. Could he simply gather the bones up in his arms?

There was a sudden rustle from the reeds nearby. A shawled form came to stand near Moses and Serach on the bank. It was Yocheved, the mother of Moses, who had nursed Moses as a baby, who had saved his life. Serach nodded to her.

"Then it has happened as my father told me it would," Yocheved whispered. Moses remembered that Yocheved was a daughter of Levi, of the same generation as Serach, privy to many secrets. He raised his eyes and saw that in his mother's hands was a worn, woven basket, pitched with bitumen, with a blanket nestled inside.

THE LEAST OF THE
HANDMAIDS

*The Israelites went into the sea on dry ground, the
waters forming a wall for them on their right and on
their left.*

—EXODUS 14:22

*At the Sea of Reeds, the least of the handmaids saw
what all the prophets together did not see.*

—ADAPTED FROM *MEKHILTA* SHIRAH 1

Bereishit bara Elohim et hashamayim ve'et haaretz—
In the beginning, God created the heavens and the
earth. Read this another way: "For Reishit, God
created the heavens and the earth."

t midnight, the people fled from Egypt, their sandals slapping, their timbrels jangling, their thin goats bleating. The
Egyptian army followed them with its thousand wheels.
The Israelites who fell behind screamed or sat down sobbing, and
were pulled along by others. The people camped before Pi-Hahirot,
facing the sea. The pillar of cloud was all around them. Everything
in their vision became blurred: the ivory sheep, the brown children
and goats, the gold necklaces glinting around the necks of women.

The sand under their feet was unformed and void. Darkness was over the surface of the deep and a wind from God was sweeping over the water. Then God said, "Let there be light," and the pillar of light appeared. God separated the pillar of light from the pillar of cloud and darkness, so that the pillar of cloud stood behind the Israelites and hid them from the Egyptians. The bright chariots were no longer visible.

At the edge of one of the camps was Reishit. She had been a Hebrew slave until midnight. She had been called Reishit, beginning, because she was the first fruit of her mother's body, but her mother had died before Reishit learned to speak. She had never known her father. She had been, her whole life, the servant of a slave who ground grain for bread in an Egyptian prison. All day she had carried dirt and chaff to the prison refuse pile, and all day walked wearily back again to the grinding pit. She slept in a pile of husks near the grinding stone. She ate burned bread thrown away from the oven. No one had ever paid the slightest attention to her except when she was too slow. Then she was threatened with being thrown into the Nile, of which she was terrified. She had never seen the Nile.

Now she sat at the edge of a small fire and stared at a single grape. A woman in a bright red headcloth had given it to her. She bit into the grape. It was juicy and sweet and tart at once. Reishit began to weep. The people around her were not watching her, they were watching the pillar of fire moving through the camp. They cried out as it passed though the hands and feet of children and the heads of sleeping elders. The pillar of fire whirled and turned and came to stand by Reishit. It was radiantly gnarled like the massive trunk of a giant olive tree. Golden rays whipped around it like leaves in the wind.

"I am for you," the pillar said to her. "Remember."

Reishit whispered the word again, "remember," and reached out to touch the pillar's shining bark. She curled up in a cleft among its thick, smooth, massive roots, dreaming of bunches of grapes. When she woke a few hours later, curled up next to her was a small girl who was cold. "My name is Achat," said the little girl when asked. It was the first full sentence someone had spoken to Reishit in a long time. Achat would say nothing else. Around them, other Israelites were waking. Some people stared at Reishit as if she might be special. One came and touched the hem of her dirty blue dress. She did not know what to make of it.

The pillars had disappeared. In the blue pre-dawn, the people could see the spears of Pharaoh's army. They ran toward the shore of the sea and stood looking at the crashing waves. Moses stood on a high peak with his staff. "Were there not enough graves in Egypt that you brought us to die in the wilderness?" the people cried to Moses. They said many other things Reishit could not hear.

While the people wailed, a tanned man with scars on his broad shoulders scrambled down the cliffs onto the beach. He waded into the water. Foam surged up his arms and back as he took step after step. Others began to follow him. Reishit was afraid. She crouched where thin gauzes of water wiped the sand. Achat stood a little in front of her. The child's chubby knees were splashed by salty wavelets. A pregnant woman stumbled in the depths.

Then God said: "Let there be an expanse in the midst of the water, that it may separate water from water." A white line appeared in the sea, beginning at the beach crowded with Hebrews. It stretched out toward the opposite shore. Wave after wave receded from this line, rapidly, in unexpected directions, as if the water were running off the back of a rising dragon. Other white lines appeared in the sea. Waves surged from them as well. Soon there was a maze of glowing tunnels, each reaching from one shore of the sea to the other. Some of them intersected with each other at strange angles. The curved walls of the tunnels almost, but not quite, joined each other at the top, leaving a bit of starry sky.

The crowd moved forward, randomly bunching into each circular opening. Reishit was afraid of the tunnels of bubbling glass. The crowd pushed her forward. As she entered the nearest of the sea's strange mouths, clear tendrils began to reach out from the walls. They splashed her face and dress with their foaming tongues, cleaning away the dirt of the prison and the grinding place. She giggled—her laughter was a sound she had heard only a few times before. She giggled again. Some of the passing people patted her wet hair. At an intersection, she saw the tall man with scars on his back who had first run into the sea. He grinned at her and swung her to his shoulders, grasping her small feet. She could see the huge mass of people and animals swaying and swerving in the tunnels. Their steps left shallow prints in the white light of the seabed.

"My name is Nachshon," he said to her before putting her down again. He pointed her in the right direction. "Find me if you need me. Be careful. Don't get trampled underfoot."

That was the second sentence someone had spoken to her that day.

The people continued to move through the labyrinth. They prodded trembling bulls, shushed infants, tore their tunics on the sharp edges of their packages. Their legs began to shake from exhaustion. Then God said, "Let the earth sprout vegetation, seed-bearing plants, fruit trees of every kind on earth that bear fruit with the seed in it." Vines began to sprout on the floor of the sea. Saplings came through cracks in the floors and walls of the tunnels. They grew tall in minutes, pushing their bright blossoms through the open spaces at the tops of the passages.

In her tunnel, with its narrow skylight of stars, Reishit picked a bunch of grapes. It was as large as her arm, almost too heavy to hold. Each grape tasted different. She fed several to Achat. Then Achat took a branch of figs, which had sprouted in the path, and brought it to a sad-looking woman who had stopped and sat on her baggage. The almond-skinned woman embraced the child with deep feeling. Reishit looked away, embarrassed. She could not remember anyone touching her that way.

"I lost my own children to Pharaoh's decrees," the woman said to Reishit. Reishit nodded sadly. Then the woman embraced her too. Reishit opened her arms and fingers and squeezed back. It was a good, warm feeling, like the roots of the pillar of light. "I was almost too tired to go on walking," the woman said. "Thank you for giving me a little rest."

There was a trembling through the web of tunnels, like an earthquake. Achat clutched at Reishit's hand. The almond-skinned woman put her arms around both girls. The Egyptian army had entered the tunnels. Soldiers swarmed through its mouths like bronze bees.

Then God said: "Let there be lights in the expanse of the sky to separate day from night." The sun rose. The frothing skin of the tunnels turned purple and pink and green and gold. The sun's rays beat down. The moon stood in the sky like an archer's bow. Their rays stung the eyes of the Egyptians so that they could barely see. Chariots careened into the tunnel walls and became stuck in them. Soldiers winced as their eyes watered. Yet still Pharaoh came, his determined officers beside him.

Frightened, Reishit ran to an orange tree. She had climbed the old fruitless palm tree in the prison yard a few times. The orange tree growing in the sea was easier to climb. In the branches, Reishit closed her eyes so that she could not see Pharaoh's army. She felt the sun and the moon caress her face. Reishit listened very carefully and began to hear a faint song rising from the channels below her. The song came from the water itself.

Reishit felt a tug on her skirts and woke from her trance. A stooped, gray-bearded man in a long violet robe was pulling her from behind. He had half-climbed into the tree with her.

"You must keep moving," he said as he set her on the ground. "The Egyptians are getting closer. We must all hurry to the other side of the sea. Go with your family now."

I have no family, Reishit wanted to say, but the almond-skinned woman was taking one of her hands and Achat was taking the other. "That was Aaron, Moses' brother," the woman whispered to Reishit as the man with the long gray beard disappeared into the apple orchard ahead of them. The three of them ran along with the rest of the Israelites. The tunnels shook terribly. They slipped and slid as it shifted minutely beneath them. The chariots were coming.

Then God said, "Let the waters bring forth swarms of living creatures, and birds that fly above the earth." In the water the Israelites began to see fish of all kinds. Some had white teeth and great red fins. Some had huge gray bodies. Some had glowing tails. The Israelites clutched at each other in wet huddles. Small brown birds flew among them, singing, and the Israelites were no longer afraid. Sheep and goats moved smoothly next to schools of darting fish. Behind the Israelites, birds of prey swooped upon the Egyptians, stabbing with their beaks. Some of the soldiers ran away, out of the tunnels. As Pharaoh's chariot rounded a turn, an enormous green shape appeared in the curved side of the tunnel. Its tail jutted out from the wall and lay like a mountain in Pharaoh's path. It was Leviathan. Leviathan opened his mouth. Pharaoh's chariot halted.

Reishit had seen only a few fish in her life, cooked ones the men at the prison ate. Sometimes she had eaten the skin or the tail of a fish. Now she laughed at the prancing creatures in the water, each one more fantastic than the next. Where she poked her finger into the fizzy body of the tunnel, small brilliant blue and green fish gathered and nibbled her fingers. Achat tittered shyly and clung to Reishit's legs. Reishit could tell that the fish were making words with their bodies. *Remember us*, they said, although Reishit was not sure how. Other children paused to watch the fishes' antics.

"Shua, is that you?" A young man wearing tanned skins and carrying a bow stopped to greet the older woman who walked with Reishit. His hair was black and wild and curling. Reishit wanted to touch it.

"Betzalel!" the almond-skinned woman exclaimed. "I thought you were with Moses."

"I doubled back to check on you stragglers," the young man said. "And I wanted to get one more look. Who knows? I might want to build something this beautiful one day." The tunnel lurched. "Pharaoh must have started his horses again. I need to get back to Moses. Shua, if all goes well, come to my tent when you reach the other side. I'll give you a place to sleep."

"Is there another side?" whispered Reishit.

Betzalel turned to Reishit, who stood near the sheer wall where she had been making faces at a bright yellow fish. She hid her face because he was so handsome.

"Don't fear, little one, you're not far now," Betzalel said. Reishit smiled at him, and he tousled her curls. "You make a light all around you," he told her, and that compliment was also a first for her.

Shua beckoned to Reishit and Achat to follow her. As they moved with the shoving crowds, Reishit saw the path was becoming wider. The space at its top opened to reveal more and more of the morning sky. The floor of white light beneath them was becoming gritty. Abruptly, the sides of the tunnel ended. A high white bridge led out onto the sand of the beach. They were on the other side of the Sea of Reeds. It was like being on the other side of the world. The beach was covered with Israelites, their livestock, packages, wheelbarrows, sweaty robes. Reishit could barely see any sand.

Theirs was the final rush off of the bridge. Someone reached out a hand to help Reishit step onto the ground. It was the woman in the red headcloth who had given her a grape. Now the woman had a timbrel in her hand. As Reishit stepped from the white arch, the sea began to churn and boil. Clouds rose from the water's surface. The curved tunnels shook and shivered where they lay spread across the face of the sea. Reishit stared. She thought the Egyptians were about to ride out onto the beach. The last Israelites hurried onto the pale sands. As Reishit watched, the tunnels began to collapse, their narrow openings to the sky closing, their walls bowing and breaking. Water rushed into the hollow tubes inside the sea. The tumult was immense. Froth shot toward the heavens. Then, slowly, all was still. The Egyptian army, the chariots, and Pharaoh and his men were no more. All along the beach, there was a tremendous sigh of relief.

Then the woman in red raised her timbrel and chanted in a ringing voice: "Sing to our God for he has surely triumphed: The horse and the rider has he thrown into the sea." There was cheering from every spot along the beach. She sang the words again, and others joined in.

The woman called Miriam held her hand out to Reishit, and they began to leap about together. *This is dancing*, Reishit thought, as her feet wheeled crazily around. *This is what is called dancing*. Then Achat joined them, and Shua, and many women, and many more women, with gray hair and red hair and black hair, with blue dresses and green vests and black trousers. The joy went on and on, long after Reishit was exhausted. The sun rose higher and higher, its hot skirts falling over the dancers.

Then God whispered, "Let us make man in our image." A single Egyptian soldier washed up on the beach. His face was gray and still. Miriam stopped her dance and walked over to the body, hips swaying. Reishit thought she might be about to kick him. Then she reached down. Very tenderly, she touched the man's face. There was an awed sound from the people, up and down the crowded sand.

It was all over. As if everything had been a dream, the people went about the business of pitching tents and cooking soup and spreading unleavened bread with butter. It was almost as if no one could remember what had happened.

Reishit remembered. She shut her eyes and saw the tunnels perfectly formed in her mind. Then she opened her eyes, saw the hundreds of knots of people on the scuffed sand. She knew she needed to find a place to sleep. There seemed to be nowhere. She sighed. She turned around. She saw before her the knob of a great wooden staff. The staff was in the hand of a man with flashing eyes.

"I have been told that you will remember everything," Moses said to Reishit. "You will remember the walls, the vines, and the fish. You will remember Nachshon's courage, Aaron's kindness, Miriam's dance. I have chosen you to sit in my councils and represent the least among my people. When I forget, you will speak to me of what has happened here."

Reishit bowed her head low. Moses raised his hands over her like clouds over the sea. Then Moses stepped away. Reishit saw Shua and Achat together beneath a palm tree. Betzalel was bringing them a flame on a long stick, for a cooking fire. Betzalel's grandmother Miriam waved from her red tent nearby. Aaron looked out from the tent's opening. Nachshon smiled at Shua as he walked along the beach. Reishit ran toward them. As she ran, a pillar of soft rosy cloud burst from the earth at the spot where Miriam had danced.

"For you," said the cloud to Reishit "for you I created the heavens and the earth."

And God saw all that he had made, and found it very good. Then God blessed the twenty-first day of Nisan and called it holy, for on it God finished the work of Creation that God had done.

THE HOUSE OF
THE PROPHETS

We are your subtlest instruments:
no music branches to your breast
that does not sound in us,
no music dies away from you,
that in us lives not,
and even in your absence
your cadence journeys...

—ALLEN MANDELBAUM, *Chelmaxioms*

I left a trail in code
goats could trample.
Nothing gets lost in these hills,
no ink blurs from a sudden rain.

—LINDA ZISQUIT, "Mt. Ardon"

MIRIAM UNDER THE
MOUNTAIN

Moses led the people out of the camp toward God,
and they took their places at the foot of the mountain.
Now Mount Sinai was all in smoke, for the Lord had
come down upon it in fire, the smoke rose like the
smoke of a kiln, and the whole mountain trembled vio-
lently. The blare of the horn grew louder and louder.
As Moses spoke, God answered him in thunder. The
Lord came down upon Mount Sinai, on the top of the
mountain, and the Lord called Moses to the top of the
mountain, and Moses went up.

—EXODUS 19:17–20

And Miriam remained at the foot of the mountain. There were those among the women with her who turned their necks upward like swans to gaze at the fire, and their eyes glowed like garnets, so passionate was their desire to join with the flame. There were others among the women who hid their faces with their hair, for they were afraid to look at God. And there were some who crouched down and touched the sand beneath them, which glistened as if with tears. But Miriam fixed her eyes on the very foot of the mountain, where rough faces of stone met the sandy earth. She waited, although she did not know what she waited for.

She waited and looked, looked and waited. She ran her eyes over the sharp edges of stone, gray and brown and red and blue. She

traced with her eyelashes the wriggling line of earth that ran along
the foot of the mountain as if along the roots of a tree. Time passed.
When a very long time had passed, Miriam saw that the lines in a
jagged gray stone had formed a forehead. There was a mound of
boulders that slowly became an aged cheek. Miriam looked and saw
in the mountain a wrinkled brown stone like an eyelid. As Miriam
watched, the eyelid opened. The stone wrinkled and lifted as if
pulled by a muscle, and behind it was a door into the heart of the
mountain.

Miriam looked around her and saw that everything in the
camp had become still. There was no bird song, no infant's cry, no
splashes of water from jugs. The women around her stood fixed,
their bright eyes directed upward, or downward, or covered with
curtains of hair. No one saw the door into the mountain but
Miriam. She straightened her purple robe and her headdress of silver and blue. She slung her tambourine on her back and a jug of
water at her waist and she went in.

Inside the round tunnel there was darkness and silence.
Miriam walked a long time in that tube of darkness. She thought
that this must be what the world was like when Creation began:
smooth and dark and narrow and round. She walked, and then,
ahead of her, there was a light like the Sabbath, a golden light. After
a few more steps, the tunnel opened into a cave, and the cave was
filled with brightness.

Miriam closed her eyes against the glare, then opened them
very slowly. She saw that the light came from jewels scattered and
piled across the floor of the cave and on its walls and ceilings. There
were jewels of every color: pearl and sapphire blue, emerald green
and rose. Each one cast its own particular variety of light. Alone,
each was magnificent. Together, they were dazzling.

Miriam looked more closely and saw that each jewel cast a

shadow onto the floor or onto one of its fellows. Yet the shadows were not round or faceted like the jewels. Rather, they were angular, thin and branching, and they were as black as night. She looked more closely and saw that the shadows were letters. Miriam began to string the letters together, but she did not know which letter to start with.

Then Miriam turned and saw an old woman watching her, an ancient woman, with hair white as lightning and eyes gray as smoke. Miriam knew that she had seen this old woman before, but she was not sure where. Perhaps near the Nile as she laid her brother's basket on the water. Perhaps while dancing at the shore of the Sea of Reeds. Miriam was sure that this old woman would know the answer to any question.

"What is this place?" Miriam asked.

"You are in the hollow of the mountain," the old woman said. "Inside the words. The stone tablets that your brother will receive—if he broke them open, this is what he would find. The Torah is the shadow and the shell of this place."

Miriam trembled. "How am I worthy to have come here?" she asked.

"You who tend the wombs of Israel are worthy to tend the womb of Torah," said the old woman. She smiled a sweet smile at Miriam. "Now you will bring back my gifts to the people, just as your brother will bring back gifts."

And Miriam turned again and saw within the cave a hundred chests, carved of cedar and acacia wood and ivory, inlaid with aquamarines and banded with gold. And the old woman walked with her to every chest, and threw each one open and revealed its contents to Miriam, but every chest was empty.

And Miriam wept and said, "I am not worthy to receive a gift for Israel."

But the old woman smiled and said nothing.

When the final chest was opened, it too was empty. Miriam wailed as she had while her brother floated down the Nile in a reed basket.

"Do you reject my gifts?" asked the old woman sternly.

"What have you given me?" Miriam cried.

"Empty spaces," said the woman with hair as white as lightning.

"Empty spaces?" asked Miriam, confused.

"I have given you all the empty places in the Torah," said the old woman. "Every place there is no ink, every place there is no word, I give to you as my gift."

"That is no great gift," said Miriam.

"Consider," said the woman to Miriam. "Of what is a river made?"

"Water," Miriam answered.

"You are wrong," said the old woman. "A river is an empty channel. Without this hollow the water would have nowhere to flow. And when the form of this hollow changes, the river changes and becomes a new shape. Now tell me: Of what is your tambourine made?"

"Of silver and wood and skin," Miriam answered. "I know, for I made it myself."

"Again you are wrong," said the old woman. "It is made of emptiness. Without the hollow in its throat, the skin would not chant and the silver would not chime. When you put more or less space between the instrument and your hand, does not its sound change?"

Miriam nodded. "And if you were to ask me of what a dance is made . . . ?"

"Yes?" said the old woman.

"I would tell you that it is made of spaces."

"When the world was created," the old woman told Miriam, "it began with a space."

Miriam smiled. "I will take your gift, old woman. But I do not yet know what I will do with it."

"That is exactly as I wish," said the old woman. "Hold out your water jug."

Miriam did so. The old woman blew into the jug, and it made sweet, hollow music such as one hears when the wind passes through the reeds. The old woman blew and blew. Miriam felt herself lifted into the air and carried through the long, dark tunnel like a blade of grass into a well. She flew through the tunnel and was set gently down at the spot where the mountain met the earth, exactly where she had begun. Around her women were standing just as they had been standing before she entered the mountain, gazing up at the fire or down at the earth or into their own dark hair. As she took her place among them, a shofar blast sounded. Movement stirred in the camp.

A woman in long red skirts took Miriam's arm and pointed upward. The fire on Mount Sinai burned brighter and brighter. From within the fire came a voice: "I am the Eternal your God, who brought you out from the land of Egypt." Miriam listened to the voice, and she listened to the silence within the voice, and she heard the command of the silence. She brought out her water bottle and poured it on the ground, where it formed a river, and when the voice had fallen silent, all the people came and drank from it.

THE MIRRORS

He made the laver out of copper, and its base out of copper, from the mirrors of the serving women [tzovot] who served at the entrance of the Tabernacle.

—EXODUS 38:8

Miriam was a teacher of women.

—TARGUM MICAH 6:4

When the Israelites received the Torah, they did not, at first, know what to do with it. Parts of it were law. Parts of it were story. Parts of it were poem. They began to read it, and discovered that every time they read it, it had a new meaning. They also discovered that the new revelation seemed more clear if they studied it together. The people were occupied with the task of building the Tabernacle and all its furnishings as a dwelling place for God. Yet they also knew that it was an equally important task to study the words that they had been given at Sinai.

So, at night when the work of building the Tabernacle had ceased for the day, the people began to gather in groups to learn Torah together. Miriam, the prophetess, called together the women who had worked hard all day to spin blue, purple, and scarlet thread for the Tabernacle's curtains. They wound their threads into skeins and came to sit in Miriam's tent, where she taught them Torah for hours, until their eyes drooped. The very beginning of the Torah fascinated them. They spent many days on the six days of Creation, probing its mysteries, for they too were engaged in a work of creation. Finally, when they came to the creation of humankind, the women became confused, for they had read this verse: "God created the *adam* in His own image, in the image of God He created him, male and female He created them." They argued about the meaning of this verse. How could God create one creature that was also two? And how could God create a mortal creature, of any gender, in God's own image? They had seen on Sinai that the Eternal was a consuming fire. No mortal could approach that presence and live.

Miriam listened as the women argued. The debate grew more and more heated. Finally Miriam said to her disciples: "Go home and fetch your mirrors."

The women did not understand this strange request, but they hastened to follow Miriam's request. Each went to her tent to find the mirror that she looked into when she braided her hair or painted her eyes. Some opened carved chests of olive wood given to them by their mothers. Some unwrapped bundles of rags. Some begged from neighbor women or from grandmothers. Some brought two or three mirrors so that others could share. Soon all came back to Miriam's tent, carrying the precious bronze circles. The firelight reflected in the many mirrors made the tent blaze like a palace of light. Then Miriam told the women to look into their mirrors.

"What do you see?" she asked.

"I see myself," each woman answered. "I see my eyes, which reveal my soul. I see my mouth, which speaks and sings. I see that I am different from everyone else."

"Each of you is made in the image of God," Miriam explained. "Your soul and your speech are like God's, and your body is God's dwelling place. Each of you embodies the divine Presence in a different way. When you look into your mirror, you see a woman, but you also see the Divine image. If a man were to look into your mirror, he would see a man, but he would also see God. This is what the Torah means when it says: 'God created the *adam* in His own image, in the image of God He created him, male and female He created them.' God is like the mirror: God remains the same but reflects each of our images differently, men and women, young and old. This is why, when we study together, we can reveal different facets of the Torah to each other. Each of us is a different reflection of the One."

The women were silent, and for a long time they looked into their mirrors without speaking. Then one of the women said: "These mirrors are holy now, because each of them has held God's image. We can no longer use them for ourselves. They belong to everyone."

Some of the women were angry at this, for their mirrors were precious to them, but another woman said: "The people are all donating their most precious possessions for the building of the Tabernacle and its instruments. Let us give our mirrors to become part of God's dwelling place. Then their holiness will be honored by all the people."

Miriam smiled, for she was very pleased by her students' words. Then Miriam said: "Let the mirrors be used to make the bronze laver that the priests will use to wash their faces and feet and hands. At each washing, they will look into the water, and they will see God's image. In this way, the mirrors will teach the priests what they have taught us."

Even the most grudging of the women consented to this plan,

and each one gave her bronze mirror to be smelted for the priestly laver. And when the Tabernacle finally was finished, Moses arranged the Tabernacle, its curtains, its altar, its incense, and its lamp. The divine Presence settled upon the Tabernacle and shone radiantly throughout the camp. The women gathered and peered into the courtyard where the polished laver stood before the door of the Tent of Meeting. They made a covenant with one another to return again and again to the door of the Tent of Meeting, to pray, to study, and to see their faces in the basin made from their mirrors. And in that company Miriam was often heard to teach: Because of the one God's many images, the Eternal is called *Adonai Tzevaot*, "Lord of Hosts"—and some say, *Adonai Tzovot*, "God of the women who serve the divine dwelling place."

THE DAUGHTERS OF
TZELAFCHAD

*The daughters of Tzelafchad, of Menashe's family,
son of Hefer son of Gilad son of Machir son of
Menashe son of Joseph—came forward. The names of
the daughters were Machlah, Noa, Choglah, Milcah,
and Tirtzah. They stood before Moses, Elazar the
priest, the chieftains, and the whole assembly, at the
entrance of the Tent of Meeting, and they said, "Our
father died in the wilderness. He was not one of the
faction, Korach's faction, which banded together
against the Lord, but died for his own sin; and he has
left no sons. Let not our father's name be lost to his
clan just because he had no son! Give us a holding
among our father's kinsmen!"*

*Moses brought their case before the Lord. And the
Lord said to Moses, "The plea of Tzelafchad's daughters is just: You should give them a hereditary holding
among their father's kinsmen; transfer their father's
share to them."*

—NUMBERS 27:1–7

MACHLAH

The night my father died, I dreamed of reeds. A riverful of
reeds, green and swaying in the wind. I broke a stem off in my hand,
sucked at it with my teeth. It was sweet inside. That was what my

father wanted all along, that sweetness you can find by a river when the soil is thick and the land is good. My mother was an orphan who used to cut flowers in an Egyptian nobleman's garden. She brought my father the little blue hippopotamus figurine, the one painted with lilies that she had stolen from her master. They would sit and admire it in the narrow shade of their tent, and try the words out on each other. Blue. Lilies. River.

They would do that once or twice a month even when we five girls were growing up. We'd crowd around them and stroke the cool blue skin. We would fight and throw sand, and our parents would threaten to put it away. Then my father would tell us how we would all have a piece of land in Canaan. The same river would run through each of our farms, so if we wanted to send a message, one of us would just drop a note in a basket in the river, and the others would find it. When we were old enough, they explained to us how Moses had told them they would die in the desert. They wouldn't be joining us on that river. My heart began to break that day, like an eggshell breaking to release a chick. It went on breaking when my mother died of a bite from a fiery serpent. I became the woman then, the one who scrubbed the pots, the one who fought with my father and warned my sisters about the boys with wolfish smiles.

We buried my father just a few months before the Promised Land came into sight. One morning when we'd been walking for a while, brown and blue mountains appeared on the horizon. The priests blew silver trumpets. The men cheered and lifted women and children onto their shoulders so they could see the land we were entering. That was the day my heart broke all the way through, and the chick inside me began to emerge. I knew that the priests' law ordained that daughters could not inherit, but that was going to change. I went to the place where we kept the painted hippopotamus in a little blue velvet sack. I took it in my hand, clenched my eyes shut, and I told my father and mother, whose spirits I carried inside me, that we would have our river with the five farms alongside, and they would have it too because their names would live in us.

NOA

When some of the Israelites gather together after the Sabbath and roll their ivory dice, I love to join in. I keep a bag of copper nuggets just for that purpose. That is why I was pleased when my older sister, Machlah, sent me to watch the lots being cast. Moses and the new high priest, Elazar, were assigning the fields of Canaan to each tribe and each family. The men clustered around, men in their twenties and men in their forties, and the lots were cast, first for the larger families, then for the smaller ones. A roar went up each time, as if the winner had won his own private kingdom.

As I followed Moses and Elazar through the camp everywhere, women watched. Eager wives and daughters wanting to know what claim would hold their cattle. Young mothers holding the hands of their tiny sons. Orphan girls with huge eyes and tangled hair. Daughters who had never married, who were weavers and potters and midwives. Earthy sisters wearing aprons, watching their laughing brothers sell their inheritance for gold as soon as Moses left. Hanging back, childless widows who took in laundry from morning till night. I leaned on my staff just outside the circle of men, wondering how I could get Moses to look at all those women.

I went to Machlah and together we began to put together our arguments. I knew we had to speak carefully, to sound brave but not too bold, eloquent but not cunning. Tirtzah ran in and out of the tent, on her way to or from her new lover. She claimed it would never work. Moses disliked women. He barely even spoke to his own wife. Choglah knelt in her corner and chanted prayers for our success. Milcah the poet sat in our circle and crafted words: death, wilderness, promise.

We went to see the judge who had been appointed to mete out justice to our clan. As we spoke, his lips thinned, like sleeves do when you pull your arms out of them. He didn't like our questions. But then Machlah spoke to him about our father, and Milcah pronounced the words to him: river, soil, justice. When I began conferring with his wife, he became nervous, just like I hoped he would. He refused to rule on our case, passing us on to the judge above him. We were on our way.

The funny thing is that I wouldn't know what to do with a farm if I had one. I like to move from place to place rather than to root myself in one spot. I like to give my wooden staff new views, let it see the world. But if one thing infuriates me, it is a game of dice where they refuse to let everyone play. Everyone should have a chance to try her luck.

CHOGLAH

Is that really what he looks like? I have not been so near to him since he passed by here on his way from the Tent of Meeting six years ago. He looks tired. The lines around his mouth are engraved like letters in stone. Is this the man who speaks to God face-to-face, whose covenant I want to enter?

I have told myself that if I believed, this moment would happen. I imagined it fourteen nights running. But now that it has happened, I cannot believe it. Moses has called every chieftain from every tribe. The priests have come out of their holy places to listen. The whole nation is gathered around this small open space. I am afraid that my sisters and I will say something wrong, that we will sound angry or spoiled or bitter, that people will whisper to each other that we want this for the wrong reasons. I am afraid that all the women secretly hate us—or even worse, that they are all counting on us, that we are their last chance.

The crowd begins to quiet. Machlah walks forward with delicate steps. Her head is as high as a pillar of cloud. Machlah speaks before Moses: "Our father died in the wilderness. He was not one of the rebels, Korach's faction, who banded together against God, but died for his own sin. He has left no sons."

Silence. Machlah cannot say more. Tears fall from her cheeks and make dark spots on the ground. Noa clears her throat, but says nothing. A chieftain mutters something under his breath. My heart is pounding. Inside my body a gazelle runs from a lion, but I am the gazelle and I am the lion. I step forward without feeling my feet.

"Let not our father's name be lost to his clan just because he had no son! Give us a holding among our father's kinsmen!"

A wave of startled sound crashes over us. I am shaken by it as I step back. Have I said the wrong thing?

Moses begins to speak. I struggle out of my thoughts to hear his words. "I do not know the answer to your question," he says. "I must inquire of the Holy One. Go to your tent. Tomorrow I will give you God's answer."

He turns and disappears into a wall of priests. I step into the arms of my sisters. The crowd buzzes. I am elated, tense, exhausted. Now it is not Moses I must hope to influence. Now it is God. I walk my sisters home, laugh with them, share their triumph. They prepare an impromptu feast, but I do not eat. I wrap myself in a red veil and go to the Tabernacle. I will sit at the entrance all night and pray. Maybe the Holy One will hear me, and grant us a share in God's promise.

MILCAH

Naturally, I cannot sleep. All night I compose little songs in my head, songs of the-women-will-dance-for-us, songs of how-it-feels-when-they-stone-us. I sing these songs instead of wondering how much longer it will be until daylight. I take my sisters' names and weave them into acronyms. I compose acrostics with five verses, one for each of us. Tirtzah begins to snore and I want to kick her. But what difference does it make if she snores? I cannot sleep.

I don't know what will happen to me if we are left without land. There will not be a place in the new villages for a woman poet. I cannot imagine Moses wants one in his retinue. He never even comes to the drumming festivals the tribes hold once a month. If I am given a piece of land, I can live on it and grow grapes and dates and grain. I will not need to marry a man I don't want just to have a roof over my head. I can light a lamp in the evening and spin new words in the darkness. I do not mind being alone. It is being poor that I fear. I don't want to harvest someone else's fields and spin someone else's wool and sleep with ten other women in a barn. I want to plant my own words.

As dawn creeps up over the horizon, I pull my robe of fine gray wool closer around me. I sit up suddenly in my bed, turn my head to the sun. A figure stands at the opening of our tent. I rise like a sleepwalker and go to the man who has come to our small, poor home. His eyes are deep and wise and full of years. "The daughters of Tzelafchad have spoken rightly," he says to me. "You are to have your father's share of the land."

I do not want to wake my sisters yet. I want to be alone with the man who talks to God. Later today, later in my life, I will speak many words. In this moment, I put my hand out to the cloak of the prophet, like a little child who has been given a present and is afraid to be trusted with so much love. It is no longer the land that matters. What matters is that I am heard. Moses places his palm on my forehead. We are a bridge across silence. I know from the ache in my chest that I will never be alone again.

TIRTZAH

All the brotherless daughters in the camp gave us a party like no one has ever seen. They wore three skirts apiece and poured nine different kinds of wine. They even found inventive ways to prepare the manna. Not, of course, the ones without heads for business. For them, we are nothing but a bellyache. They stayed home. But it was their loss. Two hundred women danced with oil lamps balanced on their heads. I would not have missed it for the world.

It was weeks later that we heard how our male cousins in the tribe of Menashe had gone to Moses and demanded a change in the new inheritance law. We inheriting daughters are enjoined to marry men from our own tribe, so that we will not transmit our land to sons from a different tribe. Of course, this is not a problem for Machlah, who is sensibly engaged to our cousin Boaz, or for Milcah, who does not want to marry, or for Choglah, who lives so high in the clouds that she will not notice whom she marries. But for me it is a problem, because I know who I want to marry, and I do not wish to change my mind.

So, my dear Eitan, I have arranged for you to be adopted by my favorite uncle. That will make you a full-fledged member of the tribe of Menashe. I hope no one decides to oppose me. I do not intend to let my cousins, or even Moses, decide whom I marry. My sisters and I are getting used to choosing for ourselves.

The House of the Judges

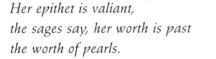

Her epithet is valiant,
the sages say, her worth is past
the worth of pearls.

  —Allen Mandelbaum, *Chelmaxioms*

Each of us has a name
given by our enemies
and given by our love.

  —Rachel, "Each of Us Has a Name"

AND THE WALLS CAME TUMBLING DOWN

The men said to her: Our lives are pledged for yours,
even to death! If you do not disclose this mission of
ours, we will show you true loyalty when the Lord
gives us the land. . . . When we invade the country,
tie this length of crimson cord to the window through
which you let us down.

　　　—JOSHUA 2:14,18*

Rachav the prostitute converted and married Joshua. . . .
Joshua did not have sons, but he had daughters.
Eight prophets who were also priests came from
Rachav the harlot.

　　　—B T MEGILLAH 14B

They fought all the time. They fought over what to name the coconut brown cows that the Israelites herded through the wilderness. They fought over what to call their daughters. They fought over whether it was too hot to use the red woolen blanket that Joshua had taken from Egypt. They fought over whether it was wrong to have sex for money; whether it was wrong to attack Canaanite villages without warning; and whether it

---

* Author's translation

mattered, in the greater scheme of things, whether she went to the ritual bath or not.

The truth was, they liked fighting. It seemed to address some deep need they had. It gave them something to do in the evening after Joshua's generals had gone home. But in the spring, around the time of the anniversary of the battle of Jericho, it always seemed to get nasty. Joshua would disappear for days in the hills around the camp, scouting, or so he said. Rachav would sulk in the tents of her relatives, claiming her mother was ill or that her younger sister needed advice on how to deal with Israelite men. Their daughters would go and hide with their friends or they would bring poppies from the fields, hoping to smooth things over. For both Joshua and Rachav, springtime stirred up harsh memories.

Joshua began to remember his youth. He thought of his days in Moses' tent. He thought of the massacre of the Golden Calf. And he thought of how ten of his good friends, the men with whom he had gone to scout Canaan, the men with whom he had shared waterskins, had faded away, become shadows, and died while he and Caleb remained healthy and strong. That had been their punishment for not trusting God, for claiming the Land was full of giants. Joshua sometimes wondered if his friends just hadn't had the stomach for war. Because of their bad report, the people had wandered in the wilderness for forty years. Joshua's own father had died sometime during those years. Joshua couldn't forgive himself for having been so unconvincing to the rebels. If only he had been able to make them listen to him.

Rachav had other problems. In the spring, she began to think about Jericho. She thought of all the people she could have warned of the Israelite attack if she hadn't been so concerned with saving herself and her own family. She had been so grateful that she'd discovered those Israelite soldiers, that she'd been able to make a deal.

She had lied to her friends, her family, for weeks. She hadn't even told her sisters. She had invited all her loved ones to her inn for a family celebration. Uncle Orev, who was mad at everyone and who disapproved of Rachav's profession, refused to come. She'd heard from an Israelite soldier how he died.

At the last minute, Rachav had opened her door and gathered in everyone she could find: the neighbors' children, the man delivering goat's milk to the elderly woman down the street, the tax collector, the midwife, and the new mother in the shanty leaning against the city wall. She'd still been ashamed when the Israelite soldiers marched them out of the city in front of everyone else, in front of all the people of Jericho who were about to be killed. "Traitor," one young boy had yelled at her. "Collaborator!" It was Joshua who struck down the boy, and it was Joshua who cursed anyone who ever tried to resettle Jericho.

Afterward, the Israelites had not known what to do with Rachav and her family. Their presence seemed to put a damper on the victory celebrations. The priests treated them like one of the mixed multitude, and the mixed multitude treated them like foreigners. The zealous treated them like proof of God's existence. They tried to rebuild their lives at the edge of the Israelite camp. They learned about their new god, their new history. They tried to imagine Sinai. They tried to imagine Egypt.

When Joshua began to court Rachav, she thought it was the most bizarre case of displaced aggression, or displaced guilt, she'd ever seen. Still, she was attracted to him. Apparently she was displacing something herself. She married him. She even fell in love with him, although she would never admit this to her mother, who was angry enough as it was.

Rachav and Joshua couldn't talk about their past, so they fought. Rachav had daughter after daughter after daughter. Joshua thought this some kind of revenge against the war effort. On this particular occasion, Rachav was pregnant for the fifth time. They'd been fighting over what to name the baby, a common flash point. Their other daughters had gone out to the well to escape their shouting.

"I will not name my child after Moses," Rachav insisted. "Even if it's a boy."

Joshua threw down the leather scabbard he was mending. "He was my teacher. He was like a father to me. Can't you understand that?"

Rachav began wiping out a speckled stone cooking pot. "He brought you people here."

"What's that supposed to mean? Where's 'here'?" Joshua was shocked. Neither he nor Rachav ever spoke about the conquest itself. They fought only about details. Rachav was breaking the rules.

"Canaan. My home. Or have you forgotten?" Rachav scraped the bottom of the pot with her fingernails.

Joshua winced. "It's my home now too," he insisted. He picked up the scabbard again and jabbed a needle into it.

"Because you stole it." Rachav went on scraping.

"God gave it to us!" Joshua shouted.

"That's very convenient." Rachav went to the door of the tent and turned the cooking pot upside down and shook it vigorously.

Joshua threw the scabbard down again and followed her. "Rachav, you believe in God! God saved your life."

Joshua's wife sighed. "Yes, I suppose I believe in God. But I don't feel saved."

"Why not?" Joshua asked. He lowered his voice. "Don't you want the life we have together?"

"Of course I do. But, Joshua, you know what I should have done."

"What should you have done?"

"I should have told them. I should have warned my people about the invasion."

Joshua took a deep breath. "Rachav, we've been through this. If you had warned them, Jericho would still have fallen, and you would have been killed too."

"That's not the point. I would have been doing the right thing."

Joshua began shouting again. "How can it not be the point? You saved yourself and your family. Not to mention assorted other people I didn't even agree to save."

"Well, thank you for sparing a few more lives," Rachav said sarcastically. "Don't tell me what to think. It's your fault Jericho was destroyed!"

Joshua crossed his arms over his chest. "They should have negotiated with us."

Rachav threw the cooking pot onto the ground, where it burst like a noisy grape. "Why couldn't you have been afraid like everyone else?"

"What?" Joshua shoved at the pieces of the pot with his foot.

"Like all the other spies. Why couldn't you and Caleb have been afraid too? Why couldn't you have told Moses you were afraid of the size of our armies, or something? Isn't that what the other ten spies did?"

"Then God would have destroyed *my* people!"

"Why is God so interested in destroying people?" Rachav bent double. "Oh, my God." A stain appeared on the front of her linen dress.

"What is it?" Joshua put his hand on his wife's shoulder. "Rachav, what's wrong?"

Rachav crouched down and put a hand on her back. "I'm in labor."

"I'll get the midwife."

"No! I'm having the baby *now*. The midwife from Jericho is all the way across the camp."

"I'll get a different midwife."

"Stay here!" Rachav moved gingerly to the slate blue rug that covered the floor of the tent. "I need you to catch the baby."

Though Joshua had felt comfortable on many battlefields, the idea of delivering a baby made him feel very nervous. "What do I do?"

Rachav gripped her husband's shoulders and began to bear down. "Do you mean to tell me you've never seen me deliver? After four children? You never even peeked?"

"Childbirth should be attended by women," Joshua stammered.

"It wouldn't be a bad thing if you saw how hard it is to bring someone into the world," Rachav gasped. "Maybe then you wouldn't remove people from the world every time they get in your way."

"The people of Israel need a place to live, Rachav." Joshua's forehead was running with sweat, but he couldn't wipe it. He was supporting Rachav by the waist.

"I know that, Joshua, I know that. I just want you to think about what it's like to be me and my family—" Rachav's face squeezed into itself until it looked like a red sponge. She bore down harder. "Oh, God!"

Joshua would never understand how he knew to dip his broad hands down and catch the baby before she fell. There was a high-pitched cry. Rachav's smile split her face.

"Is it a girl?" she asked.

"It's a girl," he said to her. He held the crying baby in his arms and gently cut her umbilical cord with the knife from his belt. He tied off the cord with a red thread he pulled from the old rope Rachav still used to tie her belongings together. Then he wiped the newborn with a linen cloth.

"Good," Rachav said. "I prayed for a girl."

"So did I," said Joshua.

"You did?" Rachav squeaked as she reached out for her daughter. "After four girls?"

"I have a hard time getting close to my disciples," Joshua admitted. "We talk only about war." He put the baby on Rachav's chest. "Somehow, it's easier with my daughters."

Rachav thought for a moment. The baby nuzzled Rachav with her tiny nose and began to nurse. "So what are we going to name her? I told you, I'm not naming her after Moses."

"What if we called her Yareach?" Joshua asked gently.

"After the moon?"

"After Jericho," Joshua said. "As a remembrance."

Rachav looked at her husband, her eyelids puffy and swollen. "I love you very much."

She was still sweating. Joshua went to the door of the hot tent and threw it open. Clouds stretched across the reddening sky in thick, fleecy yarns. As a sign, it was even better than a rainbow.

Miriam's Heir

And Caleb announced: I will give my daughter Achsah in marriage to the man who attacks and captures Kiriat-Sefer.

—Judges 1:12

She dismounted from her donkey, and Caleb asked her: What is the matter? She replied, "Give me a present, for you have given me away as Negev-land; give me springs of water."

—Judges 1:14–15*

The tent was cramped. The dirt floor smelled of blood. Achsah pushed her black hair out of her sweaty face. She longed to be outside in the spring air, but her father needed her attention. Although wounded, he directed battle plans from his bed. Men shouldered in and out of the tent flap day and night, relaying plans for the conquest of Kiriat-Sefer. Kiriat-Arba had already fallen before the tribe of Judah. Now there was to be another battle. Achsah carried another bowl of dried herbs to her small work space.

"Will Caleb be ready to go to war?" a Judahite patriarch asked her brusquely from his place on the floor. Having asked, he lowered

* Author's translation

154

his dark eyes. According to the new tribal covenant, she was a chieftain's daughter, a woman to be respected. She had not needed such titles in the wilderness.

"I do not know," Achsah replied. She turned away, and endured the sharp ache that meant that she missed her mother. Miriam had been gone some years now. Like her brothers Moses and Aaron, Miriam had not seen her beloved patchwork of tribes enter the Land of Canaan. She had gone to the well one day and fallen asleep beside it.

Achsah never asked her father about her mother, so as not to grieve him. Caleb and Miriam had been deeply in love. He dared her fierce temper and praised her long black hair, which did not gray even under many seasons of desert sun. The old women used to tell how, when Caleb had gone to spy out Canaan, Miriam waited anxiously for his return, her feet twitching on the sand. Achsah was not yet born.

Now Caleb had new women to wait for him. Caleb's two concubines, Eifah and Maacah, worked beside Achsah in the tent or slipped outside to the cooking area to boil water for bandages. Eifah and Maacah were cousins from the tribe of Naftali. They had the uncanny habit of speaking the same words simultaneously. Achsah was fascinated by them. They cared for her father, their children, and each other with gentle hands. At night they sat watching the cooking fire with deep, secretive eyes.

The afternoon wore on. Leaders debated Joshua's division of the Land. Messages arrived from Caleb's brother, who had camped on another height. Caleb reviewed the information and sent out spies and scouts, moving slightly so that Eifah could change his bandages. Achsah sharpened her father's spear and scrubbed his bloody linens. Her father's injury, she surmised, was more serious than he wished to admit.

It was evening before Achsah found a moment to step outside.

The silver ornaments in her ebony hair sparkled in the last rays of the sun. As she had hoped and expected, Otniel arose from the place where he had watched her tent and came toward her.

Otniel, son of Caleb's brother Kenaz, smithed bronze for the tribe. In his spare time he studied the lore of Moses. Many came to him for arbitration or advice. Indeed, many called him "Judge," and deferred to his wisdom. Even Caleb sought out Otniel's judgment before making important decisions. When Achsah was a girl, she had been afraid of Otniel, of his dark shape against the glowing forge. When she had grown older, braver, she began to seek him out. On the day Israel crossed the Jordan into Canaan, she and Otniel had fallen in love.

Otniel was smiling. "Will you walk with me, daughter of Caleb?"

"I will, if you do not object to my smell. I have been tending my father's wounds all day in a hot tent."

Otniel breathed deeply, his chest moving in and out. "Then take in the smell of the spring. What a good land this is!"

Achsah frowned. Otniel had reminded her of the bloody war the nomads were fighting. Both they and the Land's inhabitants believed the country was theirs by right.

"I would rather be back in the wilderness," she said.

"We cannot raise our children under a senna bush, Achsah," Otniel said. "For the last five years people have streamed into my tent with arguments about theft and inheritance. We do not have enough wealth to go around. This place will change that, Achsah."

"What if it does not? What if our thefts only grow larger?" Achsah asked.

"Then my judgments will be even more necessary," Otniel replied. "If I listen to you, I will always be a busy man."

Achsah regarded him appraisingly. "See that you continue to have time for me," she said.

Achsah took Otniel's arm, and they walked until they came to the shade of an ancient oak. They embraced each other, twining like the great brown limbs of the tree.

"Is everyone thinking of the battle?" she whispered to him.

"Of course they are. They have been trailing into my tent all day asking questions about the division of spoils."

As stars dripped into the darkness, Achsah told stories of the wilderness journey. With Otniel's head in her lap, Achsah spoke of the bubbling spring set in white stone that Miriam always seemed to find near the Israelite camp, no matter where the twelve tribes wandered. Some whispered that the moving spring was witchcraft, but Achsah would look at her mother's shining face and know that the well was a gift. Miriam held Achsah in the spring's waters to bathe her and taught her how to use the plants that grew up at its edge, how to make pipes from reeds and dye from flowers. Miriam also taught her daughter how to dance the undulating motion of the water. *Water is life, never forget that*, Miriam would say to her daughter. People said it was the well that gave Miriam her inexplicable fertility. Achsah had been born long after her mother's menses ended.

"Do you think we will ever see the spring again?" Otniel asked Achsah seriously.

"I hope that I will someday see the well again, but I do not know the way to find it," Achsah answered. "I am afraid the secret is lost."

To cheer her, Otniel told of his hopes for the Land. At midnight, the two made their way back to their nomad homes.

When Achsah woke the following morning, Caleb was awake. With one eye open, he grunted, "How is my favorite daughter?" It was a joke between them, since Achsah was his only daughter. Maacah and Eifah had borne only sons.

"I'm well, Father." Achsah smiled, slipping her bright red tunic over the white shift in which she had slept. She combed out the tangles of her hair with her fingers.

Caleb sat up and propped himself against a pillow. "I have realized," he said slowly and with a kind of grudging shame, "that I will be unable to fight in the coming battle."

"I'm relieved to hear that, Father," Achsah said, settling down at his side and stroking his forehead. "I do not want you to fight in this condition."

"Yet someone must lead this charge for me," Caleb went on in a solemn tone, "and I must make sure that man succeeds. Kiriat-Sefer will be difficult to overcome."

There was something strange in her father's voice. Achsah began to become nervous.

Caleb continued. "Achsah, I have summoned the best fighting men of the neighboring camps to our tent. I will proclaim to them that whoever conquers Kiriat-Sefer will have my daughter's hand in marriage."

"You're going to make me a spoil of war?" Shaken by her father's decision, Achsah pulled back her hand. She looked around the tent for allies, but Eifah and Maacah had their backs to her. Apparently, they had decided not to interfere. Caleb snorted angrily.

"Achsah, it's time you acted like a leader, not like a child. The Canaanites have fought against us fiercely. If Kiriat-Sefer isn't taken, our presence in this land will never be secure. You are Miriam's daughter and your hand is highly coveted. You must be aware of the men who come to me daily to ask for you. You can help win this war and fulfill the promises Moses made to us. You owe your people that much."

"But Otniel . . ." Achsah stammered. She had assumed her father would assent when Otniel asked for her hand.

"Otniel is a fair judge of the law of Moses and a fine smith, but he is not a warrior. Achsah, I know this is difficult for you, but I ask no more of you than I have asked of myself. I too had to wed for duty, not for love. I grew to love your mother, and I know you will grow to love your husband. After all, he will be a war hero."

As her father finished speaking, several men came through the tent flap. Her father had summoned them, she realized, so he could announce his challenge. This time, they looked her full in the face. Achsah was embarrassed and confused. Maybe her father was right. Back in Egypt, Miriam had been willing to risk death to save her people. If this were the best way Achsah could help the tribe of Judah, she should make the sacrifice. Her heart ached as she stood by her father.

The tent filled with men, some old, some young, some familiar to her, some not. Some were minor chieftains of her tribe. Some were princes of the tribe of Shimon, camped nearby. Caleb raised a hand for silence. "I welcome you and wish you victory in the name of God who fought for us in Egypt. Make it known throughout the camps: I will give my daughter's Achsah's hand in marriage to the man who attacks and captures Kiriat-Sefer for the tribe of Judah."

A cheer went up. *Now I am truly a chieftain's daughter,* Achsah thought, her heart breaking. *But I would rather be as common as the dirt and have the lover I want.*

"I must speak to Otniel," Achsah said to her father in an oddly hard voice, once the men had filed from the tent. "It is only just."

"Go," her father replied, trusting her. Yet when she came to Otniel's tent, he was not there.

"He cannot see you now, Achsah," Otniel's brother, Seraya, said to her. Even though she wept, no one would tell her where he was, not Otniel's friends, not his mother. She returned to her own tent, defeated. She did not even raise her head when Eifah and Maacah went out to gather medical supplies for the coming battle. Nearby, maidens tuned instruments for the dances that would celebrate victory. As Miriam's daughter, it was Achsah's duty to lead them, but she did not have the heart.

At the end of the day, a messenger came to tell Caleb that there were three different groups of soldiers in the camp, each backing a promising leader. Achsah knew the two Judahites. One was young, ruthless Aziz, who had desired Achsah for years. The other was an older, seasoned warrior named Raam, a man who already had two wives. There was also an ambitious Simeonite prince, Tomer, who had sent Achsah a formal letter of courtship around noon. The three groups had agreed to attack the city from different angles, and accord victory to the one who breached the wall. The attack would proceed the following dawn.

Eifah and Maacah arrived, shrugged off their black robes, and put down baskets of gathered figs. "We did not find Otniel," the women said to Achsah, although she had not asked them to look. They seemed oddly pleased. Achsah fell asleep angry and confused. She worried about the many warriors who would be killed in battle the following day. Why did the Israelites want the Canaanites' land? She had been happy in the wilderness, with Miriam and the well.

At dawn, Achsah awoke to Eifah and Maacah shaking her shoulders, one on either side. "Come out and see," they whispered. Caleb was not in the tent, and his staff of leadership was gone.

Achsah was alarmed. "Father is too ill to be up," she

exclaimed, but Eifah and Maacah pulled her out of bed and helped her slip on her robe.

"Come," they said.

Achsah let herself be led to the rough square at the center of the clan's cluster of tents. She saw immediately that there were many angry warriors gathered there, warriors who should have been preparing for battle. Caleb stood near the center of the square, trying to establish order.

"Treachery!" cried Aziz from a knot of young fighters. "Someone has betrayed us!"

"Caleb," demanded Raam, who was among a group of men with clenched fists, "is this a trick? Where are our weapons? We may be attacked at any minute!"

Tomer and the Simeonites were ominously silent. The tribal lord's elaborately engraved saber was missing.

Caleb raised his hands and asked over and over again for quiet without success. Suddenly, silently, Otniel appeared at the corner of the square. With great confidence, he walked to its center. The crowd grew still.

"I have hidden your weapons," he stated calmly, "and I will not return them until you agree to let me lead you in battle."

"Traitor," yelled Aziz. "You are no warrior. I will not let a thief give me orders!"

Otniel ignored him and went on. "How can we stand, divided into three? If we must fight, then we must fight as one. Have I not been a leader to you? Have I not solved your most tangled disputes? Israel is a people of justice. Let a judge lead you, and God will not let you fail."

Now Caleb moved to the center. "Otniel," he said in a stern tone, "I have promised Achsah to a warrior who can conquer Kiriat-

Sefer. We value you for your wisdom, but you cannot lead us because you are not a soldier. Trickery and thievery cannot change this. You must accept your place in the tribe and return the weapons to those who properly own them. Do it now, and we will forgive your foolishness." Hundreds of angry warriors murmured assent to Caleb's words and began to close in on the two men.

Achsah stepped out into the square and stood beside Otniel. Her loose garments flapped in the wind as the crowd around her again fell quiet. "You cry out 'thievery'! But who owns swords if not the smith?" she shouted. "Who is the hero of battle but the one who makes the weapons? Could any of you fight without the help of Otniel? Why then do you lift yourselves above him?"

There was no reply to her challenge. Some of the men looked ashamed. Achsah turned to her father. "You claim that a warrior must lead us. Moses was no warrior, and yet he led us forty years. He was a man who cared for his people, a good and honest judge, a judge like Otniel. In your lust to conquer this land you have forgotten what makes Israel strong." She caught the eyes of many in the crowd. "Do you wish to become like any other people, conquering others by strength?" she asked them. "Do you wish to be a nation forever at war? Or do you wish to be led by those who will know when the time of peace has arrived?"

There was a roar of approval. Achsah was astonished to see that behind the lines of warriors, the rest of the camp had arrived: women, craftsmen, elders, and children. It was they who cheered her. After a moment, some of the warriors joined in. Other warriors looked as if they might turn on the crowd. Achsah gasped in alarm.

Caleb raised his staff. "My daughter is right," he said. "In my grief at Miriam's death, I forgot my wife's teachings about the way to live. Achsah has reminded me. Otniel, here are your troops. Prepare them for battle. May God protect you all."

Achsah was sitting with her father when Otniel's brother, Seraya, ran up to her, covered with the blood and dust of the battlefield. "Achsah, come quickly. Otniel was struck down by a man of Kiriat-Sefer while offering terms of peace. I am afraid that he will bleed to death."

Achsah grabbed her sacks of herbs and linens and ran behind Seraya. They raced down into a valley Achsah had seen only from a distance. The walls of Kiriat-Sefer stood, still intact. At the city gate, men sliced each other with swords. A circle of Israelite warriors stood around the gate. Off to one side lay a dozen wounded men. Achsah could see Otniel among them, his shoulder wrapped in a sheepskin.

"Otniel offered Kiriat-Sefer a place in our tribe," Seraya panted, "if they would agree to give up their weapons to us and open their city to our folk. But a soldier among the Canaanites struck him with a spear. Fighting broke out."

Achsah crouched at Otniel's side. She assessed the damage. He was bleeding heavily. Her mother had taught her how to stanch a wound with leaves. She worked quickly. Then she gave Otniel an infusion of herbs to drink. Very slowly, the color returned to his face. After a time, he coughed and opened his eyes. Achsah said nothing, not wanting him to waste his strength in speaking, but she squeezed his hand. Slowly, carefully, he squeezed back. Seraya sagged with relief.

A soldier came from the battle at the gate and bent down to Otniel. Achsah noticed that it was one of her former suitors. "We have broken into the town," he reported to Otniel. "The elders of Kiriat-Sefer are once again asking for terms. Should we listen to them, or should we burn the place?"

"Send them to me," Otniel rasped. "Only this time keep them at a safe distance."

The whole camp burst into cheers as they heard of the new treaty with the people of Kiriat-Sefer. Women went out to dance. Men beat on drums and gongs. Eifah and Maacah whirled around each other like twin suns. A few chiefs of Kiriat-Sefer stiffly entered the camp, and were seated next to Otniel at a feast.

Away from the victory fire, Caleb called his daughter. Achsah came and crouched next to him.

"Achsah," Caleb began, "I owe you an apology, and an explanation."

"No, Father," Achsah said, but Caleb put a hand on her shoulder.

"Let me speak. When I married your mother, I was still mourning for my first wife, Azuvah, who died of disease in Egypt. I didn't think I could ever love someone again. My father insisted that I marry Miriam because she and I were leaders of the people. Our marriage would cement the alliance between the tribe of Judah and the tribe of Levi. Miriam was the joy of my life. I thought you too would come to love a husband I chose for you. Now I see that you chose better than I."

Caleb closed his eyes. Achsah saw that her father needed to sleep. She tiptoed over to where Maacah and Eifah pounded grain for the next day's bread. What mysterious pull drew Caleb to these strange women after Miriam's death? Caleb's concubines looked at Achsah with identical eyes. Achsah wondered what they thought of marriages, arranged or otherwise.

"You never said to my father that what he was doing was wrong." she said to the women abruptly. "He might have listened to you."

"Otniel needed to grow," they answered together. At that moment, the sound of rams' horns echoed throughout the camp. Maacah and Eifah handed Achsah her tambourine.

After a week of wedding feasts, Caleb arose on his staff to see Achsah and Otniel off to their new tent. Even after the victory, even after her wedding, Achsah felt that something was unfinished. Water is life, she remembered Miriam saying.

As Caleb walked the line of camels, Achsah leaped off her she-camel and knelt at her father's feet.

"What is the matter with you?" Caleb cried out, startled.

"Father, you have given me away as Negev-land, dry and fruitless. Give me as a dowry a piece of the good land we have entered, and my family will have a place to grow."

It was an audacious request, since land was so valuable. The crowd standing around them held its breath. "Take Upper and Lower Gullot," Caleb replied after a minute. "It is empty of inhabitants and is rich in water. I can think of no one who would care for it better than you."

Achsah and Otniel spent many weeks exploring their territory. There was enough room for a small clan. Several Judahite families asked to join the pair on their claim. In a small valley, the couple built a house, the first house either of them had ever lived in.

One morning, Achsah set out to find the source of the stream that ran through Upper Gullot. As she hiked upward, the foliage grew lusher and more fragrant. Achsah was intoxicated. There was an indefinable presence in the air. Achsah came to the crest of a hill and was suddenly able to identify the sweet scent in her nostrils.

Below her, a deep blue pool of water, perfectly round, perfectly clear, sparkled in the sunlight. Healing herbs and flowers grew around it. The spring was set in pale gray stone. It bubbled at one end, where water welled from deep inside the earth.

Achsah plunged into the cool water with a shout of joy. "Mother's well!" she cried. "It's Miriam's well! It's here!" But only when she brought Otniel to the spring and saw his battle scar disappear in its ripples did she really believe it.

Many years passed. Otniel and Achsah had two children, a son called Hatat and a daughter whom Achsah called Meyonotai, "my wells," in honor of Miriam's waters. Israelites all over Canaan heard of Otniel's wisdom and made him a judge over the twelve tribes. It was said that he restored all the teachings of Moses that the Israelites had forgotten. Caleb died, and Achsah became the chieftainess of the Calebites. Achsah guarded Miriam's wisdom and Miriam's well, passing down to her children and children's children the secret of renewing life.

THE SONG OF
DEVORAH AND YAEL

*In the days of Shamgar, son of Anat, in the days
of Yael the paths ended, and travelers walked on
roundabout paths.*

   —JUDGES 5:6*

*Sarai who is in Issachar was with Devorah, and
Issachar was like Barak.*

   —MODELED ON JUDGES 5:15

*Listen, this misshapen boulder.
Listen, smell of sage burning.
Listen, these broken bronze axles.
Listen, this Mount Tabor.
Listen, the echoes of this hammer.
Listen, the echoes of this song.
We have a story.*

*In the beginning, there was covenant.
The covenant of Noah.
The covenant of Abraham.
Of Sinai.
Of Ruth.
And our beginning
was covenant.*

* Author's translation

Great gusts of laughter stormed across the campfires and rippled the vats of wine. Veterans jested with their peers, slapping the scabbards of their swords and the taut drums of their chests. Bits of song broke out here and there, echoes of the afternoon's glory. Men of Zebulun laughed with men of Issachar. Benjaminites saluted drunkenly at men of Naftali. Barak walked from fire to fire, pounding men on the back. He joked about their bits of Canaanite spoil: leather vests, iron swords, arrowheads. A miracle, everyone said, a miracle, how the river flooded against nature, how the ruthless chariots jammed their wheels in the mud, how the little Kenite woman put a tent pin through the head of her husband's ally. Inexplicable. Devorah's prophecy had come to pass. There would be no raiding of Israelite villages next harvest.

"The Canaanites must be whining now!" Barak cried as he approached the center of the camp. He was answered with a shout. He cried again, "The stars in their courses fought against Sisera!" The answer came. Men lifted their swords, signing what they would do to Israel's oppressors. Youths raced to set gathered pine branches aflame. The fires sputtered and roared.

"The men are ready to take the Philistine capital," Barak confided in a whisper as the hoarse voices died down. Devorah stood alone on a flattened boulder, staff in hand. Her black hair was streaked with white. Her face was striped in blackness and flickering light. The song lingered on her lips. She crouched down so that her head was level with Barak's.

"Yes. A few days to rest. Then we will go to the plains. King Yavin's people will not have regrouped within that time. God will give us victory."

"Just as in your dreams." Barak laughed up at her, mocking her even as he honored her. Resenting her? Suddenly she was tired of his laughter. She retreated to the center of her stone. Barak wandered off toward a gathering of Naftali soldiers, to be at home among the roasted joints and wine of his own tribe. He was unconcerned by her silence. He had not asked to share her life, only her greatness.

Devorah watched him go, her hands clasped behind her back, thoughtful. Her brown robe billowed in a sudden wind. A hand fell on her shoulder. She reached up to clasp it gently.

It was Sarai of the tribe of Issachar. Devorah could tell by the smallness and strength of the fingers she grasped. Sarai was inheritor of her father's chiefdom. Her father had no sons, and she had strength and subtlety of mind in a time when strategy was necessary for survival. On her account, the people of Issachar were called *yodei itim*, "knowers of times," for she always seemed to know the right time for an attack, a question, a shift in tribal law—or a romance, Devorah thought. The tribe of Issachar, like Barak, had followed a woman into battle, and so Devorah had not been lonely.

"You are my life's comfort, Sarai," Devorah said quietly as the slender form arranged itself near her.

"Nonsense," replied Sarai, tossing her dark red hair. "What is between us will end when the campaign ends—but that is not why I came from my tent to speak with you."

"Why, then?" Devorah asked.

"There is a man coming," Sarai told her. "My scouts have seen him, as have Barak's. He is allied to the enemy, but they give him safe passage here because he seeks your justice. He is searching for his wife."

Devorah yawned elaborately, feigning unconcern. "Hever the Kenite."

"Yes, and he will want Yael returned." Sarai's eyes abruptly moved to scan the line of trees around the clearing, then returned to Devorah's face. "We must stop Barak from giving her to him."

Devorah frowned. "Yael broke Hever's treaty and ran away with his enemies. For that, Hever might beat her or kill her, it is true. Yet if we, as victors, make a new treaty with him, he has lost nothing. He may thank her instead. In that event, will she not be better off among her own people, rather than among these Israelites about whom she knows nothing?"

"Devorah, have you looked at this girl-creature? As she left the tent with our soldiers, she took her festival robes on her shoulders and her crockery in her arms. Treaty or no treaty, she does not want to go home!"

"Of course I looked at her," Devorah snapped, but she knew she was lying. She had been looking at the corpse at Yael's feet. She had praised Yael in song—but she had not even asked the woman why she had killed Sisera. Now Devorah looked at Sarai. The young chieftain's eyes were set wide and asymmetrical in an oval face. Devorah stroked her smooth chin with aging fingers.

"If I lie to Hever when he comes," Devorah argued, "our men will betray Yael. They cannot keep themselves from telling the story. But if we keep her, there is war between his tribe and ours. Barak will be reluctant to ignore Hever's claim. She is his wife. If women go killing their husbands' allies and running away with foreign armies, how will we keep from chaos?"

Sarai's voice was steady. "Betray the killer of Sisera? I think not. Barak and the others may be sympathetic to Hever's rights, but they are not ingrates. They will not return Yael to her husband if she does not want to go. We can hide her. Come, Devorah, would you wish, having been a hero, to return to carding wool and gelling yogurt?"

"After miracles have been done for us, I would not wish to fail in justice to Yael, through whom the miracles came. Yet, Sarai," Devorah lowered her voice, "I am judge because I accept the way things are. It is one thing not to have a husband, as we do not, but she has one!"

"I think she will have him no longer," Sarai said with gravity. She leaped off the boulder toward the Issachar camp, for Hever the Kenite had arrived. Barak was escorting him toward Devorah. The noise around the fires died down as men strained to hear. Hever was clearly surprised to see Devorah there among the blunt spears and the wine. He gave her gestures of respect in accordance with his tradition. She sat calmly with her staff, thinking of miracles. Barak looked up at her slyly, suspiciously. What did he see?

Hever's face was sweaty and dirty. He had come a long way, following the army's trail, Devorah thought. She signed for someone to bring him water. "Lady," he said when he had drunk, "I have heard a hundred rumors today in a hundred camps. That my wife was raped by a Canaanite general. That she seduced him and defiled herself. That she was killed by Israelite men pursuing the enemies' spoil. That she has become a concubine to Barak. That she is dead. I credit none of these words as proof, but there are bloodstains on the rugs of my tent and on the tools of my camp. I found the footprints of your men in the dust. If you know where she is, I ask"—he looked around into the faces of soldiers—"that she be brought to me in safety. I have been her husband since she was a child. She knows no other protector."

Devorah had lived a long time and she had not lied in many years. She saw this man as still married to a child, not understanding his wife's womanhood. She saw that he was earnest in his care. She saw that he was tired and had come a great distance. She was silent for a long time. Then she rose to her feet. The smile she gave to Hever was a rare smile, a smile of humor and sympathy and loss and invitation. It was the smile she had given Barak when he had said: If you will go with me, I will go. Devorah began to sing, quietly at first, then with great energy and passion. "Listen kings, hear princes, I will sing." She sang the song of anger, the song of victory, the song of revelation, the song of Yael and her tent pin and her bowl of curds, the song of Sisera's mother. It was the truest thing she could say.

Hever bowed his head. His face, a mountain range of leathery creases, wrinkled further. She wondered if he had understood. She knew that he had when he asked: "And now? What happens after the song?"

"Now she is the instrument of God. What touches her will be consumed with flame."

Barak stared at Devorah, startled. There was an intake of breath from around the fires, quiet, yet the flames guttered in the desert air.

"Your god has stolen her, then," Hever said heavily.

"You will be repaid in measure for her loss," Devorah replied, but she did not offer him money. She did not want to insult him, whatever he might be.

Below the mountain, Canaanite soldiers lay unburied. Shallow graves had been dug for the few Israelites who had died under the wheels of the chariots before the mud had conquered the iron wheels. The wounded lay by a far flame, wine in their mouths. A woman tended them. She had wide hips and a gently rounded face, with wide-set brown eyes peering out under a thatch of silver hair. Her full body made her look like one of the stone fertility goddesses seen in temples and city shops in the Canaanite capital. Each blanket-wrapped body reminded her of her son, Shamgar, an Israelite judge who had been wounded in battle years before. She had come to witness the defeat of the Canaanite men who once had come to her temple when she was a Canaanite priestess. It was a considerable irony, she reflected, smiling. She had left her priestly calling to follow the Israelites. Now she was a healer among the Hebrews, healing their soldiers. Another irony. It was not the only irony present tonight in this camp, where women fought men and fell in love with other women.

She was known by her son's name. Anat, mother of Shamgar. Mother of the stranger. Goddess of love and war. Invisible, contradictory presence. As Hever passed, Anat carefully drew the blanket up around a rounded shape. Anat patted the girl's head of hair, black and thick as goats' wool, and took away the half-finished cup of healing tea she had brewed. Hever looked, perhaps by chance, toward Anat before walking on.

When Devorah finally came to the crag where the soldiers of Naftali had pitched her peaked black tent, the woman Yael was squatting outside the entrance. Her bloody clothes had been taken away. She was wearing a white robe, far too big for her and no doubt given her by Anat, mother of Shamgar. Her wild black hair had been combed. It fell unbound about her shoulders, framing her catlike face. Yael looked up at Devorah with deep, rich, pale brown eyes like floodwaters. Devorah was oddly stirred. The moon was half full.

"Have you no place to sleep tonight?" Devorah asked. Her speech seemed abrupt to Yael, although she had meant to be kind.

"My tent is closed to me," replied Yael.

"Did you not want . . . ?" Devorah was disturbed.

Yael shook her head. "No, prophetess, you did me a favor tonight. Half a favor, in any case. I wanted to speak to you, before the day is over."

Devorah spread her arms wide, though she was exhausted and

past ready for sleep. "My tent is yours. Come in. Forgive me if I do not light a lamp."

Yael entered and sat comfortably in the manner of tent dwellers, her long limbs poking into the coarse cloth walls. Devorah settled more slowly, not being as young as the girl. She pushed her long black-and-white streaked hair behind her ears, laid her staff down flat on the tamped earth. She offered Yael some milk. The Kenite accepted and drank deeply, fingering the bowl, laughing suddenly at the irony. There was some horror in her laughter, some strange triumph. Devorah stroked the wrinkles in her earth-colored robe and examined her striking guest.

Yael flashed white teeth. "I enjoyed your song even more the second time."

"Because of it you cannot go home," Devorah said bluntly. "I have named you God's possession, so that no Israelite man will look at you. What can I do for you? I will provide you with a house and servants here in Naftali country, or with a ship of Zebulun to take you where you please." Devorah tasted her own guilt. This was the woman who had saved her people, and Devorah had not thought about what Yael needed until now.

"Devorah, I want to stay with you." Yael enunciated each word with a profound force.

With me? Devorah wondered. *Under my lonely palm tree? With hordes of Israelites lined up from dawn until dusk?* No one had ever wanted to stay with her for long. Anat could not bear the hordes that milled about her and made every day hot and sour with people's pain. Sarai, who was leader of a tribe, had her own matters to mind. Barak—Barak could not live comfortably with what she was.

"My life is difficult," she demurred.

"I have been a shepherd in the summer heat and drawn cold water in winter when it rains," said Yael. "I am used to hardship. I would be of use to you. I know you have no one to help you."

And how did Yael know that? "But why?" Devorah asked. "Why kill the Israelite enemy? What have we Israelites done to deserve your loyalty?"

Yael shook her head. "I am not loyal to the Israelites. I am loyal to you. I first heard you speak in the hills of Ephraim when I was on the way to my wedding. My father and I met Shamgar and his mother, Anat, on the road. They invited us to come and see the festival of the new judge in Israel. I drank sweet milk and watched the flashing of your eyes. I have loved you ever since."

Devorah sat back. "Yael," she said gently, "you are very young." *Full of hope*, she thought, *full of barbaric longing*.

Yael shook her head. "Less so after today."

Devorah nodded.

Yael spoke more urgently. "When Sisera came into my camp, running from your army, it was my chance, my first, my only opportunity to do something for you. Perhaps you are shocked by what I have done; but before I struck, I filled myself with you. Even if you do not want me, I am glad to have defeated your enemy. I am glad to have shared your tent, if only for an hour."

Yael was quiet. She had said what she had come the long way of her womanhood to say. Devorah, judge over the twelve tribes, was very still beneath her black-and-white-streaked mane. It had been an age since anyone had looked into her eyes and seen revelation. It had been an age since she had felt what she was feeling: this pull like that of a tide, slow and irresistible. Maybe she never had, before now. Yael's too-large tunic slipped off one shoulder. Moonlight from the tent's opening glanced off her date-colored skin.

Devorah pushed at the air with her hands. "How can I lie with you? I have said that whoever touches you will be consumed with flame."

Yael threw back her head and laughed, bold laughter like the calling of a bird. "Is 'flame' another word for 'desire'? I will see that your prophecy comes to pass."

Devorah set her staff aside. Yael took Devorah's hand in hers. She began to stroke the calloused fingers, then the palm. "Awake, awake, Devorah. Awake and utter a song."

"Most blessed of women be Yael," the older woman whispered. "Most blessed of all the women who have entered my tent."

At dawn, Anat changed bandages. In the branch of a pine tree Sarai sat peeling twigs. The full sleeves of Sarai's quilted red coat touched the ground beneath the tree, where giant pinecones lay.

"Your warriors will wonder where you are," said Anat.

"They will think they know," answered Sarai. "They will think I am with Devorah."

The two continued in companionable silence. The wounded men did not waken. The sun rose higher, piercing holes in the thin air.

"You should sleep," said Anat. "What is between them is. You cannot change it."

Sarai considered. "Anat, do you know when I began to love her? I watched her from across the battlefield, as I held an arrow to the string. I saw her laugh as it began to rain. She let down her hood and lifted her forehead to be blessed by the first trickles of a miracle. I see that moment now, it is true, but she is not why I am awake. I am awake because the war is not over."

"Ah," said Anat. "There is still the city of Harozet-goyyim."

"That city and its people." Sarai snapped a rubbery twig in half. She smiled. "Now that I have convinced Devorah to save Yael from her husband, I must confront a whole capital of husbands and wives."

Anat wrung out a piece of linen. "Do you hope to meet Sisera's mother behind her lattice?"

Sarai chuckled. "I had hoped to be the woman in Devorah's prophecy, the one who killed Sisera. Now I must find new dreams."

"May they be of ripe grain and calves no one will steal." Anat wrung out another discolored square. Behind the healer, chariot ruts stretched toward the horizon. Sarai shielded her eyes and looked down the path where Sisera had run.

"How things coil in upon themselves," she said.

"Yes," replied Anat. She was thinking that before long she would be asked to assume her title of priestess in order to perform a single quiet marriage ceremony. The sun kept on rising in the pale blue sky.

> *God has come down to me among the strong*
> *   branches of your arms and in your blossoms.*
> *I will be fire and food to you*
> *   and I will be the harp of your black hair.*
> *Wherever you arise, O mother*
> *   in Israel, I will rise, and where*
> *   you sing I will sing.*
>
> *I will pitch my tent with you*
> *   and share your thunder and your prophecy*
> *woman of flames*
> *   and I will tell the truth you need.*
> *In every place we walk*
> *   the land will yield up peace for you*
> *   and God will choose new things.*

THE HOUSE OF THE QUEENS

The sages sighed.
They looked again:
the Song of Songs
was in the canon.

They were wrong:
the canon should
have been within
the Song of Songs. . . .

But those who always found their force
within the blackest reach of forest
would always wince in brusque disgust
beneath the light of lakeside quays

(where some savants would scan the sun
and softly gloss the Song of Songs)

and, having winced, would conjure us:
The canon should have been within

Ecclesiastes.

> —ALLEN MANDELBAUM, *Chelmaxioms*

. . . it's possible, a woman can fly off
like the night heron
in any direction.

> —JANE SCHAPIRO, "Postpartum"

179

THE KING'S HARP

*King David was now old, advanced in years, and
though they covered him with bedclothes, he never felt
warm. His courtiers said to him, "Let a young virgin
be sought for my lord the king, to wait upon Your
Majesty and be his attendant, and let her lie in your
bosom, and my lord the king will be warm." So they
looked for a beautiful girl throughout the territory of
Israel. They found Avishag the Shunammite and
brought her to the king. The girl was exceedingly
beautiful. She became the king's attendant and waited
upon him; but the king was not intimate with her.*

—1 KINGS 1:1–4

There was a silence in the round chamber. A wrong silence.
It pervaded the dry air and clung to the bed curtains. It
swept over the open books on the cedar table and
strummed on the strings of the harp that stood at the head of the
bed. Avishag stood in the half-circular doorway and peered into the
darkness where there should have been a lit candle. Her hands were
braced against the doorposts as if she tensed for some great gust of
wind. Opposite her, three stars were framed in the arched window.
The Sabbath had ended.

King David needed her on the Sabbath as on every other day.
He was old, lean, and chilled. Even when he was covered in blan-

kets, only the warmth of her body kept him from shivering. That morning, as they awoke from the bed they shared, he had clung to her as if to a mother. He was too weak to do with her what he had done with so many women, yet she felt tender toward him, as toward a beloved who had gone away years ago. She stayed with him and saw that he ate, not taking the repose to which she was entitled on the Sabbath. When a few ministers came to see him, she had shooed them off. She reminded them that in the afternoon, David studied the sacred writings and could not be disturbed. The king himself had seemed content to read and pray in the peaceful quiet of his chamber. Avishag had napped for three hours in the large room David had insisted she have. She used it rarely, except to bathe or to practice on her own small harp. The Angel of Death had visited while she was gone.

The old king lay crumpled near his table. His curls had lost all trace of color years ago. Now his face was colorless too. His hand was clasped to his heart. A parchment had unrolled at his feet. David's handmaiden felt tears roll down her cheeks in a steady stream. There will be no more music, she thought. David has written his last psalm.

Avishag knelt down by David's side and tenderly touched his body, checking to make sure he had died of natural causes. David's house had always been full of violence. That was its curse. But Avishag did not expect to find anything suspicious. The king had known he was dying. Only two days before David had given Solomon his final instructions: who to kill, who to reward. Now Avishag's fate, Israel's fate, was in Solomon's hands. Avishag covered David with a regal purple cloth from a cedar chest. She lifted him, bit by bit, onto pillows she had taken from the bed. She did not like to think of him on the cold stone.

Many men had perished in the struggle to succeed David.

Many had waited for this day, mouthing "O king, live forever." Many had dreaded it, and now it had finally come. Avishag knew she must tell someone. She wanted to wait just a little longer. Just a few more moments before the world changed.

Avishag lay down on the bed where she and David had spent so many nights together. She wanted to weep, but also she wanted to feel the silk she had lain in for over a year. It was certain that she would not sleep in this bed again. This place was David's, not hers. Solomon would insist that she remain part of the household, but as a relic of David's reign, not as the companion of a king.

She was roused by the sound of harp strings—David's harp strings. David's harp was a nine-stringed wonder. Not only was it the voice of heaven in David's hand but, when he slept, the harp hanging at the head of his bed would sound the notes of the wind. It awakened him each midnight to make more songs for God. The wind must be mourning now, picking out tender chords in the darkness.

Avishag raised her head to watch the invisible plucking. To her astonishment, she could make out a silhouette near the harp. A candle flared. As Avishag struggled to adjust her eyes, she saw that a woman dressed in a colorful patchwork gown stood by the king's harp, strumming it with a sensual hand. No doubt it was a daughter or a wife, come to ask a favor of the king. Now that she'd found him dead, she was staking claim to her share of David's wealth. Vulture. Couldn't she wait until David had been decently buried?

"No one but the king touches that harp!" Avishag said. Let some princess order her beaten for her insolence. If her last duty to the king was to fight off the predators, so be it.

"I mean no disrespect," the red-haired woman replied calmly, "but this is my harp. I gave it to David, and now it must return to me."

The king had never told Avishag where his wonderful harp came from. Avishag could not prove the woman was lying, but there was no doubt she must be. How had she known of David's death? Perhaps she was an assassin. The woman's bearing was strange: She held herself with the assurance of a sage, but moved as lightly and flamboyantly as a traveling songster. Avishag was almost sure she had never seen this particular face in the palace before.

"Forgive me," Avishag said shakily, "but this instrument is a treasure. It holds the memory of the king's music. I cannot simply hand it to a stranger. You must bring some proof for your words."

The woman stroked the base of the harp. Slowly it split in half. Its gold overlay and smooth blond wood neatly cleaved into two harp-shapes. The strings seemed to dance between the halves, as if they did not know which owned them. Avishag stared in horror at the broken instrument, which seemed bizarrely alive, opening its halves like the pages of a book. Three solid gold forms, imbedded in the base of the harp, emerged as the two halves spread apart. The woman took them into her hand. They were letters: *shin*, *reish*, and *chet*.

The woman showed Avishag the three letters, then replaced them in their niches. The harp swung shut, so silently and completely that Avishag could barely remember what it had looked like when it was open. The woman regarded her calmly: "I am Serach, daughter of Asher," she said. "This is my harp."

"Oh," Avishag said in a breath. She knew legends of Serach, Jacob's granddaughter. Serach had lived hundreds and hundreds of years as a reward for her harp playing. There were elders from the city of Avel who claimed to have seen her, mothers from camps in the wilderness who claimed to have been delivered by the hands of Asher's daughter.

"Is it true that you played for Jacob?" Avishag asked.

Serach smiled as if Avishag were a child who had asked for the same story a dozen times before. "It is true," she said. "When my brothers returned from Egypt, knowing that Joseph was alive, they did not know how to tell Grandfather. He had lost his parents, and Rachel, and Joseph, and Leah. His heart was weak. Jacob's sons were certain that if they told him that Joseph was alive, he would die on the spot. They were even afraid to tell him they had returned, for Shimon was with them, and Grandfather believed that Shimon had been killed in Egypt. So they came to the outskirts of camp at night, and sent for me.

"I learned to sing from my grandmother Zilpah, and to play the harp from my mother, Yonah. From my father, Asher, I learned gentle speech. In myself I carried the fire to melt all these things into art. So my brothers asked me to sing Jacob the news of Joseph's rise to power in Egypt. They believed that I could soften the blow so that Jacob would not die."

Avishag listened with rapt attention. "What did you sing?" she asked eagerly when Serach paused. "How did you tell him?"

Serach placed her fingers on the harp and strummed a simple lullaby, a folk tune to soothe a tired patriarch. The lulling sound changed slowly to lament. She sang of loss and trouble, her high voice sweet and strong and sad. As the aching swelled, it became a hymn. She sang of miracles, of Noah's storm-tossed ark, of Isaac's birth. Her song dipped and soared like a bird, thrummed and piped like a frog. It made anything seem possible. Then, in a soft voice, she sang the following words:

> *Yosef sar beMitzrayim*
> *yuldu al birkayim*
> *Menashe ve'Ephraim.*

> Joseph rules Mitzrayim
> and in his arms are lying
> Menashe and Ephraim.

Serach paused a moment, as if she could still hear her grandfather say: "Where did you hear that story?" The tears shone on Avishag's face. Serach ended her song.

"Is it true," Avishag asked through her tears, "that Jacob blessed you with centuries of life?"

Serach suddenly seemed subdued. "I did not know then what that blessing would mean. When our tribe first traveled to Egypt, I saw Joseph seated on his golden throne. He seemed eternal. But I saw Joseph's funeral, and his sons' as well. I was a slave in Egypt for three generations. I was one of the redeemed. On the night of the tenth plague, the Israelites left Egypt, and only I was old enough to remember where Joseph was buried. I pointed out the bones of Joseph for Moses to carry into the wilderness, for my family had promised Joseph we would not let him lie in Egypt for eternity."

"How strange," Avishag said, "to do such sad work on a night of joy."

"It was strange, but no stranger than tonight, playing the harp above the body of a king."

Avishag clapped a hand to her mouth and cried for David. Serach touched her face. "The night we dug for Joseph, Moses asked me to play the harp for him, to give honor to our task." Serach moved her fingers. Wailing chords filled the air. She played a sweet dirge, rich with Egyptian undertones, spun out of slaves' liberation songs. Avishag's grief found a voice. She sang wordlessly with the music. Then Avishag found words, taken from ancient prophecies:

> *Darakh kokhav meYaakov,*
> *vekam shevet meYisrael;*
> *ashurenu velo karov.*

Out of Jacob came a star,
A staff arose from Israel;
I see him, but he is very far away.

Serach wove her chords in and out of Avishag's voice. The duet swelled and filled the night. Avishag thought that David himself would have been pleased. Avishag felt a chill creeping over her. Soon Serach would leave for hidden places, and the king's harp would be no more. She lapsed into stillness, clasping her knees to her chest.

"Avishag, you have heard more than most living have heard. I have not played these songs in generations. I have been glad for these moments with you, but now it is time for me to take my harp from the world." Serach hoisted the harp to the curve of her hip.

"Wait," cried Avishag urgently. "At least tell me what will become of it."

"I will open it and empty its melodies," Serach explained. "You see, one of the gifts my grandfather gave me was the secret of how to climb the ladder to heaven. I will weave David's prayers into a crown for God."

"Is that why you gave David the harp?" Avishag asked.

"I met David through his mother, who was a midwife. He was the youngest of the family, but he had a voice that sounded like Paradise. When I heard him singing in the hills of Bethlehem I knew he would be a great psalmist. I gave him the harp as a coming-of-age present. Imagine my surprise when Samuel anointed him king!"

"God had so many plans for him," Avishag mused. "But I loved his music best."

Serach sighed. "Avishag, you are stalling. You need to face the fact that the world is different now. David is no longer in it. There is no one now who can play the harp the way he did."

Avishag took a deep breath. "I can."

The ancient woman in the patchwork gown regarded her coolly. "You?"

"When David became ill," Avishag said steadily, "there was little for him to do. Solomon had taken over the governing of Israel. But David's music was still like the light of morning. So he taught me to play the harp. He taught me everything he knew. I do not want to waste the gift he gave."

Serach shook her head. "David sang of God, of wars and repentance, joy and despair. You are a maidservant, a child. Of what would you sing?"

"I would sing of David," Avishag whispered, and a single tear coursed down her cheek. "I would sing of what might have been between us, had he still been a young shepherd. In my eyes he would have been a king even if he had herded sheep his whole life. I want to sing of him. Please let me try. I swear that I will keep your harp safe as long as I live."

"David has more heirs than Solomon," Serach said. She smiled an ancient smile. "You and I have made music together, and I have not shared my music in over a century. I am in your debt. I will leave the harp with you. See that you use it well."

Serach hefted the harp with a nostalgic reluctance, then placed it in Avishag's soft hands. Avishag cradled it as though it were a child. A dry breeze riffled through her blue-black hair. There was silence.

"But someone will take it from me—" Avishag gasped suddenly. She still lived in the royal court, and there were many poets in Israel.

"No," Serach said. "I will see to it. No one will ask about the harp. They will forget it exists. It is yours now."

Avishag sighed with relief. She sat down on the purple coverlet of David's bed. Then, tremulously, her fingers touched the nearly invisible strings. A slow, luxuriant melody rose from her lips, as if it had been waiting there:

> *Tell me, you whom my soul loves,*
> *where do you pasture your sheep¿*
> *Where do you rest them at noon¿*
> *Let me not be as a lost stray*
> *beside the flocks of others.*

> *Like an apple tree among trees of the wood*
> *thus is my beloved among men.*
> *I delight to sit in his shade,*
> *and his fruit is sweet in my mouth.*
> *Refresh me with apples, for I am faint with love.*

Serach moved to the doorway, but Avishag did not notice her. She was entranced by the throbbing, living tones of the harp. She would soon stir herself to find Solomon or some other kin of David, but for now she was alone with her lord, who lay peacefully on the floor, as if asleep. It did not matter to her that one of David's heirs might steal her song and name it for himself. It was the song that mattered.

Serach looked back at the woman bent over the gilded harp. "O king, live forever," she whispered. Then the rungs of a ladder appeared at her feet, and she climbed into the sky.

SOLOMON'S BOX

Ben-Avinadav was governor over all of Nafat-Doar,
and Tafat daughter of Solomon became his wife.

—1 KINGS 4:11

Achinadav ben Iddo was governor over Mahanaim.
Achimaaz was governor over Naftali; he also took
Bosmat daughter of Solomon to wife.

—1 KINGS 4:14–15

W hen Bosmat, daughter of Solomon, returned from the house of her first husband, her younger sister was waiting for her in the oval courtyard of their father's palace. A few months before, the tender-hearted Tafat had wept as her sister departed to be the wife of Achinadav, governor of the district of Mahanaim. Now Bosmat had returned home, quietly and discreetly, with no official welcome by the king, only a word whispered in Tafat's ear by her tutor-guardian. Tafat ran over the floor mosaic to hug the black-cowled girl who came through the gates. She could not decide whether her sister looked sad, or angry, or merely serious. Her face shone beneath the cowl like the moon of another world, mysterious, uninterpretable.

Servants hustled baggage into the palace. "Bosmat," Tafat whispered into her sister's ear, "what happened?"

"Not now," Bosmat whispered back. "I need to go in and see Father. Meet me just after nightfall in the herbarium. I'll tell you the story then."

Bosmat kissed her sister and turned toward the tall, heavy carven doors to the throne room. Tafat looked after her and thought that her gown fell differently—or maybe it was her walk. A flurry of maids brought Bosmat's rosewood chest into the cool hall. After a moment, Tafat followed them, her feet cold on the smooth stones. Her stomach leaped a little, as if someone had prodded it from the inside.

When Bosmat arrived in the throne room, Solomon rose and dismissed all of his courtiers and servants. They made for the cedar doors like branching lines of ants. None of them dared to look at Bosmat. She paced to the foot of the throne, which stood seven steps above her. Her black cloak swirled at her feet, then was still.

The king folded his hands behind his back. "I have received word from Achinadav ben Iddo that you are divorced. He rejects any possibility of reconciliation."

"As do I," said Bosmat.

"You have disappointed me, Daughter." Solomon descended a step.

"Have I? But I have been your faithful student," said Bosmat. "It is because of my dowry that I am no longer married."

Solomon descended another step. He placed his hand on the carved lion that stood to the left of the step. "You opened the box."

"You knew I would," Bosmat answered. "Like God in the Garden of Eden, you know the nature of your children."

"That box was meant only for dire need," Solomon insisted angrily.

"Don't our needs always seem dire when we first have them?" Bosmat put her foot on the first step of the throne. "Marriage was difficult for me. I thought your gift might help."

"And now it has ruined you." The king turned from his daughter and paced upward two steps.

Bosmat stood on the first step with her head bowed. "It has opened my eyes to a new world."

"May that world comfort you," the king said. He seated himself on the throne. "You will get no reward in this one for what you have done."

Tafat pinched a mint leaf and inhaled its fragrance in the darkness of her father's herbarium. She was once again waiting for her sister. Through the window she could still see the Temple. She heard the whisper of silk on limestone. Bosmat slipped through a narrow arch to meet her sister. She was still wearing her cloak. In her hands she held an olive wood box.

"Here is my story," she said to Tafat. "I should not show it to you, but the secret wears on me."

"I want to know everything," Tafat whispered. Bosmat crouched down and sat next to her sister. The two huddled on the floor together as they did when they were children and there was a lightning storm. Bosmat leaned into Tafat's arms for a moment.

"On the day I left Jerusalem to be married, Father called me into his private chamber and explained to me the duties of marriage. Living as a wife in a new place can be lonely, he said. Maybe he learned that from my mother, Adah—she always missed her home in Edom.

Then he opened a chest and took out this box. He told me that he wanted to protect me always, so he was giving me a dowry. He told me that if I ever truly needed anything I should open the box, and I would find help there. But, he said, there was sorrow inside it also. I should only use it in desperate need."

"Weren't you tempted to open it right away?" asked Tafat.

"Of course I was." Bosmat smiled. "But I was also frightened. I climbed into my litter planning never to open the box. I didn't want to cause myself or my new husband any sorrow."

Tafat looked up into her sister's face. "Did you love him?"

Bosmat smiled wistfully. "I didn't know him. He was handsome and quick and proud and selfish, like Father. I admired him. He was very cultured and well educated, but somehow I found him boring."

"That sounds awful!" Tafat cried.

Bosmat paused again. "The truth is, many women do worse. Achinadav was a good husband. He didn't make me happy, but I don't think that was his job."

Bosmat fell silent. Tafat picked up her hand. "What happened next?" she asked.

"Boredom can do strange things," Bosmat said quietly. "The house in Mahanaim had enough staff to do the work, but not enough guests to need a hostess. I poked about in ponds, collected herbs, made dyes, but soon lost interest. Achinadav was governor of the province; he didn't have time to entertain me. I couldn't seem to get pregnant, so there were no children to occupy my time. I cried often that year, and Achinadav began sleeping in another bedroom. I made myself miserable. The servants were afraid to talk to me. Guests didn't stay long. Finally, in the dark of one particularly difficult night, I decided I was unhappy enough. I crept over to my dowry chest, and I took out the box and opened it."

"What was inside?" Tafat gasped.

Bosmat seemed deep inside herself. "I don't know what I

expected, maybe a new personality to pop onto my husband like a hat. Or a horse to ride away to distant lands. Or a powder that would make me sleep the days away."

Tafat held her breath. She looked at the box. The only light was a lantern she had brought, which cast a few shafts of light on a bunch of parsley near where the sisters were sitting.

Bosmat moved her hands as if the memory of opening the box were still with her. "There were demons inside."

"Demons!" Tafat shrieked. She knew her father made trips to the underworld. The governesses and concubines told hair-raising stories.

Bosmat, to Tafat's surprise, was smiling. "They didn't seem threatening at all. I knew Father was playing around in the other worlds, but he must have been in God's darkest basement to find creatures like this. One was all bedraggled fur and horns and little squinty eyes and ears. There was a dried bay leaf that floated up out of the box on a night breeze, and a glass nose with legs, and a blue fluffy ball. They were all wedding demons; they used to entertain at the weddings of the demon king. They would dance and juggle. At least that's what Balthasar told me."

"Balthasar?" Tafat queried timidly, wondering if her sister were playing a joke on her.

"The demon in charge of the little tribe. The one with horns. He uncurled himself from the box and asked me very solemnly what I needed. I was speechless. I had no idea what to say. The notion came to me that I should tell him to get rid of my husband and leave me a rich widow. Of course, I didn't say it, but after a thought like that, there was bound to be trouble."

"Mother always says that demons are God's creatures too," Tafat ventured. Her mother, Naamah, was Solomon's chief adviser and seemed to know a lot about esoteric matters. Naamah had told

Tafat many stories. Now Tafat wondered if they were real.

"That may be true," Bosmat said, "and the truth is that my demons can be very good-hearted when the spirit takes them. They certainly were that first night. There I was, with furry, horned Balthasar staring earnestly up at me with enormous teeth, and I'm trying to think of a task for him to perform that isn't a capital crime. So I say the next thing that pops into my head, which is that I'm lonely. The little demon bows and summons his bizarre troop together; they all go over to the fireplace, polish up a kettle, and brew me a cup of tea. Recipe from fifteen feet underground. The bay leaf hopped in and took a bath. I was cheered up just watching them. And then they all came and sat next to me on the bed. I didn't feel lonely anymore."

"What was in the tea?" Tafat asked, inspecting her sister for signs of poison.

"I didn't ask. It helped, though. Happuch, the blue fluffy ball, sat on my head while the tea started to work. I had hallucinations of Leviathan all night—and of you, and the people at court. Very entertaining. I was a different person in the morning. My husband didn't recognize me. I giggled all the time."

"Maybe Father picked creatures that would make you laugh," Tafat suggested.

Bosmat pondered. "Maybe," she said. "But my laughter upset my husband. He shushed me in front of the servants. 'Stop cackling like a witch!' he said. I was so angry I vowed I'd never share my secret with him. Maybe that was my mistake."

"Didn't the demons make you happier?" Tafat asked.

Bosmat frowned. "They did. What I can't understand is why my happiness didn't improve my marriage. I had so much to do, all of a sudden. I could sit with Zog on my lap—that's the glass nose—and look through him at flowers or bees. Or I could hold Ee, the bay leaf, over a flame and watch her give off colorful sparks like fireworks. Balthasar would snuggle up next to me at night and tell funny stories about disastrous wedding parties. As long as I hid them from Achinadav, I could play with the demons forever. I loved their willful ways. I helped them spy on the rest of the household, laughed with them over what they learned. The demons taught me the languages of the seven demonic worlds. We dipped our fingers in wine and painted runes on the floor of my bedroom. We summoned spirits and learned their secrets. Ee even took me flying with her on moonless nights. My life began to change—but not always for the better.

"Sometimes when I sent the demons away so I could be alone, they'd come creeping up to the windows, just to show me they could reveal themselves to everyone in the house if they wanted. Sometimes Balthasar would let out heart-rending howls. I was nervous all the time. They'd leave things on the stairs: a leaf, a red thread—just to remind me they were there. I never felt as if I were by myself.

"When I left my room at night to have sex with my husband, Balthasar and Happuch would roll around on my bed making noises, pretending to be me and Achinadav. They made it look ugly. Sex with Achinadav stopped appealing to me. I began fantasizing about the human-shaped demons Balthasar described to me. I stopped being able to concentrate on my daily tasks. I resented the time I had to spend with guests, because I could hear my companions calling to me in my mind.

"One night, after I'd denied him for far too long, Achinadav came to my room. I was half-asleep. There was a fire in the fireplace. He sat on the corner of my bed and asked me why I was so unhappy as his wife."

"What did you say?" Tafat held her breath.

"I don't know what I would have said. Maybe I would have

tried to explain. Maybe we could have found a way to come together again. But at that moment, Balthasar appeared next to the fire. My husband saw him and ran away shouting, calling me a witch. I became frightened and threatened to set the demons on him if he told anyone. The next day, he called a scribe to write out my divorce. When I went to pack my things, the demons hopped into the box and closed the lid. They've been there until now. To tell the truth, I've missed them."

Tafat was seized with a dual desire; to see the demons, and not to see them.

"I told them all about you," Bosmat said. She opened the box.

The inside was lined with green velvet. There was a strange darkness within the velvet, like a folded veil. Tafat leaned back, suddenly frightened.

A clear glass nose-like wedge was climbing out of the box. It had four black legs on its bottom and two small black dots on its top which looked like the heads of stamens. Those were its eyes, Tafat supposed. It whispered quietly, but Tafat wasn't sure how. Then it disappeared, and reappeared in Tafat's lap. It seemed a bit sad. Perhaps it was disappointed about the divorce. Tafat felt world-weary as she looked at the creature, a little jaded. She roused herself. She might never get another chance to touch a demon.

Tafat picked up Zog and placed it—him—on the mint leaf she had been smelling earlier. She could see details where her fingers had bruised the leaf, the delicate patterns of its veins. Zog stomped a bit on the leaf with his thin legs. Tafat stared. The creature seemed to magnify everything that was near him.

When Tafat looked up, it was into the huge brown eyes of a gnome-like creature with two curling horns and enormous ears. Its tail forked into five sharp ends. Its fur was a gray greenish color. "This is Balthasar," Bosmat said. The creature stood up straight and bared his teeth. Bosmat smacked him lightly on the head.

"Solomon's child, Solomon's child," chanted Balthasar. He upset a dish of pumpkin seeds out of spite, then poked at Bosmat, making her shriek. Balthasar's purpose was clearly to inspire mischief. Tafat felt itchy just looking at him.

Bosmat tugged at Tafat's sleeve and pointed to the box. A bay leaf floated up past the pomegranate lid, dangled on the breeze that was blowing through the window, then traveled around the room on swirling currents of air. After a while, it seemed as if the leaf called Ee were dancing. Bosmat clapped her hands happily. Tafat watched in wonder as the leaf's flights grew more and more intricate. What evil purpose could this lovely creature have?

Balthasar ran to the box, drew a pipe out of some unknown drawer, and began to play a bouncy, lusty tune, a devil's jig. Ee cavorted on invisible waves, quivering with delight. She began to grow, spreading into a leaf-colored flying carpet. The carpet flapped like a manta ray, beating about Bosmat's shoulders playfully. As Balthasar's playing slowed to an eerie whine, Ee's movements grew slow and sensual, even erotic. Tafat found herself drawn to her feet by the wailing pipe. She danced around the room, dodging Ee, holding Zog in her arms like a bouquet. Finally, Ee grew small again and settled into one of Solomon's dishes, at Bosmat's elbow. Tafat too settled into her seat, flushed and delighted, her hair tumbled about her shoulders. She felt free, somehow, as if she were a tree that had been uprooted and given the ability to dance. Zog scuttled under a table.

"Now for the shyest one," Bosmat said. She reached into the box and brought out a shivery sphere. Soft blue fuzz entirely covered the fleshy form except for a small pink area, which might have been a mouth. Tafat stretched out two fingers and stroked the thing carefully.

"This must be Happuch," she crooned. The sphere made a soothing, cooing sound. The rumbling trill entered Tafat strangely, making her feel quiet, thoughtful, distanced from her surroundings, as if a frosted glass wall had been erected around her. Happuch dissolved slowly into the air as Tafat stroked her, then reappeared on Balthasar's shoulder. He shrugged her off, jumping around as if she had bitten him. Bosmat laughed indulgently. Tafat picked up Zog again and examined her sister playfully through the creature's magnifying flesh.

Both princesses heard the golden trumpets that announced a visitor at court. Neither of them had heard that Solomon would have a guest that evening. Tafat had been hoping that Ben-Avinadav, the governor of Nafat-Doar, would come to the palace. She ran to the wide-silled triangular window to look into the courtyard. Bosmat hurried to pack the demons away into their box. Balthasar yelped as Bosmat picked him up. At the window, Tafat saw a lanky, handsome man in gold and blue was bowing to the king. Solomon had come out to greet his visitor personally, even though it was already night.

"It's Achimaaz, the famous runner," Tafat cried, disappointed. "The governor of Naftali province."

"It isn't the holiday season, and taxes aren't due. Could he be meant for your husband?" Bosmat wondered, putting an arm around her younger sister. "Father might have invited him to look him over as a potential match. You're about the right age to be married."

But Tafat was not surprised when a chamberlain found the two sisters in the hallway and announced that the king had sent for Bosmat. Bosmat gave her sister a rueful glance.

"Father must want to get rid of me quickly," she said. "I have been such a trouble to him." Bosmat straightened her robe before heading through a gauze curtain and down the stairs.

Then, unexpectedly, she burst back through the curtain and handed Tafat the box. "Keep it until I come upstairs again," she whispered. Then she was gone in a whirl of black silk.

Tafat sat quietly, thinking hard. She was sure her sister had not lied. But Tafat had an instinct for the truth, and she knew something was wrong with Bosmat's story.

Later that evening, King Solomon came to the new chambers of his daughter Bosmat with an olive wood box in his hand. It was identical to the one he had given her on her wedding day. He began to look around the room for Bosmat's dowry. Surely she had not abandoned it at her husband's house. Solomon lighted corner after corner with his oil lamp but saw no box. He began angry, then agitated. Where were the demons?

"They are with me, Father." A high voice came from the last unlit corner.

"Tafat?" he called. "Daughter of Naamah, what are you doing here?"

"Bosmat is my dearest friend," Tafat said. "I am guarding her property." She showed her father the olive wood box.

Solomon was enraged. "Child, do not meddle with what you do not understand," he hissed.

"I understand more than my sister," Tafat answered him. "I remember that Bosmat told me the demons you summoned for her were the demons that used to entertain the demon king at his weddings." Tafat paused. "But in a story my mother told me, the demon king always divorces his bride in the morning. These creatures are for breaking lovers apart, not joining them together."

Solomon turned pale as Tafat went on. "When I understood

that, I realized that you wanted Bosmat to be divorced. You never intended that she should stay with her husband. You only wanted her to scare him, so that he would be loyal to you, so he would fear the king whose daughter can summon demons. You chastised her only so she would not know what you have done. Now you can wed her to yet another husband, and play the same trick. That is why you brought Achimaaz here tonight."

Tafat took a deep breath. "You knew Bosmat would open that box. What you didn't know was how it would change her. She will be as powerful as you one day. I do not want her to be alone in her power. Do not destroy this marriage. Let her be."

The king's eyes glittered with anger. "I have already summoned new companions for her, even more powerful and frightening than before. The demon king will be offended if I send them back."

"If you give these new creatures to her, I will tell her everything that you have done," Tafat threatened. "She will be devastated at your betrayal. She will run into the netherworld and we will never see her again—and from there, she will fight you."

"What would you have me do?" Solomon thundered.

Tafat thought for a long moment before speaking. "Let her keep her old companions. Give me the new ones."

"You?"

"Yes." Tafat said. "That is the price of my silence. That, and I wish to be married to the governor of Nafat-Doar. He is called Ben-Avinadav because he is as brave as Nachshon ben Aminadav, who was first to walk into the Sea of Reeds. Perhaps he will not be afraid of demons."

"My children have defeated me," said Solomon. He nodded his assent, and gave Tafat the box.

Tafat did not open her box for many months. She waited until

Bosmat remarried and rode to her new home with Achimaaz. She waited until Bosmat confided in her that it was possible to maintain an uneasy balance between one's husband and one's demons. She waited through her own wedding ceremony and through her wedding night. After her husband had fallen asleep, Tafat went to the window and lifted the lid of the olive wood container she had extorted from her father. The first creature to emerge had silvery scales and a long tail. It twisted its head to look at her. Her face was reflected in its polished forehead. Ben-Avinadav snored gently on the bed. Tafat saw other shapes begin to move in the shadows of the box. *Now I too have demons*, she thought. Outside, night spread starry wings over Solomon's kingdom.

THE SCRIBE

The children of Solomon's servants: the children
of Sotai, the children of haSoferet (the scribe), the
children of Peruda.

—EZRA 2:55*

Silence within silence, says Soferet. Silence within
silence, all is silence. What profit does a woman get
from all the words she speaks beneath the sun? One
generation goes, another comes, and the earth remains
the same forever. The moon waxes and wanes, and
returns to the place where she began. . . . Only that
can be said which has already been said; only that can
be heard which has already been heard. What is new
is rendered inaudible, so that it is as if nothing new is
whispered beneath the moon.

—SOFERET 1:1–5,9

I Soferet, was Solomon's scribe in Jerusalem. When I was
young he sang The Song of Songs, and my ink was like the
wing of a bird against the sky. When I was a mother of young
men and women, he declaimed the Proverbs, and I wrote in thick
liner. My letters were the branching pillars of a cedar house. Now I

* Author's translation

203

am old, and he writes as if I were not here. Now my letters are like the spindly cracks in a thin skin of ice.

My mother, Batrinah, was the lowliest of concubines. She was one of those David set aside in living widowhood after his son Avshalom raped them. During the days when David had fled and Avshalom occupied Jerusalem, Avshalom took the king's concubines, who had been abandoned in the palace, and lay with them as a sign that the king's authority was now his. When David returned, he set the ten women aside in a guarded place, nevermore to embarrass him by seeing daylight. There were ten such women, closed into a stone box as if they were jewelry too precious to be thrown away but too much out of fashion to be worn. Their house was quiet. They walked heavily from room to room, redecorating, remembering. In the evenings they would tell stories or drink or both. Some nights one or two of them would cry, wordlessly, or laugh with a sound like mustard, hot and powerful.

My half brother, Sotai, and I were the only children born before David fled Jerusalem and left ten concubines in the palace to face Avshalom alone. We shared our father's chin and fleecy hair; but in other respects, we took on the character of the house, which ignored David as much as possible. The priests came to educate us: It was a sop to our mothers, who would have no new children to lay at their breasts, no men to warm them, no palace intrigue to occupy their minds. Early in my life I discovered that I loved words. I loved the clean feeling of setting unambiguous shapes down on paper, shapes with meaning. The pen was my adventure.

When I was twelve I rejected the name I had been given, Peruda, and insisted on being called Soferet, the scribe. After six months of argument I had my way, even with my mother, Batrinah, who had named me for someone she held dear. I was the most stubborn of children, but I could learn. Long after my half brother,

Sotai, had gone to serve as a clerk in the king's palace, the priest Azarya continued to visit me with his scrolls and tablets. I think perhaps he did not want this, but my mothers insisted, and Azarya was too polite to let his feelings show. They were all my mothers, of course, all feasting their eyes on me, their one daughter. In a stoic way, I loved them back.

Azarya showed the words I formed to other priests. No one paid attention to the brusque poems I wrote or the parroted fragments of history, but they did note the perfect form of my letters. I was praised throughout the city: a girl scribe, a supernatural novelty. I had a great ear for dictation. I did not forget words or misspell them in haste. When I was seventeen, I dressed in the finest robes available to me, turquoise castoffs from a once-favored concubine, and asked to be presented to the king as a clerk.

No one had heard of such a thing as a woman clerk, but I pleaded with Azarya until he agreed to take me to court. Perhaps he agreed so that he would not have to teach me anymore. I would succeed in David's eyes and be granted my petition, or the king would be so angry that he would banish me to the gray reaches of my mothers' house. Either way my lessons would be over, and Azarya would be free.

David met my humble prostrations with fatherly praise. He ordered his scribes to accept me as an apprentice, whether out of admiration for my skill, out of curiosity, or out of guilt, I could not tell. He was a hard man to read. I moved from my mothers' house into a small palace room, not in the scribal complex, due to the complications of my gender, but no longer behind a locked gate. My position was enviable among women. I learned all there was to learn from the scribes who kept the nation's knowledge. I wrote exactly what I was asked to write, not wanting to call attention to myself. I worked day and night, and took meals with my half brother, who chattered about foreign trade routes. I visited my mothers, for whom I was eyes and ears, though not a voice.

I was twenty when my father died, an old king who could not get warm even though the beautiful Avishag pressed her body close to his. Perhaps he was missing the warmth of his ten concubines. I was brought to his side like the other children, to bid him farewell as he panted for breath. Some asked him for rank or for a large inheritance. Some asked him to tell how he loved them. I asked him just one question: "Why did you abandon my mothers?"

The old king looked at me with shock in his misty eyes. Perhaps it was his impending death that compelled him to lean close to me, disarranging his thick blue robes, and whisper. I bent my head of carefully arranged ringlets to his mouth.

"God cursed me for taking Batsheva; he said my women would be grabbed by other men. God's curses always come to pass. Would they take Batsheva, or fiery Michal, or cool, collected Avigayil? I didn't want to lose any of my prizes. I won against Goliath with a stone. When my son Avshalom set himself up as a rival king, I saw that I had my chance to win even against God.

David coughed. "I bent God's curse away from my true family by leaving ten of my women for Avshalom. He took them on this palace roof, all ten at once, they tell me. When I returned, I couldn't keep them anymore. I built a house for them to set them apart, to show God that I was sorry for stealing the women of other men. That house was a sign of my shame. Now the Lord says that Solomon will build a house for God. The curse is paid off. After all this time, God forgives me for my sin."

David left me a large sum of money upon his death. I am not sure if it was a bribe to guarantee my silence, or God's. He left me and my services to the new king, my half brother Solomon. When David was buried, Solomon gave the order: My ten mothers still were not allowed to leave their house of stone, for fear that one of the king's rivals would steal one of them, marry her, and secure his legitimacy through her body. My mothers watched from behind black-tapestried windows as the funeral procession left the gates. I watched with them, thinking the question I did not ask my father: "Why did you leave me to be eaten by silence?"

> *So I loathed all the wealth that I gained under*
> *the sun, for my wealth was in the hands of the*
> *man who would succeed the king, and who knew*
> *whether he would be wise or foolish? He would*
> *control all the wealth that I gained by toil and*
> *wisdom under the sun. This too leads to silence,*
> *and so I came to view with despair all the gains*
> *I had made under the sun. For sometimes a*
> *woman whose fortune was made with wisdom,*
> *knowledge, and skill must hand it on to someone*
> *who did not toil for it. This too is a kind of*
> *silence, and a grave evil. For what does a woman*
> *get for all the toiling and worrying she does under*
> *the sun? All of her days her thoughts are grief*
> *and heartache, and even at night her mind has*
> *no rest: that too is silence.*
>
> —SOFERET 2:18–23

Solomon at once set about strengthening his kingdom through trade, but he also was interested in the making of books: lists of animals and plants, collections of sayings and poems. He wanted the best scribe available, and I was the best. I was made the king's chosen recorder, dressed in fine silks—new ones this time—and shown off to foreign dignitaries. My fate pleased me and made my mothers proud.

During those first years, my blood ran high. I braided my hair, wore crimson robes, and took dictation from Solomon beneath myrtle bushes and beside willows. Solomon was wise and witty. He made peace with many nations, even that of Queen Sheba, who once gave me an approving glance as she charmed Solomon into her bed. Solomon's many wives flattered me and gave me presents. They thought I had influence, and perhaps I did then, for Solomon often watched to see if I smiled at what he said. For my part, the king captivated me. I thrilled to his love poetry and nodded thoughtfully at his lists of beasts and birds. I followed my brother the king's example and took lovers. The powerful courted me shamelessly.

That I was permitted to marry was a miracle, but when Yoram, an important landowner who was an officer at court, asked to wed me, Solomon did not wish to be impolite by refusing him. Although I was a daughter of David, I was only the female child of a minor concubine and would confer no status on my husband that would threaten Solomon. If I had ever lain with a king, that would have been another matter.

In the brief winter months I visited Yoram's estate, and the vistas over the Judean hills blinded me: I was accustomed to walls with right angles, like the letters with sharp corners I could form with ease. In the summer we returned to the palace. I worked overtime to write down Solomon's thoughts. I was wealthy and learned and sought after by many as a patron, yet every time I saw the tall, narrow windows of my mothers' house, every time I thought of one or two of them weeping in the night, I could not rest easily on my cushioned couch. There did not seem to me to be anything I could do for them.

When I told my sorrow to my mother, Batrinah, she counseled me, saying: "Go, eat your bread in gladness, and drink your wine in joy, for God has approved your actions. Let your clothes always be freshly washed and your head never lack ointment. Enjoy happiness with the man you love all the fleeting days of your life that have been granted to you under the sun—all your fleeting days. For that alone is what you can get out of life and out of the means you acquire under the sun." I took her words to heart and wrote them down on a scroll: It was the first attempt I made to write anything but what the king commanded.

I lived happily with Yoram for eleven years and bore him two children, a son, Talmon, and a daughter, Raza. Yoram was killed while quashing a riot at one of Solomon's forced labor sites. I miscarried my second daughter out of grief. I went to the place where my husband had died, and there I saw that I was not the only one in Israel who suffered. Solomon had commissioned beautiful roads and buildings, but along with them came broken families and camp disease. When I returned from the labor site, I knew I could not ask Solomon to stop the forced labor. The work meant too much to his growing state. I had to ask him something, and I determined to ask him for the freedom of my ten mothers, who had lived in their high-walled house for over thirty years. I was his sister and his loyal servant, and he was a generous man. Perhaps he would grant my request.

"And if I free them, usurpers will seek them out and marry them, thus becoming contenders for David's throne," the king replied angrily. "So my brother Avshalom meant to do, and my brother Adoniyahu after him. And you, is there some man you would rather see as king?"

I was afraid that if I mentioned the matter again I would be accused of treason. Yet my mothers were old and peered out of their windows with painful curiosity. I went, quietly, to Azarya, my old tutor, and asked him to find a way to let them out into the world. He rolled out scrolls and showed me the fate the law decreed for the king's widows. I was silent. The scrolls were stones in my mouth, and their neat letters were like stitches across a bleeding void.

The king was a good king, and I wrote his Proverbs with an agile wrist. I cared for my children and arranged marriages for them. Once again, I took male and female lovers, attended lusty festivals and dances, ate delicacies from the royal kitchens. I was profligate with my wealth, which could not buy the things I wanted. My fellow scribes watched me suspiciously and waited for a chance to replace me in the king's favor. I composed my own words in silence:

> *I further observed the oppression that goes on under the sun, the tears of the oppressed, with none to comfort them, and the power of their oppressors, with none to comfort them. Then I accounted those who died long ago more fortunate than those who are still living, and happier than either are those who have not yet come into being and have never witnessed the miseries that go on under the sun. I have also noticed that labor and skilled enterprise often come from men's envy of each other—another root of silence, and a holding of breath.*
>
> —SOFERET 4:1–4

We are old now, and he has never asked my opinion. He is, after all, the king, ruler of a wealthy nation full of roads and palaces, a nation with a giant temple in its midst, a temple he ordered built. Solomon makes lists of stars and demons. He is a legend. The many queens step quietly through his halls. He calls himself Kohelet, the preacher, and in the manner of a preacher he speaks to me, droning without a pause as I wriggle my scratchy pen.

"I find women more bitter than death," I write for him in spidery script. Sheba left him for the warmth of her throne, and the daughter of Pharaoh was arrogant in his bed; therefore, he rails against women. He is a fool. I have lived with women more bitter than death. I *am* a woman more bitter than death. I asked one thing of him in all my years of service and he would not grant it.

I dip my pen in ink and wait for the king to continue. "I found only one human being in a thousand, and the one I found among so many was never a woman." Is he baiting me as he did when we were young? I no longer care. I write his words into existence, blot the pen cleanly on an old brown cloth. My daughter, my light, died many years ago in childbirth. She wrung my hand, released it slowly, painfully. She placed the child in my arms as our ancestor Ruth did for Naomi. Peruda, I named her, "Divided," as the world is divided into living and dead. When my daughter's husband came to take the child away, I turned my face to the wall. In my blurred sight it became the gray wall of my childhood, come with its thick stone fingers to bring me home.

It is springtime. The palace orchards are in bloom and pollen fills the air. My breath comes harder. Soon Solomon will replace this ailing old woman. The scribes who have been my brothers in craft conspire not only to supplant me but to erase my name from their records, so that I shall not embarrass them in future generations. I have seen them whispering when I pass by, my cropped hair gray, my robes no longer crimson. It rankles, knowing another will have credit for my work. Why must the deceitful prosper while the upright are forgotten? If I went home now, only my mothers' graves would greet me, but if frail humans could wish, I would wish to find the house I knew as a child, its corners full of praise and secrets and unambiguous shapes.

> The almond tree may blossom and the caper tree
> bud, but women search for their eternal home. . . .
> The dust returns to the ground as it was, and the
> soul-breath returns to God who gave it. Silence
> within silence, says Soferet. All is silence.
>
> —SOFERET 12:5,7–8

Vashti and
the Angel Gabriel[*]

On the seventh day, when the king was merry with
wine, he ordered . . . the seven eunuchs in attendance
on King Ahasuerus to bring Queen Vashti before the
king wearing a royal diadem, to display her beauty.

—ESTHER 1:10-11

I could not tell you now the color of his eyes, nor the length of
his hair, although he seemed a man to me then. With men I
was always observant of such things, for men's vanities were
useful in devising flattery and misdirections of all kinds, but in that
hour, my eyes learned to see some inner thing, with neither hair nor
eyes. With Gabriel, I learned, beauty of face, beauty of speech,
meant nothing. I learned, also, that in an hour everything can
change.

Beauty had meant a great deal to my father, who was a Persian
nobleman of impeccable taste. I was his prize ornament. When I
was a simpering child, my father brought me sweets and praised my
lovely face. As I grew, he brought me jewels and praised me still
more. Of that within me that was simply Vashti, he was unaware.
This was painful but commonplace. Had I been an adult, I would

---

* This story of Vashti is misplaced in time, because it is followed by a story
about the prophetess Huldah, who lived well before Vashti. Of course, according to the Sages, there is no before or after in the Torah, so perhaps the story
does belong here after all.

not have minded so much. I would have been grateful for my beauty, which won me privilege and indulgence. As things were, it took me too long to learn to manipulate him. By the time I was seventeen, he had become fixated on the idea of marrying me to the king Ahasuerus, ruler of all Persia, who had recently lost his frail queen. I could remember her crown and her dress but not her face. The idea of being faceless terrified me.

Indulged as I was, the simple fact was that my father owned me. After some coercion on his part I appeared at court. It was not long before the king owned me. Although my wedding night and the many subsequent nights were unpleasant, at least I had the satisfaction of outranking my father. He made the attempt to advise me from afar, but now I had other advisers. The king, his time often occupied by concubines, restrained me far less than my father had. A woman must get used to anything. I often told myself that my lot was better than almost any other woman's, for I did not need to work and I would never starve.

Perhaps, being a bird in a gilded cage, I admired the gilding for too long. As queen of the land and mistress of the household, my whims were answered as long as the king took no notice, so I grew adept at escaping his notice. In Shushan, vanity was a survival skill. I possessed it in plenty. When feasts and celebrations were announced, I paid little or no attention, beyond my contemplation of the young noblemen who might ease my boredom. Imagining the uses of the flesh filled my days, for the spirit that had been nurtured in me was the spirit of flesh, hungry and never satisfied. I became devious and cunning. I sought ways to indulge myself, to outdo in majesty and popularity the king's concubines and the wives of the powerful. I was unhappy, as are all who feel love neither for themselves nor for others. I blotted out my unhappiness in wine, pleasure, and what mean power was allotted me. And so I passed the years.

In all that time I only engaged in one worthwhile pursuit. I spent my private hours studying books, satisfying a passion all but denied me as a child. In the books, I found descriptions of many other worlds, some fanciful, and some entirely beyond my comprehension. I absorbed what I could, ignored what I did not understand. I read tales of romance and epics of the gods, stories of war and histories of ancient Persia. I read the legends of the Jews, their prophets, and invisible God, but these were alien to me, for in them was little that I could touch. I was always grasping for substance, images to fill my eyes and mind. The tomes I pored over held my attention because I believed that arcane knowledge would gain me more influence, but even when I saw that my influence had not increased, I continued to read. The books were solace for some wound I could not name.

I do not remember many of the hours I spent in the palace, but this one I remember, for during that hour my fate was rewritten. Having been given permission from the king to hold my own banquet for the noblewomen on his chosen feast day, I was as merry and haughty as a spoiled child. I impressed the wives of the ministers with my exquisite gown, with the elaborate ornamentation, the succulent food, the glamour and style of each detail. Then the messenger arrived.

When I heard the king's summons, I was shocked. It must have been shock, for nothing but shock would have upset my composure in front of my competitors and opponents, the other ladies of the court. Walking, then running, from the room, I dashed along the corridors until I could no longer hear the voice of the king's herald demanding my answer. I sought a place where my maids-in-waiting would not think to look for me.

I happened upon a small earth-colored chamber that looked out on the lush gardens. It held nothing but pots, vases, and flowers. I realized that it must be the room where the servants arranged the palace flowers every day, but I had never seen it before. I gazed on the fresh, new, rosebuds with envy: None could pry them open before their time.

The demand of the king was that I appear nude, wearing nothing but my crown, before his gathered male guests. It was a direct order, and I had never defied a direct order. To anger the king would only have weakened my position as queen. I did not think that I should refuse him now. He was the king. He had the right to command, even when he was drunk and obscene. Yet my skin crawled with rage. Perhaps it was not modesty that caused my rage but my sense of the unfairness of my position. The king need never accede to my smallest request, but I must degrade myself if he wished. The entire court would be reminded that I was the king's chattel, no less than the lowest concubine.

I tried to be philosophical—at least the king would protect me from any drunkard who sought to abuse me. His protection would not out be of concern for me but for his reputation, yet I was grateful for it. I plucked a rose from a vase and sniffed it, squeezed my eyes shut, trying to regain my composure. When I opened my eyes, I had crushed the blossom in my fingers.

A young man rested his elbow against a wide-lipped urn, watching me. In his belt were tucked a scroll and a sheathed weapon. I drew up angrily, imagining that another herald had dared to invade my privacy. Then I sighed, resigned. It seemed that my privacy was not guaranteed, so my indignation on its behalf was foolish. Also, I did not quite want the unfamiliar man to leave. His form, features, and garments were lovely, but it was not that—it was his presence that was extraordinary. Perhaps I should have known what he was.

"Do you, too, come to shame a queen?" I inquired icily.

"I have not come to a queen but simply to Vashti," he said gently. He surrendered the bright sunshine that cast its golden light over the urn and slowly approached me in the shadows.

Had I been deposed? Or was this one of the pleasing young gentlemen who had noticed my roving eye and become too bold? My curiosity increased, but also my irritation. "Which Vashti is that?" I rapped out sharply. I hoped to remind him that my title as queen superseded my identity as an individual. If he wanted to be insolent, he was talking to the wrong woman.

"The Vashti who paces the gardens in the evening and reads late into the night. The Vashti who feeds herself treasures to satisfy her hunger. The Vashti who keeps her father's gifts hidden away as a remembrance of her childhood," he replied. His voice was like a waterfall heard from far away: peaceful, yet commanding attention.

Any man who knew—who noticed—this much about my life was interesting and, perhaps, dangerous.

"Who are you, and for what reason have you approached me?" I demanded.

"I am Gabriel. I have come to plead with you to commit an act of sacred rebellion." The youth spoke with extraordinary self-possession in spite of his strange words. His eyes glowed softly, full of strength. I became afraid of him. I strove not to show my discomfort.

"Rebellion?" I laughed derisively. "Are you an assassin or merely a failed diplomat?"

"I am a messenger of God."

"Which god?" Religious fanaticism sustained many at the palace, but it did not interest me in the slightest, as it often seemed to conceal a futile lust for power. I prided myself on good judgment. I sincerely hoped my curiosity had not been captured so easily by a pious maniac.

"You might perhaps call my god the god of the Jews." Still the expression on the lovely face did not change.

I had read of the beliefs of the Jews, and they sometimes did business at court. At another time, the man's joke or delusion might have amused me. Today, on the day of my impending disgrace, his claim enraged me.

"Have you nothing better to do than mock me with your god!" Once I allowed myself to feel, my emotions of helplessness and fury became uncontrollable. I vented my anger on everything in the room, smashing crystal vases I vaguely remembered having seen in the dining hall. I gathered up flowers and tore at them in my fury, scattering petals, leaves, and fine grains of pollen everywhere.

Gabriel bent and with great care picked up each one of the torn blossoms. As he handled them, they returned to their original state. Their colors were even more rich for having been repaired. He is a magician, I thought; but then he himself blossomed, became filled from within with a pure light, which blinded me. He was an angel. I had read about them late at night, almost believing. He was far more than I could have imagined. I knelt on the floor, more from distress than from humility, but he took my hand and helped me to my feet. The light he held within seemed to adjust to my eyes' need. His voice, although strong, held music.

He said to me: "Vashti, be comforted. Soon you will be free."

I laughed harshly. "Why would an . . . an angel speak to me about freedom, I who will be wed lifelong to my lord the king?"

"The time of your escape is at hand. I have been sent to guide you on your path."

"You may be an angel, but you speak nonsense. Everyone knows that rebellion is not sacred, not even among the Jews. Slaves who escape are punished, and servants who disobey their masters must pay the price." Suddenly, I could remember the punishments visited upon me when I at first refused to marry the king. These were memories I had worked long and hard to erase. I did not understand why these thoughts had returned to plague me.

"I have come to issue you a challenge," he insisted, unruffled by my discomposure. "A way to restore the self-respect that has been lost to you. A way to become more than a vain consort to a demanding king. A way to win your freedom, perhaps even your happiness."

Gabriel's words, although they resembled the blandishments of many courtiers I had encountered, fired old, charred hopes in my mind. When I was young, I had dreamed of someone I could love. It was a romantic hope. I had discarded it at a very early age, knowing that such dreams were not open to a woman in my position, or indeed to most women. The king was thoughtless, with no feelings for me other than a dull interest in my beauty and a keen one in my father's wealth. I might have wanted his affections if he had sought mine. I was forced to admit that I would rather have had no one at all. I had hoped to free myself from my bodily desires. It had not occurred to me to hope for freedom from my king.

I discovered abruptly that I had been speaking my thoughts aloud to the first sympathetic ear I had encountered. Gabriel listened quietly, intently, with all of himself. Shocked at my divulgence, I nevertheless wondered how anyone could listen like that. I wished I could listen so.

"You remind me of the maiden Istehar," he said.

I am no maiden, I thought. This, certainly, is flattery, and his listening is a sham. Or, perhaps, all women remind him of Istehar. Do angels have lovers? "Istehar?" I inquired idly.

"May I tell you a story?"

"I adore stories," I replied dryly. "Tell away."

"In the days just after the creation of the world, certain angels, others among my kind, lusted after human women and pursued them. One such angel desired the mortal woman Istehar. The angel demanded that she lie with him. She agreed, but she demanded a price: that he teach her the Name of God, which mortals do not know."

"Clever girl, to derive profit from her misfortune. What did she do, after he lay with her?" In spite of myself, I was interested in the outcome of the story.

"He never lay with her at all. Before he could touch her, she uttered the Divine Name he had taught her and flew away to the heavens. She was transformed into a star as a reward for her pure heart. One can see her shining among the Pleiades to this day."

"A charming tale. Regrettably, in Persia a mortal woman cannot fly away from her admirers."

"But she can fight those who would coerce her."

I was more moved by the story of Istehar than I cared to admit. I had often wished for a way to escape from the king. Yet Gabriel's offer of freedom seemed preposterous to me, a child's notion, easily dispelled by the realities of life.

"Women do not fight," I pointed out. "They depend on men for safety." I thought of my mother, who always waited eagerly for my father to return home. He, for his part, adored her and kept her from any trouble. I had often envied her for his kindness and respect.

"And do men always make women safe?"

It was a good question. I did not know how to answer. When the king's men came for me, my father had not heeded my cries.

"Are you not a man who is protecting me?" I inquired flirtatiously, seeking to deflect the question.

"I am not a man at all. I am the symbol of what all people might become. It is your need to see me as a man that causes me to appear as one."

"Why do you, an angel of God, question the way things are between people?"

"Permit me to tell you another story."

"Of course."

Gabriel sat cross-legged on the floor of the flower-filled chamber and began, "I once was present in two evil cities, which I had been commanded to destroy. In these cities, Sodom and Gomorrah by name, no one was allowed to help another, under penalty of death. Citizens threw stones at strangers, robbed and deceived everyone they encountered. The people of the city were so wicked that they once cruelly murdered a young woman, Paltit, because she gave food to a hungry beggar. Because of evil like this, God determined that the city should be put to the fire. Not even the righteous Abraham could dissuade Him from this course of action.

"When I arrived there to carry out God's command, I entered the house of a certain man, Lot the nephew of Abraham. I came there to save his life, for his family was the only one in the city that had not been completely corrupted. When I arrived in his house, he sought to protect me, his honored guest, from the angry mob gathered outside. Lot, the righteous man of Sodom, offered his two youngest daughters to the crowd instead of me. He heeded neither my protests nor the cries of his wife, Idit.

"I pulled him back into the house, insisted that he and his family leave Sodom right away. His older daughters did not leave. The younger ones followed in silence. I cautioned them not to look back. Later, as I led them from the city, Idit looked back toward Sodom. She was unable to leave two of her offspring in the city and equally unable to follow the man who had offered up her other two daughters to a destructive mob. I think, also, that she could not face those young girls, whom she had not been able to protect. Out of pity, God turned her into a pillar of salt. His daughters later lay with their father, suffering from the fear that there were no more men to marry and care for them."

Gabriel seemed strange to me then, a bitter angel, a sharp note beautiful in its discordance. "Lot's daughters did not understand. There were plenty of men. The problem was that there was no justice."

"Justice is the cause you offer me," I whispered softly, "but what weapon could I use to advance such a cause? It may be wrong for me to dishonor myself in front of the court"—suddenly I believed this—"but how can I defy the king? I am like Lot's wife. If I disobey, I will be destroyed."

Gabriel drew forth a mighty scythe from the sheath hanging from his belt. The curved form seemed to grow as it was revealed to the daylight. "My weapon is as old as the world itself. I formed it during the first days of Creation for my battle with Sennacherib. It is the weapon of just strength, of righteous anger." Gabriel ran his shining hand along the blade, impossibly sharp, an edge of darkness.

"The weapon that belongs to you is even older," he said, "for it begins with the spoken word. 'In the beginning,' the start of Holy Scripture, is simply the beginning of all that might be said. What would you say, if you had the voice?"

"What would I say? That my husband is a lout? That I am tired of glorifying my servitude? That I wish to belong, at last, to no one?" I threw up my hands. "These words are useless. They have no substance. They cannot be heard by anyone but me."

"They will be heard. The king himself will remember your words. Everyone will remember them. In the scroll that I will soon deliver, your words will be recorded for all time."

I eyed the scroll rolled at his waist, which appeared blank. I had never hoped to be remembered by anyone but a few cranky gossips. Gabriel's words filled me with an odd sensation. Suddenly, I was no longer lonely. I had never known that I was afflicted with loneliness, but indeed that was the pain I had hoped to blot out with my books. Feelings of anticipation and fulfillment suffused me. My gratitude was boundless, but it was sharpened by my sudden fear that Gabriel's words might not come true.

"To whom will you deliver this scroll?" I asked abruptly.

"To Mordechai the Jew, the man who refuses to bow down before Haman, the evil adviser of the king."

I had met Haman a few times but knew him mostly by reputation. He had a tremendous ego and an appetite for cruelty. I stayed away from his wife, Zeresh, whose greed and meanness of spirit made her a dangerous opponent. "He must be brave who does not bow down before the strength of a powerful man."

Gabriel smiled at me. "I think you, also, will refuse to bow down." His faith in me warmed me. I found that I was even capable of thinking of others besides myself.

"And who will be afflicted with my husband's affections, should I fall in with your plan of rebellion and refuse him?"

Gabriel sighed, if angels can sigh. "Esther is her name. She has the gift of faith. She is pious, virtuous, and courageous. She is destined to become queen in your place and save her people, the Jews, from destruction."

"And this is the cause in which you enlist me? I know the Jews only from books."

Gabriel smiled. "The cause in which I enlist you is justice."

"And, in justice's name, I should refuse my husband's command."

"Yes," Gabriel almost sang, rising to his feet in some private moment of joy and triumph.

"He will depose me," I stated bleakly. "I will no longer be queen, and my father will humiliate me for my failure."

"Yes," Gabriel acknowledged. His gaze did not waver.

"I accept your challenge," I declared, with a show of bravery I did not entirely feel. "But I place a condition on my acceptance."

Gabriel frowned but remained silent.

"Teach me the divine Name," I demanded. "If you truly have faith in me, as you have in this Esther, let me know what the angels know. Leave something inside me besides my beauty, which, when I use my voice against my husband, will no longer be my shield."

For the first time, Gabriel looked worried. "Only one Name has been entrusted to me. If I give it to you, there will be no Name for the Book of Esther."

"Esther has her piety, her virtue, and her people," I snapped. "I have none of those things." Then, imagining Esther as a friend instead of a rival, I softened my words. "You say she has the gift of faith. From her youth she has found God inside herself. When I look inward I see nothing there but a vain and bitter woman. Istehar, Paltit, Esther, these women you have paraded in front of me as examples, they had faith to make them strong. I have nothing except desperation, and your word."

"Faith is acquired over many years," Gabriel told me sternly.

"I don't have many years. I only have a few minutes, and I need to make them count. You are asking me to give up everything I know. You must give up something you know as well."

For the first time in my life, I had made a decision I would abide by, no matter what happened. Gabriel looked at me for a long time.

Then he leaned near me, and I felt the brush of wings. I heard the faint sound of a breath. On my mouth was the feeling of a kiss, although nothing had touched me. Then Gabriel was gone. Only a perfect, closed rosebud remained in the place where he had been.

I had given my word to an angel, and I would keep my promise. It was to be my last act as queen, and I made it a magnificent one. I strode out of the chamber, refusing to look back. Now that I had agreed to Gabriel's wish I was sure I had seen him for the last time. I found my way out of the servants' halls into the royal chambers. They seemed much smaller than they had the day before. I summoned the herald who waited there. He was ready to conduct me to the king's banquet, where I was supposed to strip naked and display myself. The idea that I would do this seemed ridiculous. I wondered if I was the same person I had been before.

Strangely, the courtier did not seem impatient. I realized, as at the end of a dream, that almost no time had passed since I had fled to the simple gardener's room. I drew myself up to the impossible height and beauty of a woman wearing a crown. I brushed past the messenger and entered the royal banquet hall, where the king sat with his drunken guests. The herald hastily announced me. Everyone turned to watch my entrance.

The king frowned mightily when he saw that I was clothed. I was not afraid of him. Inside myself I held a holy secret, and the knowledge that an angel trusted me. What was inside was unpronounceable, yet I found my voice. I spoke directly to my husband.

"I refuse to be paraded in front of your revelers like an exotic trained beast. I am your wife, and even if I were only your milkmaid, I would be worthy of more respect than you have shown me. Your request is obscene, and it comes from a drunken boor. I will not be commanded by you, and no one who believes in justice should obey you or heed your words." Leaving my royal spouse gaping and the entire court in stunned silence, I swept out of the hall in a wave of peacock-colored robes, the same robes I had donned for my magnificent banquet. They seemed heavy to me now, the remains of a luxury I must shed. No man would protect me now. If I did not escape I might be executed for my disobedience. Although I knew I should pack a few belongings and find a way out of Shushan, I could not imagine anywhere on earth that would tolerate a woman such as I had become. As I quickly passed from room to room, somehow I was drawn to the chamber where I had experienced the first real friendship of my life.

I was certain that when I reached the earth-colored room with its vases of humble wildflowers and modest sprays of roses, no angel would appear. My messenger had surely gone to deliver his scroll to Mordechai. To my joy, when I arrived in the small chamber, Gabriel was there. His belt no longer held a scroll. He regarded me first in satisfaction, then in concern. "Vashti, a world has closed to you, but many have opened. Where will you go now?" And at that moment I knew.

In the court of Persia, no one survives who cannot learn from a good story. Like Istehar, I rose to the heavens—the heavens of the Jews, for how could I resist a paradise of books? Gabriel, chiding and laughing, rose golden-hearted after me. I think he was glad. I *know* he was glad, for in that moment we were completely open to each other. Gaining my freedom, I had revealed myself at last. Do angels have lovers? I cannot say, for in the upper worlds no being has gender or even form. I will say this: No mortal loved me as well as Gabriel, who showed me the beauty of my soul.

In this paradise of trees and books, there are no servants, for none need be masters. There is only one Ruler, and that Rule is better than any I have ever known. Standing before the divine throne, I would have shivered, thinking myself once again in the court of my tyrant husband, but the incorporeal do not shiver. In any case, the voice I perceived was not wanton and loud, but still and small as the breath of a bird. There was no test of beauty. I, Vashti, was welcome.

I soon embarked on my second friendship. Enoch, the heavenly chronicler, also came here without dying. It was he who first called me Ofanniel, an angel's name. Though surely I was no angel in my time on earth, the name delights: "wheel of God," a reminder that in an hour everything can change. Now I, like Gabriel, am a symbol of what all people might be.

What I desired most was to give of myself. Gabriel assigned me the task of guiding the moon. The work is intricate, complicated, requiring a sure hand and keen eye. Yet it suits me, who wove my way through the king's court with grace and skill. I feel an affinity with the moon, keeper of the months, watcher of time, emblem of the renewal of life. The moon is metaphor for the Shekhinah, God's divine, queenly presence. She, like me, reveals Herself only in Her own time.

EPILOGUE

Then she remembers one—and with
insistent tenderness—who kept
a flock of scumbled images.

   —ALLEN MANDELBAUM, *Chelmaxioms*

   if we remembered it together,
   we could recreate holy time
   sparks flying

     —MERLE FELD, "We All Stood Together"

THE WORDS
IN THE SCROLL

For Alicia

*Then the high priest Hilkiah said to the scribe
Shaphan, "I have found a scroll of the Teaching in
the House of the Lord." . . .*

*When the king heard the words of the scroll of the
Teaching, he rent his clothes. And the king gave orders
to the priest Hilkiah, and to Ahikam son of Shaphan,
Achbor son of Michaiah, and the scribe Shaphan, and
Asaiah, the king's minister: "Go, inquire of the Lord
on my behalf, and on behalf of this people, and on
behalf of all Judah, concerning the words of this scroll
that has been found. For great indeed must be the
wrath of the Lord that has been kindled against us,
because our fathers did not obey the words of this
scroll to do all that has been prescribed for us."*

*So the priest Hilkiah, and Ahikam, Achbor, Shaphan,
and Asaiah went to the prophetess Huldah—the wife
of Shallum son of Tikvah son of Harhas, the keeper
of the wardrobe—who was living in Jerusalem in the
Mishneh, and they spoke to her. She responded:
"Thus said the Lord, the God of Israel: Tell the man
who sent you to me; Thus said the Lord: I am going to
bring disaster upon this place and its inhabitants, in
accordance with all the words of the scroll which the
king of Judah has read. Because they have forsaken
Me and have made offerings to other gods and vexed
Me with all their deeds, My wrath is kindled against*

231

*this place and it shall not be quenched. But say this to
the king, who sent you to inquire of the Lord: Thus said
the Lord, the God of Israel: As for the words which
you have heard—because your heart was softened and
you humbled yourself before the Lord when you heard
what I decreed against this place and its inhabitants—
that it will become a desolation and a curse—and
because you rent your clothes and wept before me, I for
my part have listened—declares the Lord. Assuredly,
I will gather you to your fathers and you will be laid
in your tomb in peace. Your eyes shall not see all the
disaster which I will bring upon this place." So they
brought back the reply to the king.*

—2 KINGS 22:8,11–20

Everyone wants to know if I wrote it. You want to know too, hmmm? Did Huldah write the Book of Deuteronomy, that inspiring, bullying tract? Did she sneak it into the Temple while the priests' watches were changing? Well? What do you think? Do you suppose I tell everyone everything the first time she asks?

I might have slammed the door in their faces, you know. That would have changed history, hmmm? How would you feel if you saw a gaggle of silk-robed administrators at your door? Administrators are boring people! They have so much ink in their ears that they cannot report what they are told in an accurate fashion, and their fashion itself is barbaric. My eyes are old! How much scarlet can they take? And they all have gray beards like the birds' nests in my chimney. Yes, birds' nests over my cooking fires—because I don't cook! I am far too busy with the needs of the common folk, that is, their need to be talked out of their foolishness. Not an easy job. No. Particularly with such bad reporting.

Yet there they were, the nervous, mouse-faced creatures with their half-nibbled scroll. No doubt one of them had been snacking on it. Achbor! Shaphan! I knew them when they were scribe's apprentices and went about with blackened fingers! I learned to read and write by hiding on the roof of the scriptorium. I peered through the skylight at their cramped scribblings on potsherds. Hilkiah the high priest I knew also, the oily autocrat. Maybe he wrote the scroll! He lifted it eagerly enough, with his proud white hand, until the hem of my old gray robe brushed against his fingernails. He nearly jumped backward. Some people think only clean laundry is relevant, not prophecy. I debated whether to get my broom and sweep the lot of them into the street.

Hilkiah, my old rival, looked down at me from his considerable height, jingled his priestly bells, and made his announcement. He and his party, at the king's suggestion, had come to inquire of the respected, the revered prophetess. Was this ancient scroll, which claimed to be Moses' farewell address, genuine?

So it was the king's idea to ask me, hmmm? Certainly not Hilkiah's. The man looked positively miffed. *He must have written it,* I thought. *Now I have the chance to foil his plans.* I was pleased about this. The gaggle no doubt interpreted my ancient giggle as a fit of divine ecstasy. I was even more pleased when I realized that they might have asked my cousin Jeremiah, who would no doubt have orated something long and dreary to which no one would pay any attention. A prophecy should never run longer than fifteen minutes, twenty on a holiday. But no, they'd asked me. A stroke of luck. Truly a stroke of luck.

"Give me the scroll!" I said, drawing myself up to my full height of five feet. The parchment was rolled up in Hilkiah's hand, tied with a leather cord. It didn't look ancient to me. He handed it to me reluctantly, a troubled look on his face. He said he knew I would scrutinize it carefully. "Come back tomorrow at this time," I demanded, stepping back onto my stone stoop. I didn't intend to invite them in for tea—I have a black cat from Egypt and I'm sure one of those fine gentlemen was allergic. Besides, prophets are always rude. Ask yourself, is it polite to call a nation names like "worm" and "whore"? If you don't want enemies, don't become a prophet. The five officials bumped into each other trying to maintain their dignity as they left. I closed my door and stepped down the four steps into my office, where I had been counseling a widow who needed to pull herself together. I'd asked her to wait, but she hadn't. No doubt kings' ministers scared her. They'd scare me too, if I had outstanding taxes.

I washed my hands and settled into my great cedar chair, my one luxury. My husband bought it for me in his days as the keeper of the king's wardrobe. I unrolled the scroll on my lap, slowly, annoyed as I realized how long it was. I had only a day to read it. Fortunately, it was written neatly in block print. This was already suspicious—could a man like Moses, with such an unkempt beard, have had neat handwriting?

Moses' farewell address began with a long history of Israel's wandering in the desert, and a good deal of chastising. I'm not opposed to chastising, but it is not interesting to read. I found my mind wandering. I skimmed through the scroll, noting that rites of sacrifice were to occur only in "God's chosen place"—the Temple built by Solomon. Hilkiah's been wanting to shut down the mountain shrines for years, I mused. This could be his work. He might certainly have thought of the financial restrictions the scroll placed on the king—kings can get out of hand, as anyone knows. Yet I also noticed the command to destroy all the surrounding peoples, and that might very well be the king's idea. He was a soldier, after all. Perhaps the king had written the scroll.

There was busy insistence on justice toward the poor, of which I had to approve. The Sinai commandments appeared, with various additions. Anyone could have copied that from a scroll in the king's library and altered it to taste, I thought. I began to doze off again, but then I read of a terrible curse. It was a curse of exile, powerfully written. It sent chills down my spine. I'd been preaching about the possibility of exile for years, if Israel didn't clean up its act. Someone else had said it better than me, put it in appallingly physical terms, as if the dust of the earth could be an instrument of God's wrath.

The thing was almost certainly a fake. But there was a blessing at the end, snatches of which I was sure I'd heard my mother singing over her wash basin. That blessing might indeed be older. *Torah tzivah lanu moshe, morashah kehillat yaakov.* "Moses commanded us a Torah, an inheritance for the community of Jacob." Catchy phrase. And then there was the death scene of Moses—after all the elaborate legends, this story was so simple it had to be true. Had God whispered in someone's ear?

I often question myself. A prophet has to question everything. I laid down the scroll, closed my eyes, and considered whether I, in fact, had any idea of how to tell whether this was a true work of prophecy. My conclusion was that I did not. I might be able to tell whether Moses had written it, but that was not at all the same matter. It could be that he had not written it at all, but that it was still a prophecy. Even true prophets plagiarize. It is one of the techniques of our trade.

I know what you're thinking. "Why doesn't she just ask God to tell her, if she's a prophet? Is the little old woman scared of the Big Voice? Or is she deaf to God and the milkman alike?" But prophecy isn't like that. Prophecy is the gift of seeing where things have gone wrong and having the courage to put them right. Talking to God, well—sometimes you sit in the sun in the afternoon and doze and a thought comes to you that starts you upright again. Is that God? I often thought it was. A prophet has to be willing to believe that what she sees is what God sees.

My cat, Hagar, climbed into my lap and settled there, purring. After a while, I opened my eyes and saw that the sun had set. It was time for dinner, but I wasn't hungry. I was immersed in the mystery, becoming nervous as I realized the potential consequences of my decision. King Josiah was straight and uncomplicated as an arrow. If I said this scroll was the genuine article, he would enact all the laws in it. No more hilltop shrines, no more ritual prostitutes, no more weavings for Asherah, no more marrying foreigners. Certainly no more foreign gods. A pure but rather harsh existence, like hard oak furniture. Maybe some people would die of that hardness.

But if I claimed the scroll was not real, the Israelites might go on joining with the nearby nations until they were indistinguishable from their neighbors. Or we might be attacked by the Assyrians, who are known to send all their conquered peoples into exile. Exile would finish us entirely, unless . . . I got up stiffly, lit an oil lamp, and went back to reading. Hagar perched on the carved arm of my chair and watched me, jealous of the parchment's weight on my lap.

It was on that second read that I saw it, buried in the theological exhortation near the beginning. "Hear O Israel, the Lord our God, the Lord is one." Famous now, but at that time no one had ever seen it. Except me. And I'd seen it the week before.

Prophets are poets, of course. We write down our turns of phrase in the hope that we will convince someone to stick his hand in his pocket and pull out a coin or an onion for a beggar on a cold rainy day. You'd be surprised how hard that is to do. In any case, that Friday I'd stopped my trek through the marketplace in search of good bread and sat down on an upended cobblestone with a scrap

of leather, to write down what I'd thought up. I was between a potter's stall and a weaver's wagon—I remember it clearly. I'd been
thinking about an argument I had with a priestess of Asherah about
the nature of the Israelite God. God has no partner, I tried to
explain, but I didn't have the right words. I'd left her house angry
with my tongue for not working properly. It was on that dusty pavement that it came to me: The Lord our God, the Lord is one. God
is alone, maybe even lonely. Maybe that is why our God seems to be
so close to people, so obsessed with covenant. There are no other
gods with whom to converse.

There it was, the same words. I checked the scrap of leather to
be sure—it was still in my pocket. Could it be a coincidence? What
fool believes in coincidences? I suddenly started to laugh. Right
then the answer seemed obvious. I'd written this scroll in my sleep.
No doubt I'd planted it in the Temple treasury while wearing my
nightgown.

Not possible, you say? I didn't think so either. If I were to say
truthfully, which naturally I would not, I would tell you that I was
more frightened that night than I ever have been before or since. To
make matters worse, my lamp smoked and went out a few minutes
later. It was as black as pitch in my house. Hagar yowled. I lit my
lamp again from the coals, my back aching as I bent low. When I
straightened up again, I quickly peeked through my narrow window
to make sure my neighbor's houses were still there. I intended to
stay up all night and make the most of the time I had, but my eyes
were heavy and I lay down on my bed to rest a while. As I drifted
into sleep, I saw the vivid flash of Hilkiah's troubled eyes as he
handed me the scroll. The same coincidence happened to him, my
fancy said. A word, a phrase. Or something like that. That would
explain the eyes.

Have you ever been horrified by the angle of the sun?

Hmmm? Not you, you bronze sun worshiper. But that morning my blood froze when I woke and saw how high the sun had gotten. I only had a few hours until those sniveling bureaucrats would return, and what would I tell them? That I would present my results the following week at a scholars' tea? I plucked the scroll from the place too close to the lamp where I had left it, opened it randomly to a passage about exemption from the army for the newly married. Did God write that? I was unbearably hungry. I slammed the scroll down, knotted my hair under a shawl, and went up my steps. I strode out into the marketplace to find a loaf of bread and some cheese. Maybe I wanted to linger again at that spot between the weaver's wagon and the potter's stall. I started, but I never got there.

The streets are where I learned prophecy. No court appointment for me: The king's adultery was not my affair. I dealt with the affairs of individuals you might meet on market day: old fat Levites, harried mothers, gruff stone masons, foreign sailors, sooty children with their hands full of stolen salty olives, slinking slave merchants and their desperately rebellious slaves. For fifty years, I've been pushing and pulling at people who are stuck in place. On my father's side I descend from Joshua and Rachav. Prostitutes are a particular concern of mine. Once I took a few twelve-year-old servant girls about to be sold for harlots and slipped them into the queen mother's kitchen. Not prophecy, you say? No one understands prophecy anymore, not even Jeremiah.

Passing along the streets that raised me, I grumbled to myself. I waved my staff about and in general kept up my image, which keeps people from annoying me. After a while I got so caught up in the sounds and colors of the city that I forgot to act my part. Everything seemed brighter that day: the rich men in wool cloaks giving out loans, which the scroll said should be given without interest; the multiple wives of merchants, whom the scroll said should be treated with equal fairness; the priests and witches and veiled priestesses of cults and shrines, which the scroll would abhor and abolish; the babies whom the scroll threatened with disease and destruction if God's will were not obeyed. The sky above Jerusalem had indescribable clouds that day, full, luminous, and layered around the horizon like towers around a city wall. Forgetting about bread and cheese, I bought a handful of dates and ate them while sitting on the rim of a cistern. I watched the local girls come and go with their pitchers, like Rebekah, their bronze earrings glinting in the sun. Beyond the nearby wall, just below the clouds, palm branches curved like knives.

I slowly became aware of a conversation to my left between a mother and her young son. The mother was standing at an open-air scribe's stall near the well, waiting for the scribe to draw up a contract. I knew her name: She was Nechushta, daughter of Elnatan of Jerusalem. She was a young, wealthy, and hardworking daughter of landowners who gave charity here and there around the city. No doubt she was buying a new field. As she waited, sweating beneath her red linen veil, she spoke to the young boy at her side—maybe her brother, not her son—who was chattering to her about a bird's nest he had found, full of eggs, in the old olive tree that stood near a well-traveled road not far from the family home.

This is the essence of what she said: "If, along the road, you chance upon a bird's nest, in any tree or on the ground, with fledglings or eggs and the mother sitting over the fledglings or on the eggs, do not take the mother together with her young. Let the mother go, and take only the young, in order that you may fare well and have a long life."

It was wise. It was just. It was moving. And, of course, it was from the scroll.

I had sat an hour by the cistern, and it was time for me to get back to my house. I would rather shimmy up a palm naked than have royal courtiers come calling while I was still sweating and puffing. As I walked home, I passed a trio of soldiers heading toward the Lebanon Forest House. I paused to look after them. What was *their* verse? "Remember what Amalek did to you on your journey after you left Egypt"? "Be strong and of good courage"? "If you see among the captives a beautiful woman"? Or—"Cursed be he who strikes down his fellow countryman in secret"?

I told you earlier, courtiers make terrible reporters. They did not tell the king exactly what I said about the scroll. But one thing they did get right. As the high priest Hilkiah was leaving for his audience with King Josiah, I told him to take the last letters of the first and last words of that sacred phrase—"Hear O Israel"—and enlarge them, in every scroll he copied from the original. *Eid*, that spells. "Witness." That is what I am, a witness to God's word. I am an old woman with a demanding job. I have a right to some small pride in my work.

And what is *your* verse? Hmmm?

COMMENTARY

A person who quotes a source brings deliverance to the world; as it is written: "And Esther spoke to the king, in the name of Mordechai" (Esther 2:22).

   —PIRKE AVOT 6:6

SOURCES

The commentary contains personal reflections on the origin and character of each story as well as the biblical references that are necessary to understand the thrust of each midrash. Biblical texts are referred to as either "base texts" (texts that are the foundation of the story) or "auxiliary texts" (texts that are referred to in the story). The notes also refer to numerous rabbinic and modern midrashim that have informed this work or that stand in counterpoint to it. Full citations of modern midrashic works appear in the bibliography. For readers who are unfamiliar with rabbinic midrash, a brief guide to most of the cited sources appears below.

While the dating of almost all of these sources is uncertain, the descriptions will give the reader some idea of when and in what form the midrashim were compiled. Many midrashic works cite or revise earlier works, so dating a particular midrashic idea is particularly difficult. I have also occasionally cited Louis Ginzberg's *Legends of the Jews*, which retells many of these midrashim in English.

In addition, I have cited a number of medieval commentators. Brief biographies of these scholars are given below. These commentators tend to collect and revise earlier midrashim, but they also innovate.

TALMUD

Babylonian Talmud

The Mishnah is a legal text, redacted in Palestine in the second century, that interprets the laws of Jewish life. The Talmud, also known as the Gemara, is an interpretation of and commentary on the Mishnah. It is the major source of our knowledge about rabbinic life. The Babylonian Talmud was composed and edited from many rabbinic statements and was compiled in the fourth to sixth centuries in Babylonia. It contains, in addition to legal material, stories, legends, incantations, and many midrashim. In this book, references to talmudic tractates of the Babylonian Talmud are preceded by the letters "BT."

Jerusalem Talmud

The Jerusalem Talmud, like the Babylonian Talmud, is an interpretation and discussion of the Mishnah. It was compiled earlier than the Babylonian Talmud, sometime in the fourth century. There are significant differences between the two collections, although some material is shared. When determining matters of law, the Babylonian Talmud is considered authoritative. In this book, references to talmudic tractates in the Jerusalem Talmud are preceded by the letters "JT."

EARLIER WORKS OF MIDRASH

Mekhilta de-Rabbi Yishmael

A halakhic (legal) and aggadic (narrative) midrash on the Book of Exodus, dated to the third century. Chapters of the *Mekhilta* quoted in this book are *Mekhilta* Be-shallah and *Mekhilta* Shirah.

Midrash Rabbah

Rabbinic midrash spans the entire Torah and certain other books of the Bible, including Ruth and The Song of Songs. Midrash Rabbah is not a single work—the books within the category of Midrash Rabbah are linked by name only. Different books of Midrash Rabbah were composed by different authors and editors in different eras. Genesis Rabbah, for example, was written in the fifth century, at the same time as the Babylonian Talmud and cites many of the same rabbis. Leviticus Rabbah is a slightly later work, composed by a single editor. Exodus Rabbah and Numbers Rabbah were also written later, perhaps in the ninth or tenth centuries. Many books of Midrash Rabbah use the classical proem (or *petihah*), a literary form in which verses from the Torah are linked to verses from other parts of the Bible through a narrative, linguistic, or thematic connection.

Midrash Tanhuma

Also known as *Tanhuma Yelammedenu*, this midrashic work occurs in various versions and is difficult to date, but it was probably composed around the ninth century. It is known as Midrash Tanḥuma because it frequently cites the statements of Rabbi Tanḥuma. This collection, organized around sections of the Torah, uses the specialized midrashic form known as the proem (see comment to Midrash Rabbah). Most Tanḥuma sources quoted here are from the standard version and are designated by the name of a *parashah*, or section of the Torah. There is also a version known as Tanḥuma Buber, after Solomon Buber, who reconstructed and edited it.

Pesikta de-Rav Kahana

This early rabbinic collection of midrash was written between 500 and 700 and uses the proem (see comment to Midrash Rabbah). It is organized around the liturgical calendar.

Pirkei de-Rabbi Eliezer

This eighth-century midrashic work is known as *Pirkei de-Rabbi Eliezer* because it begins with the statement "It is told of Rabbi Eliezer ben Hyrcanus." Unlike other midrashic works, *Pirkei de-Rabbi Eliezer* is not organized by verses of the Torah but is a midrashic narrative that reads as a story. The work cites and revises many earlier midrashim as part of its story line.

Sifrei

Sifrei is an early halakhic (legal) midrash on the Books of Numbers and Deuteronomy. This rabbinic work was compiled sometime around the fifth century.

LATER WORKS OF MIDRASH

Aggadat Bereishit

This collection of midrash on the Book of Genesis dates to the tenth century and is also known as *Seder Eliyahu Rabbah*. It contains midrashim in groups of three. The first section of a triad is on a verse from Genesis; the second, on a verse from the prophets; and the third, on a verse from Psalms. The work contains classical rabbinic proems (see comment on Midrash Rabbah).

Aggadat Shir

A collection of extracts from various midrashim, compiled in the tenth century.

Alphabet of Ben Sira

The *Encyclopaedia Judaica* describes this midrashic work as a sophisticated satire written sometime after the Muslim conquest. It contains the story of Lilith, Adam's first wife.

Midrash ha-Gadol

This medieval anthology of earlier midrashim was composed between 1300 and 1400.

Sefer ha-Yashar

This is a novel-like midrash on the Joseph story, written in Muslim Spain in the tenth or eleventh century.

Yalkut Reuveni

A mystical midrash on the Torah, written by Abraham Reuben ha-Cohen in the seventeenth century.

Yalkut Shimoni

A midrashic anthology on the entire Bible, composed by Simeon of Frankfort in the thirteenth century.

Zohar

The Zohar is the central work of Jewish mysticism. It takes the form of a commentary on the Torah, although it contains a wide variety of kabbalistic material. The authorship of the Zohar and its dating are matters of tremendous debate, but it was probably written in Spain by Moses de Leon in the late thirteenth century. The book itself claims that its author is Yochanan ben Zakkai, a talmudic Rabbi. The Zohar cites earlier midrash and invents its own midrash, using a symbolic, mystical style of interpretation.

MEDIEVAL COMMENTATORS

Avraham ibn Ezra

Avraham ibn Ezra (1089–1164) was a poet, philosopher, grammarian, and biblical commentator from Tudela, Spain. He wandered through many countries as an itinerant scholar and had a notable impact on both poetic form and biblical exegesis in the lands he visited, particularly Italy. His acute and subtle biblical commentary often breaks with the more fantastic rabbinic midrash in its explanations of verses.

Maimonides

Moses ben Maimon (1135–1204), legal authority, commentator, philosopher, and royal physician, is generally agreed to be one of the most important Jewish thinkers. He lived in Cordova, in Fez, and in Cairo and may have lived in Israel as well. His rationalist philosophy profoundly affected Jewish ideas about theology, and his legal code—the *Mishneh Torah*—became highly authoritative. He also wrote a commentary on the Torah, which is cited in this book, as well as a philosophical treatise titled *Guide of the Perplexed*.

Rashbam

Rabbi Samuel ben Meir (ca. 1080–1174) was the son of Rashi's daughter Yocheved and one of Rashi's disciples, Meir. A respected commentator on Bible and Talmud, he frequently argued with his grandfather. He strove to elucidate the contextual meaning *(pshat)* of the biblical text and to distinguish between the plain meaning of the text and the midrash on it.

Rashi

Rabbi Solomon ben Isaac (1040–1105) was one of the major biblical commentators, and his work is an essential tool for all traditional study of Bible and Talmud. He was born in Troyes, France; studied at the great academies of Mainz and Worms; and returned to Troyes, where he continued his vast writings. Rashi synthesized and summarized many rabbinic midrashim in his commentary on the Torah. Rashi had three daughters, all of whom became the mothers of rabbinic dynasties.

NOTES
TO THE STORIES

PROLOGUE

Havdalah (p. 3)

Base texts: Genesis 2:8–9, 4:1
Auxiliary texts: Genesis 1:3, 2:15–18

Isaac Luria, the great kabbalist, posited that at the beginning of Creation there was a great shattering. The vessels into which God had poured the primordial light broke, and both the sparks of light and the shards of the vessel were scattered throughout the universe. It became the task of humans to repair the vessels and the light and to return the world to its perfect state (cf. Scholem, *Major Trends in Jewish Mysticism*, pp. 266–68). Luria identified the eating of the fruit with this breaking of vessels. He called his image of God "the tree of life" and said that humans shared the attributes that made up this tree. Luria identified the tree of knowledge of good and evil as the shadow, the dark side, of the tree of life. Luria saw the Garden of Eden as a parable, a tale about the human condition and the divine purpose.

Isaac Luria has had a deep impact on my theology. I see the world as a place that is broken, that requires the partnership of humans and God in order to repair it. It is the world's brokenness that makes this partnership possible. For me, even the Torah has broken places that need repair—this is one reason to do midrash. I imagine Eve in the Garden of Eden as a woman who does not yet know that this is her task. She must somehow learn about brokenness and its repair.

Into Eve's garden, I invite Lilith. The only mention of Lilith in the Bible is as a night demon, or night owl (Isaiah 34:14). In a medieval book called *Alphabet of Ben Sira*, Lilith is described as Adam's first wife, who rebels against him, claims to be his equal, and flies away from him (23a–b). She escapes to the Sea of Reeds and refuses to return even when God sends angels to bring her back. God then creates Eve as a second wife for Adam. Lilith is told that she will become a demon and will give birth to hundreds of children a day, but that they will all perish. In rabbinic lore, Lilith is a danger to children and pregnant women and is a seducer of men. Modern feminist midrash has interpreted Lilith as the original liberated woman, untainted by patriarchal domination, and perhaps even Eve's teacher (cf. Judith Plaskow's story "The Coming of Lilith" in Christ and Plaskow, eds., *Womanspirit Rising*, pp. 198–209). In fact, Lilith, in her connection to fertility, mortality, and freedom, is very similar to Eve, who is the mother of all life, who chooses wisdom, mortality, and free will in a single bite. In my poem "Eve and Lilith," I express my sense that Eve and Lilith are actually the same woman, and they are separate only in the perceptions of others. This story stems partly from that insight.

For many years, the legend of the death of Lilith's myriad children disturbed me. Then it occurred to me that if Lilith and Eve are the same person, then their children are the same as well. Lilith's ethereal children are the souls of Eve's corporeal ones. It is written in the Talmud (BT Hagigah 13b) that at the time of Creation many souls "pressed forward to be born." Perhaps Lilith, driven by her children's need to be born, entered the garden one last time to plant the seeds of Eve's rebellion, to begin human history.

When Eve gives birth for the first time, she says: "*kaniti ish et hashem*" (I have created a man with God) (Genesis 4:1). Eve's sense of her partnership with God, her sharing in God's creative powers, has always moved me. Perhaps that partnership became possible only after Eve rebelled, for to engage in creation is to take some of God's power for yourself. To create is to assert that the world is not yet finished, that you must participate in its completion—in your own completion. Changing the world and changing the self are deeply human activities. They are sacred activities that constantly engage the people we meet throughout the Bible.

"Havdalah" is based on the legend of the origins of *Havdalah*, the celebration of the separation between the Sabbath and the rest of the week. There is a rabbinic midrash that Adam and Eve become afraid when night falls in the garden. To comfort them, God shows them how to make fire. This, according to the rabbis, is the first *Havdalah*, the first ceremony of separation, the first blessing over fire (cf. Genesis Rabbah 11:1, 12:6). Fire is one symbol for revelation, and the time of *Havdalah* can be a time of insight. Another midrash describes how Adam received a book called the *Book of Raziel*, which contains the secrets of heaven and earth (Zohar 1:55b) and the generations of humankind. The angels are jealous of this knowledge and seek to take it from him. Adam is instructed to hide this book from the angels lest they learn too many divine secrets. Like the legend of Lilith, the story of the *Book of Raziel* deals with the consequences of wisdom and generativity. I see the revelation of Lilith to Eve as a parallel to the revelation of the *Book of Raziel* to Adam.

The biblical text purports to represent Eve as subservient to Adam, saying "he shall rule over you" (Genesis 3:16), yet Eve is the one who sets the action in motion by taking the fruit. In the Bible, Eve is a deep part of the unfolding of the story. She is the beginning because she was made at the beginning, but she is also the beginning because she chose to be. May we learn, as many modern poets and prophets have learned, to revere her as the ancestor of our own free will, our own creative urge.

THE HOUSE OF THE MOTHERS

Naamah and the Hummingbird (p. 15)

Base texts: Genesis 6:9–9:19; 1 Kings 15:10
Auxiliary texts: Genesis 4:22, 10:2, 10:6; 2 Chronicles 13:1

The family of Noah is a source of fascination for me because, like Eve's family, they are firsts: They begin the human population anew. Who were the women of that family? They are not named, but their stories wait to be told. The spark for "Naamah and the Hummingbird" came from my discovery that there are two Naamahs in the Bible. One is mentioned as one of Cain's descendants, daughter of Lamech and Zillah and sister of the metalworker Tubal-Cain (Genesis 4:22). This Naamah, in one midrashic tradition, is the wife of Noah (Genesis Rabbah 23:3). Yet in some midrashic traditions, this Naamah is a demon, like Lilith (Zohar 1:55a). The other Naamah is one of Solomon's wives and the mother of his heir, Rechavam (1 Kings 14:31). That later Naamah is an Ammonite and descended from one of Lot's daughters. I began to conjecture a connection between these two women, a connection explained in a story.

Naamah, the queen of Solomon, became the teller of my story. To give her an audience, I chose Maacah, her daughter-in-law, to walk with her in Solomon's exotic garden. Maacah bat Avishalom of Gibeah, Solomon and Naamah's daughter-in-law, is listed in 1 Kings 15:10 as the mother of Rechavam's son and heir Asa. Her life must have been profoundly affected by Rechavam's ascension to the throne, which split the kingdom in two. She may, in fact, have been a granddaughter of David through David's son Avshalom (1 Kings 15:2,10). Apparently, she participated in some kind of goddess-worship later in her life and was deposed (see 1 Kings 5:13). I began to sympathize with this young woman and to imagine what kind of story she might need to hear at the beginning of her reign. Solomon's garden itself is an invention, but Solomon was known as a collector of plants and animals (1 Kings 5:13), perhaps even of hummingbirds, which do not exist in the Middle East.

The story itself is based on my own love of hummingbirds, who seem to hover between heaven and earth like messengers of color and light. It is also based on my own childhood claustrophobia—it was easy for me to imagine why someone would refuse to enter a dark, closed space, even if that space would save her life. I wanted to explain, through this story, how companionship helps us cope with our fears.

The atmosphere of the ark is midrashic in nature. The strange window of Noah's ark is called the *tzohar* in the Bible, an unusual word; and in midrashic tradition it is said to have mystical powers (Genesis Rabbah 25:2; BT Sanhedrin 108b). The separation of genders on the ark is also from traditional midrash and can be found in Rashi's commentary on the Genesis story.

Midrash itself is a story within a story—one tale, or one imaginative comment, within the larger context of the biblical narrative. The advantage of story within story is that there can be built-in layers, cross-references, intertexts. A story within a story is like an episode within our lives—it is always part of something larger. Naamah's tale of the earlier Naamah is meant to recall the gifts of midrash.

The Arranged Marriage (p. 27)

Base texts: Genesis 11:29
Auxiliary text: Genesis 20:12

This tale came out of the question: How did Abraham and Sarah meet? In Genesis 20:12 Abraham tells us that Sarah is his father's daughter but not his mother's, implying matrilineal marriage laws in their culture. We know Abraham's father as Terach. However, we never hear any more about Abraham's or Sarah's mothers, or their relationship with Terach. The midrash tells us that Abraham's father was an idol maker and/or a royal courtier at the court of King Nimrod—a king who once sought to kill Abraham. In rabbinic midrash, Abraham's mother is called Emetlai or Emtelai (BT Bava Batra 91a) and witnesses numerous miracles. I have been unable to locate any source that speaks of Sarah's mother. The Rabbis, who often identify Sarah with Iscah, Abraham's niece (BT Megillah 14a), seem to deny that she in fact is Abraham's sister, no doubt out of discomfort with what they regard as an incestuous marriage. In fact, they seem to avoid stories of Sarah's origins altogether—but that doesn't mean *we* should.

Savina Teubal, in her book *Sarah the Priestess*, suggests that Sarah was part of a matriarchal priestly tradition, and that her childlessness was part of this status. I adopted the idea that Sarah came from a priestess's family. Modern scholarship suggests that many names of Abraham's family are moon-centered names (Sarai is a name of the Akkadian moon-god's daughter, Milcah is a female deity associated with the moon, and Terach means moon). Therefore, I have made Sarai/Sarah a daughter of a moon priestess—naturally, with tendencies toward monotheism. In rabbinic midrash, Sarah is considered to be a greater prophet than Abraham, and her midrashic name Iscah can mean "anointed" or "seeing." This name is said to reflect her greatness as a prophet (Megillah 14a). She is also said to have converted many women to her new faith (Zohar 1:102a). If we imagine her more deeply, we can conceive Sarah as a priestess connected to ancient traditions and as an iconoclast who challenges what exists.

"The Arranged Marriage" contains the famous midrashic "breaking of the idols" scene, in which Abraham convinces his father of the powerlessness of gods of stone. This story is told in many midrashic sources, such as Genesis Rabbah 38:13. The parallel scene involving Sarai is my own invention. Avram and Sarai are the representatives of all who leave their past behind and begin something new. That these two people are our mythic ancestors reminds us of our own need to seek our path even when we must find the way ourselves.

Sarai and Avram are prophets. A prophet in ancient Israel meant one who carried God's message, one who spoke the truth of God's justice and compassion. In imagining Avram and Sarai, I have imagined a kind of prophecy that allows one to be in tune with the oneness of all things. From the biblical verse that I translate "Avram took Sarai his wife and Lot his nephew, and all the things they had collected, and all the souls that they had acquired, and they set out for the land of Canaan" (Genesis 12:5), I have deduced that Abraham and Sarah had spiritual connections to both people and inanimate objects. God says to Abraham: "Whatever Sarah tells you, listen to her" (Genesis 21:12). It seems possible to me that Sarah could hear things Abraham could not hear—and vice versa.

Isaac and Rebekah, Jacob and Rachel, meet in what appears to be a "fated" way. They meet their appropriate spouse on the road, as if by chance. It seems to me that Avram and Sarai must have met the same way, yet we have no legends of their meeting. But if the meeting is important, as I think it must be—for all connections are important—it is worthy of a hundred tales.

The Revenge of Lot's Wife (p. 35)

Base text: Genesis 19:26

Auxiliary texts: Numbers 18:19; Genesis 19:30–38

Lot's wife, who in the midrash is sometimes called Idit (*Pirkei de-Rabbi Eliezer* 25), was turned into a pillar of salt because she looked back toward Sodom. This is generally regarded as a punishment. Medieval commentators like Rashi and ibn Ezra accuse Idit of being inhospitable to angels. Others complain of her lack of faith. No one remarks on the anguish she must have felt when her husband offered her daughters to the howling mob gathered outside their house. In rabbinic commentary, there has been little compassion for Idit, although some midrashim do criticize Lot for his treatment of his daughters (Midrash Tanḥuma Va-yera' 12). Modern poets like Anna Akhmatova and Wislawa Szymborska (Curzon, ed., *Modern Poems on the Bible*, pp. 127–28) are much more sympathetic to Lot's wife and her reasons for turning.

We should note that rabbinic commentary, after a careful reading of the text, puts the number of Lot's daughters at four, not two (Genesis Rabbah 50:9; *Pirkei de-Rabbi Eliezer* 25). Two are saved with Lot and Idit, and two are left in Sodom with their husbands, Lot's sons-in-law. Some commentators wonder whether Idit turned because she was looking for her two older daughters, to see if they were following her out of the city after all. We are told only that Lot asked his sons-in-law to accompany him out of Sodom. We are not told that he asked their wives, his daughters. It is possible that upon learning of this, Idit panicked and looked back. Or perhaps she could not choose between her children, those on the road and those in the city. Lot had no such compunctions about his children. Even before Sodom's destruction he was willing to give his daughters to a mob in order to spare his guests. In "The Revenge of Lot's Wife," Idit has better values than her husband. It seems to me that she must have turned in order to try to bring her four daughters together.

I can only imagine what happened to Idit after she became a pillar of salt. The Rabbis of the Talmud do in fact say blessings over the pillar of salt believed to be Lot's wife (BT Berachot 54a). Was it boring being a pillar? Did she have adventures? Did she miss her daughters? What did she think about? How did she feel about her husband? Although at first her situation seemed tragic, I began to think of her "lot" as somewhat humorous. Imagine becoming a stop on the tour bus routes! What an opportunity for conversation! Then it occurred to me that salt dissolves in water . . . and Idit still had a way to escape her frozen shape and set out after her husband and daughters.

In biblical Judaism, salt is a sign of covenant. It is offered with all the sacrifices. Modern Jews still use salt in the ritual of blessing bread on the Sabbath. Perhaps this salt is to remind us of Idit. Idit is a word meaning "witness," and Lot's wife is a witness that when we are saved from danger we should not leave others behind. She is the representative of a covenant in which all are included. In Jewish tradition, Lot and his wife are the ancestors of Ruth and of King David. One of the descendants of King David, according to legend, will someday become the Messiah. It seems appropriate to me that Idit, who is an eternal witness to the world's troubles, is also related to the source of its redemption.

The Switch (p. 40)

Base text: Genesis 22
Auxiliary text: Genesis 23:1–2

Rabbi Neil Gillman, a philosopher and professor at the Jewish Theological Seminary, introduced me to the wealth of midrash written on the *Akedah* (the Binding of Isaac). This story was my own response to the *Akedah*. "The Switch" is probably the most complex story I have written. This is ironic, since it deals with one of the starkest, most terrifyingly simple texts in the Bible. Its complexity is a sign of how I have struggled, over the years, to understand the Binding of Isaac. Its pattern of role reversal is an indication of my understanding that we as humans never fully know what role we are playing, whether what we do is ultimately right or wrong.

"The Switch" is based on many rabbinic sources. First, it is based on the midrashic legend that Michael was the angel whom God sent to stop the *Akedah*. It is striking that Michael, the prince of Israel, is the one who saves Isaac's life. This led me to imagine Michael, the keeper of Israel's identity, as a conscientious objector to God's test. The midrashim in which the angels gather around the altar and attempt to stop the *Akedah*, accusing God of injustice (Genesis Rabbah 56:7; Midrash Tanḥuma Va-yera' 23), also were key factors in my reading. My insight was that Michael, as an angel of love, would have opposed the sacrifice.

Second, "The Switch" is based on the various midrashic scenes in which Samael attempts to dissuade Abraham and Isaac from continuing with the sacrifice (cf. Midrash Tanḥuma Va-yera' 22). In biblical and later Jewish tradition, Samael, or the Satan (a word that means "the accuser"), is a kind of prosecuting attorney for God. His role is to tempt humans to sin and, if he is able to corrupt them, to report on them. What is striking about the midrashim about Samael and the *Akedah* is the fact that

Samael's arguments against the *Akedah* are exactly the ones a modern person would use in dissuading a zealous father and an obedient son. "Are you out of your mind?" Samael asks Abraham. "Didn't God give this son to you in your old age?" "Your father is crazy," Samael says to Isaac. "This will destroy your mother." From a modern point of view, Samael is the voice of reason and compassion, objecting to callous acts of piety. It was this depiction of Samael, clearly not a demonic one, that led me to imagine Michael, the angel of compassion, as the speaker of these words.

Third, "The Switch" is based on Tikvah Frymer-Kensky's reading of the *Akedah*. Frymer-Kensky believes that there is an original text of Genesis 22, made up of verses 1–14 and 19, that actually condemns Abraham for his act: "I know that you are a righteous man, yet you did not withhold your son, your only one, from Me." If one reads only these verses from Genesis, one can interpret them to mean that Abraham is supposed to argue, as he did in the case of Sodom and Gomorrah, and he fails the test. In Frymer-Kensky's reading, it is a later, interpretive text (Genesis 22:15–18), added to the original, that praises Abraham for his obedience rather than condemning him. In my reading, this "later text" is Satan's devious twist on the original words God has spoken.

Fourth, "The Switch" is based on the rabbinic legends in which Satan kills Sarah simply by telling her the truth about what has happened on Mount Moriah (Midrash Tanḥuma Va-yera' 23). In that midrash, Sarah cries out with the sound of a shofar and dies of grief upon hearing that her husband has nearly sacrificed her only child. "The Switch" continues that tradition and connects the *Akedah* with Sarah's death— Michael's switch of roles leaves Sarah exposed to Satan's cruel words. Yet the story suggests that Sarah's death, by awakening Abraham's heart, partially redeems the failure of the *Akedah*. The rabbinic midrash in which an angel announces Rebekah's birth to Abraham also appears in the final scene of "The Switch." The possibility of an heir for Sarah, a wife for Isaac, constitutes another potential redemption for Abraham.

Finally, I based my work on a close reading of Genesis 22:15—"The angel of God called to Abraham a second time from heaven." I asked these questions of the text: Why does an angel call a second time from heaven? What is the meaning of the word *shenit* (second)? What relationship does this utterance have to the first one? Who is the angel involved? And why do we need to be told that the angel calls "from heaven"? Could that be because this angel is not usually in heaven? And why call the angel an "angel of God"? Aren't all angels angels of God? In the end, I chose to read the verse as ironic, pointing to an angel who in spite of himself speaks from heaven and who in spite of himself is an angel of God.

THE HOUSE OF THE MATRIARCHS

Second Blessings (p. 55)

Base texts: Genesis 26:34, 28:9, 36:1–43
Auxiliary texts: Genesis 32:4–33, 33:1–17

The middle of Genesis is overshadowed by the dramatic story of Jacob, the son of Isaac and Rebekah. As soon as he is born, he takes center stage. He grabs his brother's heel in the birth canal. He barters with his brother, Esau, for the birthright. He steals Esau's blessing. He flees his brother's wrath. On his journey to his mother's relatives, he finds a ladder stretching between heaven and earth. Later, he wrestles with an angel. But what happens behind him? What drama unfolds in Esau's life while Jacob is marrying Leah and Rachel? What does Esau do until the day he comes to meet Jacob and his family as they arrive in Canaan? The rabbis tell us that Esau plots against Jacob while he is gone (Genesis Rabbah 57:8)—an unsatisfying answer arising from their deep suspicion of Esau. My own answer is told through the eyes of one of Esau's wives: Mahalat the daughter of Ishmael. "Second Blessings" is a close reading of Esau's genealogy. I looked at that obscure genealogy to unearth the women—and the story—within it.

MAHALAT

The first thing Esau does after Jacob leaves for his uncle's house is marry another wife. He already has two: Yehudit (daughter of Beeri) and Bosmat (daughter of Elon), who are "a source of bitterness" to Isaac and Rebekah. Later in the biblical texts, the names will shift: the daughter of Ishmael will be called Bosmat, and the daughter of Elon will be called Adah. But for now, Bosmat is a Canaanite wife and Mahalat is the daughter of Ishmael.

Esau sees that his wives displease his father, and so he marries Mahalat. The rejected son goes to another rejected son to find a wife who will please the favored son, Isaac. There is an irony here, one that is surely implied in the Bible. Mahalat is both a granddaughter of Abraham and a daughter of Ishmael. She is a bridge. She carries a blessing, for her grandmother Hagar is blessed like Abraham: "I will greatly increase your offspring, and they shall be too many to count." The fact that Esau marries Mahalat in itself tells a story of a journey toward blessing.

The name Mahalat can mean "pity" or "comfort." I wondered if Mahalat might have been a comfort for Rebekah when Jacob was gone, a kind of substitute child. Mahalat shares her household with Esau's other wives, but also with Abraham's wife Keturah and with Isaac's wife, Rebekah. In Proverbs we are taught that "a threefold cord will not break," and I have imagined Keturah, Rebekah, and Mahalat as a three-fold cord of spiritual experience.

After Hagar's epiphany in the desert, she names God El-Ro'i, "God of seeing" (Genesis 16:13). She is the first human to name God. Her granddaughter Mahalat/Bosmat names her only son Reuel, "see God" (Genesis 36:4). The connection is too clear to be a coincidence. There is a shared religious spirit, perhaps a shared epiphany, between grand-mother Hagar and granddaughter Mahalat. In my story, Mahalat shares this epiphany with Rebekah and Keturah. This is another reconcilia-tion—it is a return of Hagar to Sarah's tent, for Mahalat represents Hagar and Rebekah represents Sarah.

The name of Elah, Mahalat's daughter, comes from a clan of Esau called Elah (Genesis 36:41). Several of these clans are named for women (Timna, Oholivamah; Genesis 36:40–41). I chose Elah's name, which means "goddess" as well as "oak tree," to indicate that the women of Hagar's family remained strong and powerful.

Ishmael, in rabbinic lore, is identified with Islam, and the Rabbis applied Islamic names to Ishmael's wives; for example, there is a midrash that Mahalat's mother was called Aisha, and Ishmael's second wife was called Fatima (*Pirkei de-Rabbi Eliezer* 30, 31). In modern times, we are seeking peace between the children of Isaac and of Ishmael. Mahalat is a symbolic bearer of reconciliation between two long-separated house-holds. In the commentary *Yalkut Reuveni* (36c), we find the statement that Abraham married one wife from the lines of Noah's three sons: Sarah was a daughter of Shem, Hagar was a daughter of Ham, and Keturah was a daughter of Japheth. Thus in Mahalat's time, the hope for peace between peoples dwells in Abraham's household.

ADAH

Two lists of Esau's wives are given in the Bible, in Genesis 26 and in Genesis 36. They do not match. In chapter 26 the wives are Yehudit bat Beeri, Bosmat bat Elon, and Mahalat bat Ishmael. In chapter 36, the wives are Adah bat Elon, Bosmat bat Ishmael, and Oholivamah bat Anah. The daughter of Ishmael has two names, and her name in the second list is the same as a different wife's name in the first list. This may be con-fusing to the reader. It was certainly confusing to me.

There are rabbinic solutions to this problem (cf. Genesis Rabbah 57:13, which gives symbolic interpretations of the names), but I like my own better. Yehudit bat Beeri drops out of the second list, and I learn from this that she died young. Adiva, Yehudit's daughter, appears in "Shimon's Prison" (p. 84, herein), and her name comes from the name of Shimon's wife in the Book of Jubilees (34:20).

Oholivamah appears only in the second list. I learn from this that Esau married her later in his life. This leaves Bosmat/Adah and Mahalat/Bosmat. The name Bosmat means "aromatic" or "spice." Bosmat is the repeating name. I studied the passages with Jeremy Goldman, who suggested to me that Bosmat is a title of endearment given to the chief wife in Esau's family. If this is so, what changes between the first list and the second list is not the number of wives but the identity of the chief wife: In the first section, it is Adah who is favored; in the second, it is Mahalat. Thus there are four named wives: Yehudit, Adah, Mahalat, and Oholivamah.

Timna is the concubine of Esau's son Elifaz. She is mentioned in the same verse as Adah (Genesis 36:12). It is somewhat unusual for a concubine to be listed by name in the Torah, so the rabbis wonder what Timna's story is. The text tells us she was a chieftain's daughter (verses 36:20–22). There is a midrash that Timna, a princess, desired to convert to the new Hebrew religion, but that Sarah would not accept her. Timna then decided to attach herself to Abraham's family by becoming a concubine to his great-grandson. Timna's son is Amalek, the great enemy of Israel. Through this midrash the rabbis teach that rejection of outsiders can have serious consequences (BT Sanhedrin 99b; *Midrash ha-Gadol* 1:542). Adah is the grandmother of Amalek—this teaches that while peace dwells in Esau's household, conflict dwells there as well.

OHOLIVAMAH

Oholivamah, daughter of Anah, becomes one of Esau's wives (Genesis 36:2), She is called by her mother's name: Oholivamah daughter of Anah daughter of Tzivon the Hivite (verse 36:2). (Anah is sometimes referred to as female, as in verse 36:2, and sometimes as male, as in verse 36:24; but I saw her as a female character.) Oholivamah means "my tent is at the shrine," indicating to me that she is a prophet. Some commentators believe that Oholivamah is identical with Yehudit (cf. Rashi), but since neither their names, their father's names, nor their tribal names are similar, I have dealt with the two women as separate individuals. Rashbam, a medieval commentator, agrees with this position. Rashbam further says that Esau married Oholivamah later in life, and I have concurred with this view.

In Genesis 36:24, we are given a fragment of a story: We are told that Anah discovered the *"yemim"* while pasturing his/her father's donkeys. What the *yemim* are is unclear. Jewish commentators seem to reach the consensus that Anah discovered the breeding of mules (cf. Rashi on

Genesis 36:24; Genesis Rabbah 82:14). However, the Vulgate (Jerome's Latin translation of the Bible), as well as several modern translations such as the JPS translation of the Bible, render *yemim* as "hot springs," deriving the word from *yam*, "sea." I have taken the second interpretation, to contrast the *yemim* (hot springs) of Anah and Oholivamah with the *ein* (well) of Rebekah and Miriam. Springs of water symbolize sources of spirituality. I have imagined Oholivamah as a seer, guarding her mother's legacy.

While we are privy to Jacob's spiritual transformation as he wrestles with the angel, we do not hear of any similar wrestling by Esau. However, Esau does seem changed when he meets Jacob: He is willing to let Jacob keep what is his, rather than trying to take anything back from him (Genesis 33:9). What happened to Esau's anger? My answer is that Oholivamah and her *yemim* washed it out of him. Jacob got his new name, Israel, from an angel, and Esau got his, Edom, from a prophetess, Oholivamah.

In Genesis 36:6–8, Esau moves to another land, Seir, because he and his brother, Jacob, are crowding each other. Seir becomes Esau's eternal possession (Deuteronomy 2:5), just as Canaan becomes Jacob's possession. I can only imagine that Esau somehow, finally, managed to acquire for himself an equal blessing. The women of Esau's family also deserve an equal blessing.

Mitosis (p. 69)

Base text: Genesis 35:8–21
Auxiliary texts: Genesis 29:17–28, 30:21, 35:27–29

The word "mitosis," refers to the process of cell division that results in two cells containing the exact same genetic material. It refers to Jacob's spiritual "split" in the story but also to Rachel and Leah, who, although different sisters, both carry the destiny of Israel within them.

To me, Leah is not simply a tragic character or a jealous wife. Leah has a powerful spirit. Her "tender eyes" indicate compassion and wisdom. She is the mother of six tribes and of Jacob's only daughter, and she gives eight names to her children in the course of the Genesis narrative, each dealing with a stage in her love for her husband and her own spiritual journey. In spite of her pain, she can praise God; and it is written in the Talmud and midrashim that "no one praised the Holy One until Leah came along and praised him" (BT Berachot 7b; BT Bava Batra 123a; Genesis Rabbah 7:2). The Rabbis of the Talmud claim that Leah was blessed with many children because she was righteous and merciful (BT Bava Batra 123a). The midrash names Leah a prophet who knows the fate of her children. The Zohar identifies Leah with the upper world of hidden creation. The modern commentator Avivah Zornberg equates Leah with the dynamic imagination (*Genesis: The Beginning of Desire*, p. 211). It has always been impossible for me to believe that Leah took Rachel's husband out of spite or that Jacob never loved Leah. This midrash was born of my desire to redeem Leah from her obscurity.

"Mitosis" is also a midrash on two specific verses in Genesis. First, in Genesis 35:9–13 it is written:

> *God appeared again to Jacob on his arrival from*
> *Paddan-Aram, and he blessed him. God said to him:*
> *"You whose name is Jacob, you shall be called Jacob*
> *no more, for Israel shall be your name." Thus he*
> *named him Israel. And God said to him: "I am El*
> *Shaddai. Be fertile and increase. A nation, an*
> *assembly of nations shall descend from you. Kings*
> *shall issue from your loins. The land that I assigned*
> *to Abraham and Isaac I assign to you, and to your*
> *offspring to come will I assign the land." God parted*
> *from him at the spot where he had spoken to him.*

Since Jacob has already been named Israel/Yisrael during his nighttime wrestle with the angel, why does God name him again? My story suggests that at this point, God actually separates Jacob from Israel, and sends Israel into the past to find Leah. The phrase "God parted from him at the spot where he had spoken to him" could also be translated: "he ascended from him(self)—God was in the place where he had spoken to him." I have interpreted the verse to mean that part of Jacob left his body, that Jacob and Israel became separate personalities who loved different women: Rachel and Leah.

Second, in Genesis 35:19–21 it is written: "So Rachel died and was buried on the road to Efrat, which is Bethlehem. Over her grave Jacob set up a pillar . . . and Israel journeyed on." Why use two different names for Jacob in the same sentence? Was Jacob somehow more Israel when he journeyed on than when he buried Rachel? From somewhere in my distant past, I remembered a rabbi's teaching that Jacob was Jacob with Rachel and Israel with Leah. Here, in the text describing Rachel's death, I saw that Jacob made the transition from one self to the other. Later, I looked up the source in the Zohar that identifies Jacob, Israel, Rachel, and Leah with the four faces of Israel. This mystical idea gave my understanding of Jacob, Rachel, and Leah a deeper resonance.

I liked the idea that Jacob could move between his wives not only through space, but through time. The Sages say that there is no before or after in the Torah, and perhaps there is also no before or after for the characters in the Torah. All moments are equally accessible for them. Maybe this is why Abraham was able to dream of his great-grandchildren's oppression in Egypt (Genesis 15:12–13). He too was able to move in time.

Midrashic sources tend to assert that Leah's motives for tricking Jacob were pure and holy (Genesis Rabbah 72:5; BT Niddah 31a). This is rabbinic apologia, but I have borrowed from it in writing this midrash because the rabbinic view of Leah is so compelling. In the Bible, Leah perseveres in her love. In rabbinic imagination Leah's perseverance becomes prophetic power. First, Leah refuses to marry her betrothed, Esau, and weeps until heaven changes its decree and allows her to marry Jacob (BT Bava Batra 123a; Midrash Tanḥuma Va-yetze' 4). Later, afraid that her sister, Rachel, will not have enough tribes to her name, Leah intercedes with God to exchange the sexes of Leah's and Rachel's pregnancies. It is Leah's deep and persevering desire to exchange what is for what can be that draws Israel out of the future to court his intended bride.

At the end of this story, Leah is identified as an author, who writes the tale at a later date. While this view of the matriarch is my own invention, there is a midrash by Rabbi Moses of Narbonne, cited in the modern commentary *Moshav Zekenim*, that Leah used to wear a breastplate that read: *"Torah tzivah lanu Moshe, morashah kehillat Yaakov"* (Moses commanded us the Torah, as an inheritance of the congregation of Jacob). It is the brightness of this golden plate that made her eyes dim. In this legend, Leah already knows that the Torah will be revealed. It is her hidden knowledge of the Torah that veils her eyes. Maybe it is she who begins to write the tales that will be transmitted to her descendants.

["Mitosis" was first published in *Living Text: The Journal of Contemporary Midrash*, no. 3 (summer 1998): 5–8.]

Penitence (p. 79)

Base texts: Genesis 38:1–30, 35:22

The story of Tamar is an interlude between segments of the Joseph story. Judah marries off his eldest son, Er, to a woman named Tamar. Er dies by the hand of God, leaving no sons; so by custom Tamar must marry the next son, who is Onan, so that Onan may make Tamar pregnant and thus provide a child to carry on his brother's name. Onan spills his seed on the ground rather than father a child who will not be his, and God causes his death as well. Judah sends Tamar home to her family, promising she will wed his youngest son, Shelah, when he grows up, for this is what custom demands. Judah breaks his promise, but Tamar is still chained to Judah's third son—she cannot marry anyone else. Tamar, seeing that she has not been given to Shelah as a wife, dresses as a prostitute, seduces Judah, and becomes pregnant with twins. When Judah hears that she is pregnant, he believes she has committed adultery and tries to have her executed. However, she has proof that Judah himself is the father, so she is spared. She gives birth to Judah's sons (one of whom becomes the ancestor of David), but Judah is not intimate with her again. That seems like it might be a cruel fate for a woman, because in a sense Tamar cannot marry anyone but Judah—and yet she is still alone. I wonder what Judah's reasoning was for remaining celibate and also what Tamar might have done about her predicament.

Tamar's companion in this story, Bilhah, is also known for sexual transgressiveness. Although she is Jacob's concubine, it is reported that Reuven, Jacob's son, had sex with her and that Jacob found out. Yet in rabbinic midrashim, Bilhah is Jacob's devoted wife (cf. *Sefer ha-Yashar*). The Rabbis refuse even to admit that Reuven and Bilhah had sex, preferring to suggest that Reuven merely messed up Bilhah's bed. Supposedly, he did this because he was angry that Jacob had moved into Bilhah's tent after Rachel's death rather than into the tent of Leah, Reuven's mother (BT Shabbat 55b). This story has never rung true to me. The Rabbis also say that Reuven repented for his liaison with his father's concubine by praying and fasting (cf. Rashi on Genesis 37:29). They don't say anything about Bilhah's reaction—leaving ample room for midrash.

Shimon's Prison (p. 84)

Base text: Genesis 42:24–43:23
Auxiliary texts: Genesis 34:1–31, 41:45, 46:10

Like many midrashim, this story comes out of a very simple question: Whatever happened to Shimon? As the Egyptian vizier, Joseph imprisons his brother Shimon (Simeon) as a way of chastening his half brothers and forcing them to bring him his full brother, Benjamin. The Rabbis state that Shimon must have been the original instigator of the plot against Joseph and that Joseph is paying him back. After Joseph imprisons Shimon, the rest of the brothers leave Egypt and do not return for some time, not until after the grain runs out again. In fact, Jacob refuses to make any haste in rescuing Shimon—rather, he acts as if Shimon were lost forever, saying, "It is always me that you bereave; Shimon is no more" (Genesis 42:36). We do not hear of Shimon again until the brothers return to Egypt and Joseph brings him out to them. What happened to Shimon during his time in Egypt?

While some rabbinic midrashim suggest that Joseph kept Shimon in luxury during his stay (Genesis Rabbah 92:4), this seems less than plausible to me. Joseph's anger toward his brothers is extreme; and in traditional midrash, it is Shimon who most wants to kill Joseph while he is in the pit. I could imagine that Joseph would keep Shimon in prison a long time, just as Joseph himself was kept in prison a long time.

Prison is a place where it is difficult to avoid oneself, and Shimon may have good reason to avoid his own company. In addition to whatever guilt he bears for his brother, Shimon is one of the two men who avenges Dinah's rape by conducting a massacre at Shechem (Genesis 34). Shimon has a violent past to contend with. He also has many relationships with women to consider. The Rabbis posit a special relationship between Shimon and Dinah. Rav Huna even goes so far as to suggest that Dinah married Shimon (Genesis Rabbah 80:11). The Rabbis also say that Shimon was the one to bury Dinah when she died (Genesis Rabbah 80:11). Shimon is portrayed by the Bible and the midrash as a violent man who kills (Genesis 49:5–7; Genesis Rabbah 84:3); yet according to the biblical account, Shimon also rescues Dinah from her rapist. His character is, perhaps, as complex as it is criminal.

The Rabbis criticize Dinah for being the kind of woman who "goes out," who goes exploring in public. They criticize Leah for the same "fault," saying: "As the mother, so the daughter" (Ezekiel 16:44). This seems to me more a virtue than a fault, because women who explore are more likely to discover their own freedom. I like to think that Shimon, who cannot sit still, might be sympathetic to Dinah's need for liberty. Perhaps this is another matter he explores during his imprisonment.

In a genealogical list, in addition to his other children, Shimon is called the father of "Shaul, son of a Canaanite woman" (Genesis 46:10). One midrash suggests that this "Canaanite woman" is Dinah and the child is the child of Dinah's rape, adopted by Shimon. This midrash says that Dinah is called a Canaanite woman because she has had sex with a Canaanite (Genesis Rabbah 80:11). I objected to the implication that being raped defiled Dinah in some way, so I used the midrash in a changed form. In my midrash, the Canaanite woman is named Cozbi, and Dinah adopts Cozbi's child, Shaul.

Adiva is the name that the Book of Jubilees gives to Shimon's wife (34:20). The implication that she was Esau's daughter is my own. I wondered about Shimon's relationship to his wife and to his concubine, to his sister and to his mother, Leah. I began to wonder how Shimon would deal with his past as he began to face it.

To discover this, I had to find a confidante for Shimon, and I chose his sister-in-law Asnat. In the Bible, Joseph marries a woman named Asnat (Asenath) after he reaches his high estate, and she bears him two children: Ephraim and Menashe. Asnat is the daughter of the priest Poti-phera, whom the Rabbis identify with Potifar, Joseph's master (*Pirkei de-Rabbi Eliezer* 37). According to one daring midrash, Asnat is Dinah's daughter: for when Dinah is raped and becomes pregnant, she gives birth to a daughter, who is taken away by the angel Michael and given to Potifar (*Pirkei de-Rabbi Eliezer* 37). Michael gives Asnat an amulet, which reads "Holy to the Lord," so that Joseph can identify her later. Thus God provides for Joseph a wife of the "proper" descent. The adoption of Asnat has always fascinated me. This story explores how she might have discovered her roots through her uncle Shimon as well as how he might have come to face his past through her.

This midrash deals with one final question: Why do Ephraim and Menashe not continue the cycle of anger that surrounds the brothers of Genesis? My answer is: because of Shimon's repentance. In order to change his life, Shimon must heal his relationships, and he must teach his nephews to do the same. On Friday nights, traditional parents bless their sons by saying: "May you be like Ephraim and Menashe." Rabbi Arthur Waskow suggests that when we say these words to our sons, we mean that the cycle of violence must be broken. We must always seek to understand our past and to change our future.

THE HOUSE OF THE MIDWIVES

The Tenth Plague (p. 107)

Base text: Exodus 12:21–36
Auxiliary texts: Exodus 1:15–22, 6:23–25; Numbers 25:10–13

"The Tenth Plague" was written for entry in a contest held by the Reconstructionist Rabbinical College, the Whizin Prize for a midrash on a contemporary issue. It won the contest and, by doing so, seeded this book. At the time that I wrote this story, I was a graduate student in psychology, and was working for the AIDS Risk Reduction Project at the University of Connecticut. The word "plague" was very much on my mind. I wanted to write a midrash that would deal with the shunning of victims of contagious disease. The night of the tenth plague immediately came to mind. Of course, the state of being a firstborn Egyptian isn't catching, but the Egyptians didn't know that—and maybe the Israelites didn't either. The sight of many, many firstborn Egyptians dying must have created panic among the people. I can imagine firstborn children being pushed out of their homes, shunned, even sacrificed. This image brings home to me the arbitrary nature of the plague, its unfairness. In the "Tenth Plague," I wanted to write about a character who would see this injustice and do something to change it.

Writing this midrash gave me a chance to solve a biblical puzzle that had plagued me for some time. I was interested in the character of Elisheva, wife of Aaron the high priest, named in Exodus 6:23. Who was she? Why did Aaron marry her? The Talmud teaches that she had five joys more than all other daughters of Israel (BT Zevachim 102a) and then proceeds to list her male relatives: her husband Aaron, the high priest; her brother-in-law Moses, the prophet; her son Elazar, the high priest; her grandson Pinchas, the warrior priest; and her brother Nachshon, prince of the tribe of Judah, the character famous in midrash for his leap into the Sea of Reeds. "Didn't she have any joys of her own?" I wondered. Something that would make her worthy of being the mother of the whole priestly tribe? The Talmud further suggests (BT Sotah 11b) that Elisheva might have been a midwife during the time of the Exodus and identifies her with the biblical character Puah (who is also identified with Miriam).

Immediately the question came to mind: Which midwife went to deliver the firstborn of Egypt on the night of the tenth plague? Someone surely must have. Later in the Bible it is Aaron who stops plagues sent by God (Numbers 17:11–13). I imagined that on the night of the Exodus, it was Elisheva, Aaron's wife, who stopped the plague. In Exodus 1:21 we are told that God built houses for the courageous midwives Shifrah and Puah. Elisheva has one of the most noble houses of all, the house of the priesthood. Her midwifery must have been worth such a splendid lineage. I imagined that through her sense of justice, she was able to save Egyptian lives. I am grateful to Jeremy Goldman, who helped me arrive at many of the insights in this story.

In Exodus 6:25 we are told that Elisheva's son Elazar, who will someday be the high priest, takes to wife one of the daughters of Putiel. The son of Elazar and Putiel's daughter is Pinchas. Pinchas, Elisheva's grandson, has a special status: He is zealous for God and is given God's covenant of peace (Numbers 25:10–13). The daughter of Putiel is another foundress of a priestly family. But who is she? Who are her sisters, Putiel's other daughters? And who is Putiel?

In some rabbinic midrashim Putiel is a name for Jethro, Moses' father-in-law (cf. Rashi on Exodus 6:25). Putiel's daughters are Zipporah and her six sisters—Elazar would thus have married his uncle's sister-in-law. I took a different route, in which Putiel is the Egyptian woman who is spared by the Angel of Death. In "The Tenth Plague," Pinchas, the most pure of the priestly line, is descended from an Egyptian convert. In biblical and rabbinic tradition, King David comes from a line that includes non-Israelites, even enemies of Israel. I like the notion that Pinchas has a similar story, because that kind of origin story reminds us that none of us is separate from the people around us.

["The Tenth Plague" was first published in *The Reconstructionist Rabbinical College Annual Report* (1995).]

The Bones of Joseph (p. 114)

Base text: Exodus 13:19
Auxiliary texts: Genesis 46:17, 50:25–26

Serach, daughter of Asher (cf. Genesis 46:17), is an obscure figure in the biblical text—she appears only in a genealogy—but is a major character in midrash. Her full legend is recounted in the story "The King's Harp" (p. 181, herein) and its commentary. Serach is a granddaughter of Jacob. She is a harpist, who lives an extended, some say eternal, life (Genesis Rabbah 94:15). While the Israelites are packing to leave Egypt, Moses goes to fulfill the vow that Joseph has demanded from his family: "Bring up my bones from here." Yet Joseph has died so long ago, and the Egyptians have hidden him so well, that no one knows where he is buried. Only the aged Serach, Joseph's niece, knows how to find the spot (Midrash Tanḥuma Be-shallaḥ 2). She also knows Moses is the deliverer of Israel because he uses the code phrase her father taught her: "I shall surely redeem you." Serach leads Moses to the site of Joseph's coffin and watches as he chants the incantation that commands the coffin to rise from its resting place in the Nile River.

The moment at which the coffin rises from the Nile is full of drama. "If you do not rise," Moses declaims, "we shall be free of the oath which you made us swear." Joseph's heavy, ornate Egyptian coffin bobs to the surface of the Nile when Moses calls. The Israelites then bear Joseph out of Egypt—in fact, the midrash relates that Moses himself carries Joseph's bones (Midrash Tanḥuma Be-shallaḥ 2). What the midrash does not go on to say is how Moses gets Joseph's remains from the coffin to the Israelite tribes. It is not easy to carry a lead coffin through a wilderness even if one is a prophet. How did Moses and Serach carry Joseph's bones? I wrote this brief answer to that question during a writing exercise. It is based on the traditionally midrashic principle that what goes around comes around: All things in the Bible are connected.

It is notable that the midrash portrays Serach, a woman, as the source of traditional memory for the Israelites. Like the crone or the sibyl in other cultures, Serach is a source of ancient knowledge for her people. Like the Torah, she lives forever. In the Bible, Serach has only a name, but in midrash, she has a powerful myth attached to her: Serach is the personification of wisdom and the link among generations.

The Least of the Handmaids (p. 117)

Base texts: Genesis 1:1–2:3; Exodus 14:1–15:21

When the Rabbis say that "a maidservant at the Sea of Reeds saw more than Isaiah and Ezekiel ever saw" (*Mekhilta Shirah 1*) they mean to praise the revelatory nature of the Sea of Reeds. How wonderful the miracle must have been, they say, if even a maidservant could see it. But I choose to read their commentary differently. I read it as a reminder of what has come to be called "liberation theology": The recently liberated, whether from the Bible or from our own time, have a special glimpse of God's glory, no matter how bereft and destitute they may be. I read this midrash as a promise that God is revealed in the search for freedom.

Reishit's story came not piecemeal, as some of my stories do, but all at once. I sometimes use meditation as a tool for creating midrash. I do not meditate on a particular text but simply allow my imagination to roam. On one occasion, I went on a long meditative journey in which the first prominent image was of an angel who handed me a book. The book the angel held was blank, but as I paged through it, the two texts of the Creation and the parting of the Sea of Reeds appeared opposite one another, one text on each page. These two texts were headed by a single verse, the first verse of the Torah: *Bereishit bara Elohim* (in the beginning God created). I immediately saw a parallel between the seven days of the Creation story and the stages of the crossing of the Sea of Reeds. I give credit to my subconscious—I don't think my conscious mind would have come up with the parallel.

As I looked at these two paired texts, I saw another image, this time of a girl. This image led to my reinterpretation of the first verse of Genesis, which headed the page. *Reishit* means "beginning"; *bereishit* means "in the beginning." Reishit became the name of a slave escaping from Egypt, a girl slave with no family—the least of the maidservants. It was this freed slave for whom God created the whole world. *Bereishit bara Elohim et hashamayim ve'et haaretz*, "For the sake of Reishit, God created the heavens and the earth." When I ended my meditation, I quickly wrote down the idea, which became this story.

The names of Reishit's companions are mostly well known. Moses, Aaron, and Miriam accompany her. Nachshon ben Amindadav is the famous character, a biblical prince of Judah (Numbers 1:7), who in midrash was the first to step into the sea (BT Sotah 37a). Betzalel is the artist of the Tabernacle, chosen by God for his wisdom (Exodus 31:2–3; 35:30–31). Achat comes from my own imagination. Shua, whom I also invented, bears the name of a woman of the tribe of Asher about whom I can find no legends (1 Chronicles 7:32).

The fantastic nature of the story is not my own invention. The Rabbis also imagine the parting of the sea as a kind of fantasy in which all things become possible. For example, the image of the parted sea as a network of twelve tunnels is located in numerous sources (*Mekhilta* Beshallah 5:31a–b; *Pirkei de-Rabbi Eliezer* 32; BT Sotah 37a). Each tribe is given a tunnel. Fruit trees grow in the tunnels and feed the fleeing slaves (Exodus Rabbah 21:10). The midrash that the Song at the Sea was sung by embryos in the womb (*Mekhilta* Shirah 1:35a; Zohar 2:60a) is a particularly lovely touch of supernatural wonder in a story already filled with miracles. I wanted to capture the magic in the life of a small child, and the Rabbis helped me to do that.

Reishit's journey also has dark notes. There is a well-known legend: When the Egyptians were drowned in the sea, the angels wanted to sing and rejoice because the Israelites had been saved, but God said to them: "The work of my hands is drowning, and you sing praises?" (Midrash Tanhuma Buber 2:60–61). It is this legend that is the basis for the "sixth day" of the story. I have often wondered if the Israelite women on the shore of the sea, led by Miriam (Exodus 15:20), confronted the bodies of dead Egyptians as they danced, and so I imagined Miriam leaning down to touch a dead Egyptian's face.

Throughout the Bible, we are told to care for the stranger because we were strangers in the land of Egypt (Exodus 22:20, 23:9; Leviticus 19:34). This is a cardinal principle of biblical ethics. Perhaps that is the most important message of Reishit's revelation. It is our care for the stranger that puts us closest to God's presence.

Reishit's story is about joy. Susan Windle writes in her poem "The Lost Coin": "Have you ever been lost? / Have you ever been useless? / Have you ever remembered to whom you belong?" That sense of finding one's place, of suddenly being free to become, has been one of the great miracles of my own life. Unlike Reishit, we often forget the wonder of our liberation—but we are capable of remembering.

THE HOUSE OF THE PROPHETS

Miriam under the Mountain (p. 129)

Base text: Exodus 19:17–20
Auxiliary text: Exodus 20:1–2

It is written in the account of the Revelation at Sinai that "the people stood at the foot of the mountain (*betachtit hahar*)" (Exodus 19:17). The word *tachtit* actually means "under." One famous midrash on this verse, cited by Rashi, suggests that the people actually stood *under* the mountain—that God held the mountain above the heads of the Children of Israel and said: "If you will not accept the Torah, here will be your graves." The idea that Israel was coerced into covenant is a disturbing one. However, Rabbi Michael Bernstein once pointed out to me a delicious perspective on this midrash: If God was holding Mount Sinai over the heads of the Israelites, that means the people could see what was *inside* the mountain. They were privy, as it were, to the innermost caves of revelation.

In Merle Feld's poem "We All Stood Together" (Hyman, ed., *Biblical Women in the Midrash: A Sourcebook*, pp. xli–xlii), Miriam receives the Torah just as her brother did, but she is always so busy with her womanly work that she never has a chance to write it down. Moses has a record of what he remembers, but it is all consonants (here Feld picks up on a characteristic of the Hebrew language, which is written in consonants). Miriam remembers the vowels. "If we remembered it together," Feld writes, "we could recreate holy time / sparks flying." Feld uses the opposition of Miriam and Moses to suggest a role for women in defining revelation, although the fixed consonants have already been written down.

It is, perhaps, the combination of these two insights that led to this story. I perceive Miriam not only as a figure of song and dance, freedom and rebellion, but as a figure of revelation, a source of Torah. It is written in the Targum (ancient Aramaic translation) to Micah 6:4 that "Miriam was a teacher of women"; and so she has remained until this day. In rabbinic tradition as in biblical times, water is a symbol for Torah, and Miriam is associated with the miraculous well that was said to accompany the Children of Israel through the desert (BT Bava Metzi'a 17a; BT Shabbat 35a; BT Ta'anit 9a; Song of Songs Rabbah 5:2). It is also written in the Talmud that Miriam was a midwife (BT Sotah 11b); and one who teaches Torah is like a midwife, helping others to birth new interpretations. It is not difficult for me to imagine Miriam sharing Torah with the people as she shared water—freely and with joy. The immense outpouring of modern-day midrash about Miriam indicates the affection of Jewish women for this character and their thirst for the perspective Miriam can bring to the text (see, for example, Schwartz, ed., *And All the Women Followed Her* and Adelman, *Miriam's Well*). Miriam both saves Moses as a child (Exodus 2) and challenges him as a prophet (Numbers 12). In the same way, Jewish women's Torah supports and rivals that of the tradition.

And what would be the nature of Miriam's revelation? Isaac Luria, the great kabbalist, developed the theological principle of *tzimtzum*—that God had to contract in order to make a space for the world to exist (Scholem, *Major Trends in Jewish Mysticism*, pp. 260–65). It was in this way that I imagined the space beneath Sinai, where Miriam must go in order to bring back Torah. There is a traditional midrash noting that nothing moves as the Torah is given—no bird sings, no lamb bleats. All is silent (*Midrash ha-Gadol* 2:215; Ginzberg, *Legends of the Jews*, vol. 3, p. 97). This, too, is a space, the space into which Miriam must step in order to meet God. It is common in the mythologies of many cultures to tell of women who must enter underground caverns—the story of the labors of Psyche, in which Psyche must descend into the netherworld to bring back the beauty of Persephone, is a Greek example, pointed out to me by Wendy Besmann. This journey underground symbolizes the womb, the depths of the female soul, and no doubt many other things. To me, it also symbolizes the woman's ability to invent through midrash the revelation that has been denied her.

I believe that the spaces within the Torah are the places in which God makes room for human creativity and human compassion. It is powerful to me to remember that the Torah has gaps in it as well as words. Those spaces, which are the opportunity for midrash, are also the way in which Torah remains a living text. Torah is lost if it cannot be interpreted, and we are lost if we forget how to interpret faithfully and yet with personal integrity.

It is the place where God's voice falls silent that is most crucial. I believe that silent space, where Torah ceases to speak, is the space in which we are called to meet the Divine. That is also the space in which we must consider what we truly believe to be the will of God. This is the struggle in which twenty-first-century Jews are deeply engaged. I wrote this story to sustain us in our struggle.

The Mirrors (p. 134)

Base text: Exodus 38:8
Auxiliary texts: Exodus 35:25; Genesis 1:27

E xodus 38:8 reads as follows: "[Moses] made the laver of copper and its stand of copper, from the mirrors of the women who performed tasks at the entrance of the Tent of Meeting."

What mirrors? What women? The text of Exodus, which describes the making of the Tabernacle furniture, tells us nothing to explain this obscure reference. Bible scholars have made a number of suggestions. Edward Greenstein, a modern biblical scholar, suggests that perhaps these women are being punished for some sexual sin, since in 1 Samuel 2:22 a pair of corrupt priests are having sex with these women, the *tzovot*, or "serving women." Are the women ritual prostitutes? Or are they simply pious women who want to gather and pray at the Tent of Meeting?

The rabbinic midrash on the subject tells us that these women were pious Israelites who wanted to make a gift to the Tabernacle. Moses wanted to refuse their mirrors because they pandered to "feminine vanity." God, however, told Moses to accept the gifts of the women because they had used the same mirrors to make themselves beautiful in Egypt, to arouse their exhausted and depressed husbands and to cheer them (Midrash Tanḥuma Pekudei 9). The sexuality of these women, the midrash implies, is not to be rejected as unholy. I like the midrash, but it is incomplete for me, since it addresses only one kind of pious woman and one kind of sexuality. I wanted to imagine the mirrors as coming from all sorts of Israelite women.

There is another obscure reference in this section of the Bible: to the women who spun the wool for the hangings of the Tabernacle. They are called "wise-hearted women" (*chachamot lev;* Exodus 35:25), meaning that they are skilled in artistic crafts. I was curious about these women, who had contributed their wise-hearted work to the creation of a dwelling place for God. I wondered if they might not be the same women as the *tzovot*, and I wondered if they were involved in the study of Torah, in addition to the physical labor of building the *Mishkan*, the divine dwelling place. I also wondered if Miriam was among them. "The Mirrors" was an answer to my questions about these mysterious women, in which I imagined their generous gift as being the result of their Torah study.

"The Mirrors" gave me a chance to meditate on one of the central aspects of my theology, which is the idea that everyone is created in the image of God. We are specifically told in Genesis 1:27 that both men and women have this distinction—this is a good proof text for the equality of the sexes and the right of each person to respectful treatment. Both the mirror and the water basin provide an opportunity to see the physical self—in the rabbinic midrash, this is Moses' objection to the women's donation. Yet the physical self, with its needs and desires, is also a reflection of God. Perhaps by making the laver of mirrors, the women were able to remind Moses and the priests of that fact.

The last line of the story refers to a common biblical name for God: *Adonai Tzevaot*, or "God of Hosts." The word "hosts" is spelled in the same way as "hosting women" or *tzovot*. When I hear the name of the Lord of Hosts invoked in synagogue, I remember the women who gave their mirrors to the Tabernacle, and I remember that God is their God, the God of divine images and human bodies.

["This story was first published in an anthology of Miriam stories: Rebecca Schwartz, ed., *And All the Women Followed Her* (Mountain View, CA: Rikudei Miriam Press, 2001).]

The Daughters of Tzelafchad (p. 138)

Base text: Numbers 27:1–11
Auxiliary texts: Numbers 36:1–12; Joshua 17:3–6

The story of the daughters of Tzelafchad (or Zelophehad), which appears among the many "wilderness" stories of the book of Numbers, is perhaps the most directly relevant Bible story to the cause of gender equality. At this point in the biblical narrative the Israelites are preparing to enter the Land, and each family is being assigned a piece of property in Canaan. The daughters, whose father has died, have no brothers, and they have not received an inheritance of land because they are daughters. They present themselves before Moses and ask for justice: They want a piece of land alongside their father's kinsmen. Moses doesn't know how to respond. He goes to inquire of God—the women, in fact, get a divine hearing as a result of their boldness in petitioning Moses. God speaks to Moses and says that "the plea of Tzelafchad's daughters is just" and that they and all other brotherless daughters must receive land alongside their male relatives.

In other words, the daughters win, and their victory becomes part of Israelite case law. Rashi comments that all the daughters are mentioned by name, and in multiple orders: "because they are equally wise." Since many women are not named in the Bible, the list of five names is striking, almost shocking. It implies that there was a tradition concerning these women that couldn't be erased. Rashi praises the piety and loyalty of these women, and considers them a credit to their ancestor Joseph (Rashi on Numbers 27:1).

The story isn't over, however. Later in the Book of Numbers (36:1–12), the men of Tzelafchad's tribe, Menashe, complain that if these women marry outside their tribe, men of other tribes will inherit the tribe of Menashe's land. Moses informs them, "at the Lord's bidding," that their plea is also just, and all daughters who inherit must marry men from their own tribe to preserve their inheritance for their father's clan. We are then told that the daughters all married their first cousins. Clearly, the text seeks to balance the justice of the women's plea with the needs of patriarchal society. Interestingly, in the second passage there is no verbatim communication from God.

And the story *still* isn't over. In Joshua 17:3–6, when the people have entered the Land and have begun to conquer it, the same five women—Machlah, Noa, Choglah, Milcah, and Tirtzah—appear and remind Joshua of Moses' order that they be allowed to inherit. Joshua and the tribe of Menashe comply with the law, and the daughters receive land. This third episode is yet another support for letting daughters inherit, and it makes no mention of the daughters' marriages. That there are three separate stories about the daughters of Tzelafchad suggests that this inheritance issue was a live one for early biblical readers—and the text supports the daughters' inheritance, within limits.

Rashi comments on Numbers 27:3: "If Tzelafchad had had sons, [the daughters] would have said nothing. This shows that they were wise." I regret that Rashi brings this up, but he is probably right. The daughters couldn't have won if they had brothers. This story is not an overthrow of patriarchy, but a modification of it. In fact, it uses the values of patriarchy—the rights of fathers—as a justification for the daughters' claims. Nevertheless, it is clearly a story of profoundly resourceful women who were willing to stand before a prophet, a priest, and an entire nation to get justice for themselves.

My own story about these five women began with my fascination that there were *five* of them: as many as the books of the Torah. In the Bible, only Jethro and the judge Ibzan (Judges 12:9) have more than five daughters. Not only were there five daughters of Tzelafchad, but they all seemed to work together toward a common goal. Yet each must have had a separate identity. I imagined that each woman had a different reason for her plea to Moses. Machlah is mourning her father. Noa, the gambler, is interested in fairness. Choglah has theological reasons for wanting a portion of the Land. Milcah wants to be free. Tirtzah likes women to celebrate together—and she's figured out how to marry whomever she wants, in spite of Moses' decree concerning her future spouse. Imagining each woman separately made me realize how different we all are, even when we work together toward goals we have in common.

Finally, I would like to note that I have split the plea of the daughters into two, one segment uttered by Machlah, and the other by Choglah, although the text only tells us that "they said." I like the idea that more than one daughter had to speak in order to get the job done. I also have imagined that Moses' report of the law to the daughters was private, although the text does not tell us how the daughters learned of Moses' decision.

[This story was read at the Society for the Advancement of Judaism in Manhattan in July 2000. I am grateful to my appreciative audience there. I also would like to thank Arthur Strimling, who provided incisive comments on an earlier draft.]

THE HOUSE OF THE JUDGES

And the Walls Came Tumbling Down (p. 147)

Base texts: Joshua 2:1–24, 6:22–23
Auxiliary text: Exodus 17:8–13

Opposites attract—but it is hard to imagine that they attract enough to bring together a prostitute from Jericho with an Israelite general who has just slaughtered everyone else in her city. Yet that's what the Rabbis imagine about Joshua and Rachav (or Rahab). Rachav, we must recall, saves two Israelite spies from the guards of Jericho, who are pursuing them. She does this on condition that when the Israelites conquer the city and destroy it, they will spare her and her family. Rachav believes that God is on the side of the Israelites, and her belief is rewarded: When the Israelites conquer the city, they bring out Rachav and all the people she has squeezed into her house, and spare them.

Rachav saves her family, but at the expense of her loyalty to her people. As if to point to this tension, the Bible tells us how "Rachav, her mother, father, brothers, everything that belonged to her, and her whole family" leave Jericho as everything around them is being destroyed, and camp "outside the camp of Israel" (Joshua 6:23). They have been saved by the Israelites, but they are not Israelites. Their home has been destroyed. One wonders what their presence must mean to the Israelites who had sacked their city. One also wonders about Rachav's relationship to God. Is she grateful to the God she has chosen over her ancestral traditions or is she angry at the destruction of Jericho?

There was a group of Jews in Jeremiah's time called the Rechabites. The name is spelled differently, but I still wonder whether the descendants of Rachav were set apart even then by the harrowing, Noah-like experience in their past—closed into a single house so that they could be spared while those around them perished.

Rabbinic midrash develops Rachav's character so that she is even more complex than she first appears to be. In midrash, Joshua is one of the spies who comes to Jericho and stays with Rachav the harlot. Apparently, Joshua is very taken with this harlot, because the Talmud teaches that "Rachav the prostitute converted and married Joshua" (BT Megillah 14b). That the Rabbis would marry Joshua to a former prostitute, a woman whose city Joshua destroyed, is extraordinary. It is equally extraordinary that she would consent to marry him. How could Rachav have married Joshua, the enemy of Jericho? What did they have to talk about? And there is a further surprise. The Rabbis assert, since we never hear of any male ancestors of Joshua, that Joshua and Rachav had only daughters (BT Megillah 14b). But these daughters have a lineage. Their descendants include, among many other worthies, Jeremiah and the prophetess Huldah (BT Megillah 14b). The Rabbis convert a harlot into the matriarch of a priestly and prophetic clan. Why did the Sages tell such stories about Rachav? Perhaps because of her faith in God's power. Or perhaps it is because Rachav keeps Israel honest, as she keeps Joshua honest. She forces us to remember the people who we have pushed aside to become what we are.

This story is a birth story because of the legend of Rachav's daughters but also because the time of entering Canaan was a kind of birth for Israel. Like all births, it entailed struggle and hardship. The Israelites did not enter an empty land—there were people in it, and the relationships between Israelites and other peoples were often hostile. Joshua destroyed Jericho and killed the people in it—and the Rabbis tell us he woke up every morning beside the one woman who could intimately remind him of that act. Alicia Ostriker writes in her poem "The Story of Joshua": "I give you the secret knowledge that you are doing wrong" (Curzon, ed., *Modern Poems on the Bible*, pp. 180–81). Perhaps one way Joshua might have received that knowledge was through Rachav. The Talmud does not give Joshua's daughters names, but I have called the youngest Yareach, after Jericho itself. What better way to remind him of the reality of war—and of the necessity of peace?

Miriam's Heir (p. 154)

Base texts: Judges 1:10–15, 3:8–11; Joshua 15:13–19
Auxiliary texts: 1 Chronicles 2:18–20,42–50, 4:13–14; Joshua 14:6–15

Rabbinic midrashim ascribe son after son to the prophetess Miriam, but not a single daughter. Yet their own legends about Miriam suggest that she did have a daughter. In a popular midrash, Miriam is married to Caleb, one of the two men righteous enough to live through the wanderings in the desert and enter the Promised Land (cf. BT Sotah 12a). In 1 Chronicles 2:18–20, Caleb seems to have many wives. The rabbinic reading (Exodus Rabbah 1:17) is that all of these women are Miriam, except for the two women listed as concubines, Eifah and Maacah, who appear in this story. Achsah is Caleb's daughter in the biblical text, yet no rabbinic midrash links her to Miriam. Perhaps this is because the idea of a daughter who inherits Miriam's prophetic legacy is far too threatening to a patriarchal tradition.

The link is easy to make, however, almost eerily so. In Judges 1, Achsah marries after a fairy-tale-like episode in which her father promises her to the man who conquers the city of Kiriat-Sefer (City of the Book!). Achsah demands as her dowry a land with "springs of water." The legend of the well of water, associated with Miriam, that followed the Israelites through their forty years of wandering in the desert (BT Ta'anit 9a; BT Bava Metzi'a 17a; BT Shabbat 35a; Song of Songs Rabbah 5:2) immediately comes to mind. The demand for wells of water indeed sounds like the request of Miriam's daughter.

If this were not proof enough, 1 Chronicles 4 lists the children of Achsah's husband, Otniel, as Hatat and Meyonotai. Meyonotai can mean "my dwellings" but, with a very slight twist, it can mean "my wells." The name Meyonotai is so reminiscent of Miriam that, of midrashic necessity, the child must be a daughter of Miriam's line.

According to midrash, David was descended from Miriam (*Sifrei Numbers* 78). In the Bible, however, David's father's line is traced to Judah, not Miriam. Perhaps David descended from Miriam through his mother, who in the Talmud is named Natzvat bat Adael (BT Bava Batra 91a). Natzvat means "to stand," just as Miriam stood—*nitzvah*—by the Nile to see what would become of her brother. In this midrashic chain, Miriam is the ancestor not only of Achsah and Meyonotai but also of the prophesied Davidic messiah. Dr. Marc Bregman of Hebrew Union College in Jerusalem pointed out to me that Achsah's name means "anklet" and may come from the root "to be sinuous" or "to connect." For me, Achsah became the connecting link in a chain of powerful women.

The story of Achsah and Otniel, which is told very briefly in Joshua and Judges, is clearly of the genre of fairy tale. The father promises his daughter to the man who conquers a certain city, just as legendary kings promise their daughters to the slayers of dragons, healers of diseases, solvers of riddles. Yet after the young hero receives his bride, she herself demands a gift of her father. The object of the story, the passive "princess," turns out to be an active player after all. The gift she asks for is water: the most obvious symbol of life in a desert environment. Where her father has concerned himself with war, Achsah concerns herself with the continuation of life and civilization.

The Rabbis felt the mythic undertones of this passage. The Talmud claims that Caleb's gift of "upper" and "lower" springs is a metaphor. It means that Caleb gave Achsah Torah learning as well as physical sustenance. The Talmud also ascribes spiritual gifts to Otniel: Otniel restores many of the teachings of Moses that the Israelites have forgotten (BT Terumah 16a). Otniel and Achsah are true conquerors of the City of the Book.

The Song of Devorah and Yael (p. 167)

Base text: Judges 4–5
Auxiliary texts: Judges 3:31; 1 Chronicles 12:33

A literature professor of mine once said this of Yael's murder of Sisera: "Why she did it is a mystery." Commentators have been asking for centuries about the motivation of Yael, wife of Hever the Kenite. Yael kills her husband's ally, a Canaanite general fleeing from Israelite troops, without stating any reason whatsoever. Is she simply an instrument of the Israelite God? Is she an Israelite? Is she a convert, as the Rabbis suggest? Is she a rape victim? Is she a woman who has illicit sex with Sisera and then destroys the evidence? Is she bloodthirsty or desperate? Is her action part of a longer story? My answer to these questions—that Yael killed Sisera out of love for Devorah—is only one in a long chain of musings about the mystery of Yael.

"The Song of Devorah and Yael" is a tale of four women. Devorah is the prophet, the judge of Israel, and the military strategist for Barak, general of the Israelite tribes. Yael is the unexpected heroine, the killer of the enemy general, Sisera. Both of them are unusually strong and warlike female characters and have captured the imagination of poets and painters for centuries. Although no one else, to my knowledge, has portrayed them as lovers, they are linked both by biblical narrative and by midrashic imagination. The leap from comrades to lovers was not difficult for me to make.

I also took the opportunity to explain what happens to Yael after the battle. Yael's violation of her husband's treaty probably makes her persona non grata at her husband's home, but we do not hear of her fate. Nor do we hear of how the Israelite army dealt with Yael's husband, Hever, once he discovered what his wife had done. I like the idea that Yael decided to share Devorah's life. Perhaps she also shared Devorah's judgeship: There is, in fact, a traditional midrash that Yael became a judge of the Israelites. If Devorah was to separate Yael from her husband, she would have to give him some reason: Therefore, I invented the idea that Devorah dedicated Yael to God's service.

The other two women in the story, Anat and Sarai, require some further introduction. In the biblical text, the judge before Devorah is called Shamgar ben Anat; he is famous for having killed six hundred of his enemies with an oxgoad (Judges 3:31). Normally, an Israelite man is referred to by his father's name, but Anat is clearly the name of the Canaanite goddess of love and war. This is an irony, since, at least biblically, the Canaanites and the Israelites were enemies, and the irony continues to this day: Anat is a popular name for girls in modern Israel.

I was interested by a theory of Dr. Diane Sharon, a Bible professor at the Jewish Theological Seminary. Sharon suggests that Shamgar may be a legendary figure who is somehow associated with the goddess Anat. This convinced me to think of Shamgar's mother as a bridge figure between Canaanite and Israelite culture. My other root for the character of Anat was a story I wrote for Rabbi Anat Moskowitz, who used to bemoan the pagan origins of her name. That story was based on one of Devorah's verses of song—"In the days of Shamgar ben Anat, in the days of Yael, caravans ceased, and travelers went by roundabout paths" (Judges 5:6). This implied to me that Yael and Anat met while traveling on a roundabout path. In this new story, their encounter continues on the battlefield.

Sarai, the female chieftain of Issachar, is a midrashic invention. She comes from an "aha!" moment I experienced while reading Judges 5. During her song, Devorah praises the soldiers of many tribes who come to join her and Barak. One group Devorah praises is the tribe of Issachar: "The princes of Issachar were with Devorah, and Issachar was like Barak." This appeared, on my first reading, to mean that Issachar followed Devorah bravely just as Barak did. However, I began to reread the verse with great excitement, for I had realized that the word for "the princes in Issachar" reads in the Hebrew *"sarai beyissachar."* One would expect *"sarim,"* the plural of *"sar"* (prince), but even if the word is an archaic and correct form of "princes," it is also identical to Sarai, the name of the first matriarch before her name was changed to Sarah. Sarai, like Anat, is clearly a woman's name. The verse can be read: "Sarai in Issachar was with Devorah, and Issachar was like Barak." How was Issachar like Barak? They too followed a woman leader, and her name was Sarai. I imagine that Sarai was, like the rest of the tribe of Issachar, a "knower of the wisdom of times" (1 Chronicles 12:33). Issachar, in rabbinic midrash, is the tribe most fully engaged in Torah study (cf. Genesis Rabbah 72:5). I like to think of such a tribe having woman as its *sara*, its princess.

The love poetry that appears at the beginning and end of the story was, in fact, the genesis of the story itself. As I began to imagine Devorah's loneliness as a woman in a man's profession and Yael's choice to end her old life forever by killing Devorah's enemy, I saw how Devorah and Yael belonged together. And I began to write the words they might say to each other. My feelings about them are forever changed. I cannot think of one of them now without thinking of the other.

[This story was first published in *The Jewish Women's Literary Annual*, vol. 4 (2001).]

THE HOUSE OF THE QUEENS

The King's Harp (p. 181)

Base text: 1 Kings 1:1–4
Auxiliary texts: 1 Kings 2:1–12; Genesis 46:17

A midrash tells us that David knows he will die on a Sabbath. He seeks to avoid his death by studying Torah all *Shabbat* long (BT Shabbat 30a–b; Ruth Rabbah 1:17). The Angel of Death is reduced to throwing pebbles at the window to distract the king.

In Jewish songs we say: King David lives forever. There is something about his story that is eternal. In folklore, his life is full of magic. His harp plays by itself when stroked by the wind at midnight, calling him to psalm and study (BT Berachot 3b; Numbers Rabbah 15:16). David's harp haunts me. Does it, too, live forever? What happened to it when David died?

My answer comes from my awareness that there is another great harpist in Jewish legend. We have met her earlier in this book. Her name is Serach, daughter of Asher. She was a great harpist, and through her music she earned eternal life. When Joseph's brothers returned home from Egypt knowing he was alive, they were afraid that the joyful and unbelievable news would stop Jacob's heart. They asked Serach, Asher's daughter, to sing the news to Jacob while playing on the harp. Through song, Serach was able to share the news without killing Jacob. Jacob then blessed her with eternal life, saying: "The mouth that conveyed such good tidings shall not taste death" (Genesis Rabbah 94:15). The words of that song appear in folklore.

Serach lived through slavery and on the night of the Exodus showed Moses where Joseph's bones were buried, so that they could be carried up out of Egypt (Sotah 13a; Midrash Tanḥuma Be-shallaḥ 9). She lived to enter the Land of Israel and generations later gave David's general Yoav some good advice under the guise of the "wise woman of Avel" (2 Samuel 20:15–22, as interpreted by Genesis Rabbah 94:15). In fact, she lived into the rabbinic period and told the Sages how the parting of the Sea of Reeds looked (*Pesikta de-Rav Kahana* 10:117). Some say she died in a fire in Persia, but some, like writer and folklorist Howard Schwartz, claim to have met her even in modern times. Serach, like David, lives forever. It seemed clear to me that David's harp is Serach's harp. Serach must have given it to him when he was a young shepherd. As David lies dying, Serach must surely come to take it back.

To whom could Serach give the harp? Who was as worthy as David? The obvious choice, for me, was Avishag, the woman who attended David in his illness (1 Kings 1:1–4). Avishag was never David's lover, but perhaps she did love him. There is a midrash that the Song of Songs was written by Solomon for Avishag. My midrash says that she wrote it herself, in memory of the king.

The words of Serach's songs are partly from midrashic folklore. Avishag's first song in this story comes from the prophecy of Balaam (Numbers 24:17). It is generally considered to be a messianic prophecy, but I have read it as a farewell to David. The second one is composed of verses from the Song of Songs itself. The idea that prayers rise to heaven and form a crown for God is an ancient one found in the Talmud and in Jewish folklore of all ages.

Who has the harp now? It could be anyone. I very much doubt that Serach would let it depart from human hands, now that she has seen what it can do.

Solomon's Box (p. 190)

Base text: 1 Kings 4:11,14–15
Auxiliary texts: 1 Kings 11:1, 14:21

King Solomon is well known both for his many wives (1 Kings 11:3; BT Bava Metzi'a 86b) and for his connections with demons (cf. BT Gittin 68a–b; Zohar 3:233a–b). One wonders whether the women of his household were meeting with demons as well. His wife Naamah shares the name of a well-known female demon. While bathing at the springs of Tiberias, I remembered with pleasure the legend in which Solomon commands demons to heat up the waters for the health of his people (Song of Songs Rabbah 3:8). Sometimes demons do good in the world. In fact, Louis Ginzberg informs us that some demons are Jewish and obey the Torah (*Legends of the Jews*, vol. 6, p. 86). Sometimes the work demons do is a double-edged sword.

There are several legends about Solomon's encounters with his daughters, mostly involving their marriages, and two of his daughters, Tafat and Bosmat, are named in the biblical text (1 Kings 4:11,14–15) as wives of Solomon's chief officials. Their mothers are not listed, but perhaps Tafat is the daughter of Solomon's chief consort Naamah (1 Kings 14:21), who appears elsewhere in this book. Perhaps Bosmat, who bears the same name as Esau's wife, is the daughter of one of Solomon's Edomite wives (1 Kings 11:1). I wanted to write about these women, and this story is the result.

My questions about these two daughters began with the verse

describing Bosmat's marriage: "Achinadav ben Iddo was governor over Mahanaim. Achimaaz was governor over Naftali; he also took Bosmat daughter of Solomon to wife" (1 Kings 4:14–15). Why does the text say "also" Achimaaz? Did someone else take Bosmat to wife before Achimaaz? I used the rabbinic principle of *smichut parshiyyot* (juxtaposition of texts), and concluded that the man listed just before Achimaaz also took Bosmat to wife. His name is Achinadav ben Iddo, governor of Mahanaim. My own interpretation is that Bosmat marries both of them, one after the other. Tafat, apparently, only marries once. The demons of Bosmat and Tafat are entirely my invention.

The notion of a box that one must not open is, of course, not my own: Pandora's box is the archetypal tale of this type. Yet, as we all know, some boxes are impossible to leave alone. This story is my meditation on the advantages and disadvantages of releasing demons. We keep our demons hidden so our lives may remain neat and orderly, but hiding our demons also means we must hide ourselves. Women have often struggled to keep their deep feelings and intuitions "inside the box" rather than let those unruly emotions change their lives. Sometimes, our demons grow so powerful that we cannot ignore them any longer. Then we must decide how and when to release them—and who we will trust as we explore the demons' impact on our lives.

The Scribe (p. 203)

Base texts: Ezra 2:55; Book of Ecclesiastes
Auxiliary texts: 2 Samuel 15:16, 20:3

I was reading a rather uneventful genealogical text in the Book of Ezra for a class on ancient Jewish history, when I suddenly stared intently at my Bible, let out a shriek, and ran to the computer. In those genealogical lists, which describe families who return from Babylonian exile, I had discovered a "servant of Solomon" called "Hasoferet." Hasoferet means "the scribe." The noun/name is very clearly feminine. Solomon had a scribe who was a woman? According to legend, Solomon is the author of the Song of Songs, Proverbs, and Ecclesiastes (*Aggadat Shir* 1.6; Ginzberg, *Legends of the Jews*, vol. 6, p. 301). Then this scribe might have written down whole books of the Bible! I was riveted by the idea. My ancient history homework did not get done. Instead, I wrote this midrash.

The name Soferet, scribe, for me echoed the eponymous author of the book of Ecclesiastes, who is called Kohelet, or preacher. That name too is feminine, interestingly enough. To me, this hinted that Kohelet was somehow associated with the feminine. I wrote sections of my invented Book of Soferet, parallel to those of Kohelet, that might reveal the experience of a woman who was as cynical as the man who wrote Kohelet. Rather than use the recurring theme of "vanity" as Kohelet does, I chose as Soferet's lament the theme of silence, a silence that women live throughout the Bible. The wordlessness of many biblical women oppresses me as much as the apparent pointlessness of life oppressed Kohelet, and I found that Kohelet's words were easily molded into a lament about a silence that cannot be broken because no one is listening. The forced silencing of women has ill effects and is ultimately unjust. Soferet dwells in a silence within a silence: She is silent because she knows that the women around her must be silent—but when she writes, she imagines what it might be like to break that silence.

Who was Soferet? My idea was that she was a daughter of David by one of his concubines. Not any concubine, of course, but one of the ten David had placed in living widowhood. I had long wanted to write a story about David's ten concubines, who he abandons in Jerusalem "to mind the house" when he flees from his rebellious son Avshalom (2 Samuel 15:16). Avshalom takes over the palace and proceeds to have sex with these women as an usurpation of his father's authority. Sex with the leader's women is symbolic seizure of their leadership. (Another example of this can be found in Genesis 35:22, when Reuven lies with his father's concubine.) Avshalom is later killed. When David returns, he places his concubines in a "guarded place; he provided for them, but he did not cohabit with them" (2 Samuel 20:3). To be virtually abandoned, but not given their freedom, is a cruel fate for ten women who have done no wrong.

Why does David force these women into such a situation? Surely he didn't really need ten of his women to "mind the house!" To understand this, one must remember that God has cursed David, saying that other men will take his women before his very eyes (2 Samuel 12:11). David is trying to divert this curse from his wives, Batsheva and Avigayil, to these ten insignificant concubines. He puts these women, for whom he cares little, aside. God in fact seems to go along with this charade, because David's wives and concubines are not taken by others in any other incident.

In putting this clever plan into action, David creates the first *agunot*, the first chained women, who have no real married life yet cannot be free of their husbands. My heart went out to these women in their secluded house. I wanted to give them an illustrious daughter, someone who would tell their story, someone who would expose the abuses of David and Solomon.

Soferet is witness not only to Solomon's glory but also to his forced labor decrees, which are documented in the Bible (1 Kings 5:27). She is also witness to the decree that a king's widow may not marry—which, in actuality, is talmudic in origin. (Maimonides, centuries later, says no one may marry the widow or divorcée of a king [*Mishneh Torah*, Laws of Kings and War 2:2].) Just as Kohelet is unable to find anything new under the sun, so Soferet is unable to change what she sees in the world. Yet she serves as a witness. Others may try to forget her words, but they will not succeed.

Vashti and the Angel Gabriel (p. 213)

Base text: Esther 1
Auxiliary texts: Genesis 5:23–24, 6:1–4, 19:1–38

While Vashti is not of the era of David or Solomon, I chose to include her, and by extension the story of Esther, in this section. The story properly belongs much later in time, after the fall of the Davidic monarchy and the First Exile to Babylonia and Persia.

This story was written in response to my delighted discovery of a classical midrash. In that legend, it was the angel Gabriel who convinced the queen Vashti to rebel against her husband Ahasuerus. The talmudic version of this legend (BT Megillah 12b) claims he convinced her by giving her boils, but I chose to ignore that part. The idea that an angel incites the queen to reject the king's misused authority is a work of rabbinic genius, even if the Rabbis only meant it to discredit the idea that Vashti might have acted on her own. I have built, gratefully and perhaps ironically, on their foundation. In the biblical text, the king's request is simply to appear before the king and his guests in her crown, but in rabbinic midrash the request is to appear before the king and his guests wearing *only* her crown, a very different matter, and worthy of an angel's attention.

It has long irritated me that Vashti is treated badly by rabbinic sources (cf. BT Megillah 12b; Esther Rabbah 3:2,9). Apparently the Rabbis are as uncomfortable with her disobedience as is the drunken king. They also, most probably, do not want Esther to have any rivals for the role of heroine. This is a complete misunderstanding of the story, as Esther's actions are a continuation of Vashti's story, not a break with it. Ahasuerus, who refuses to listen to his wife and expels her for disobeying, spends the rest of the Book of Esther taking orders from his new wife. A clearer example of poetic justice could not be had. Furthermore, Vashti prefigures Mordechai as a character who will not bow down. Her unspecified but worrisome fate is a reminder of what might have happened to the Jews had all not gone well in the plot against Haman. Not only is Vashti a good role model for feminists in her refusal to be ordered about but she is also a positive character according to the drama of the Book of Esther itself. Many rabbinic legends turn her into an oppressor of Jewish women, a monster who is afraid to appear in public because she does not want anyone to see her tail. My midrash was written as a countertext.

As for the angels, the name Ofanniel, angel of the moon, is taken from the Third Book of Enoch. Enoch—an obscure biblical character whom God "takes" in some mysterious way—becomes in apocryphal and rabbinic legend a man who rises to heaven without dying and becomes a scribe for God. This story also takes advantage of many rabbinic midrashim in which Gabriel plays a part, including the destruction of Sodom (Genesis Rabbah 50:2) and the annihilation of Sennacherib, an enemy general who attempted to invade Jerusalem. Gabriel is often presented as an angel of courage and strength, a warrior for God, and a supporter of justice on earth. The legend of Istehar the virgin, who convinces her angelic seducer to teach her the name of God and then uses it to fly away from him toward the stars, is from rabbinic midrash (*Aggadat Bereishit* 38), as is the legend of Lot's daughter Paltit, who dies for the crime of feeding a beggar (*Pirkei de-Rabbi Eliezer* 25). Idit is a rabbinic name for Lot's wife (*Pirkei de-Rabbi Eliezer* 25), but the commentary on Lot's wife's turning is my own. For me, Paltit and Istehar, Gabriel and Vashti have come to symbolize courage. They are mythic reminders of what ordinary people can accomplish when they find themselves in extraordinary circumstances.

["Vashti and the Angel Gabriel" was first published in Naomi Hyman, ed., *Biblical Women in the Midrash: A Sourcebook* (Northvale, NJ: Jason Aronson, 1997). It is reprinted here in an edited version with Naomi's kind encouragement.]

EPILOGUE

The Words in the Scroll (p. 231)

Base texts: 2 Kings 22:1–20; 2 Chronicles 34:1–33
Auxiliary texts: Deuteronomy 6:4, 21:11, 22:6–7, 27:24; 2 Kings 24:8, 12,15

The first version of this story was written for a bibliodrama class taught by Peter Pitzele, but the idea for the story came from a good laugh I had while studying the story of the prophetess Huldah. Huldah is an extraordinary woman. She is the only person in the

Bible who is asked to canonize a book—and the only person entrusted with the authority of determining the authenticity of part of the Torah. Scholars believe, based on the reforms that Josiah enacts, that the work Huldah judges is the Book of Deuteronomy.

The Rabbis are somewhat uncomfortable with the honor that Josiah's court shows to Huldah as a mediator of God's word. They want to know why Huldah's male contemporary, Jeremiah, is not raised above her. They claim Josiah picks Huldah as judge, although Jeremiah is more important, because she is Jeremiah's cousin and he will not be shamed if she is asked. They also say that she is chosen because women are compassionate and Huldah is, therefore, likely to mitigate the curses found in the book (BT Megillah 14b). Huldah's role is limited in the rabbinic conception, probably because she is female. The Rabbis claim for Huldah an ambiguous ancestry—Joshua, the triumphant general, and Rachav, the triumphant general and the resourceful harlot—and say that Huldah's husband's name, Shallum ben Tikvah, is a reference to the knot *(tikvah)* of scarlet thread Rachav hung in her window (BT Megillah 14b). Finally, as if to demean Huldah's considerable prophetic authority, the Rabbis make fun of her name: "There were two uppity women who had unpleasant names, one was named Devorah (bee) and the other Huldah (weasel)" (BT Megillah 14b). In fact, there is even one midrash that says that Huldah was given the gift of prophecy because her *husband* was righteous (*Pirkei de-Rabbi Eliezer* 33).

The Rabbis may be uncomfortable with uppity women, but I am not. As I read the story, I concentrated on its names. Every name of the five-man delegation sent to Huldah is mentioned. One minister is named Achbor, which means "mouse." Another is named Shaphan, which means "rabbit." The mouse and the rabbit going to visit the weasel! It is almost like the characters in one of Aesop's fables. One has to suspect that Huldah may eat these mild-mannered courtiers if nothing better presents itself. Her words are in fact rather sharp. I found in the text the uppity Huldah of the Rabbis, a Huldah with a weasel's quick bite. I liked her. I wondered how she would have made her momentous decision about the scroll. This story is one possible answer, and it also explains why the last letters of the first and last words of the verse known as the *Shema* (Deuteronomy 6:4) are written in the Torah scroll in an enlarged form.

"The Words in the Scroll," is, of course, a meditation on midrash and its place in revelation. If, as the Sages say, all of us were at Sinai, and all of us heard something different, then revelation is indeed composed of multiple voices. In fact, we cannot learn Torah without listening to each other. But it is only the prophet who can sort through those voices and come up with a coherent whole. For the rest of us, the study of Torah is mysterious, conflicted, confusing—and endlessly engaging.

Finally, let me note that Huldah is not the only prominent woman in this story. Among the verses of Deuteronomy that appear throughout the narrative, I have put the verse that speaks of the mother bird and her eggs in the mouth of Nechushta, daughter of Elnatan of Jerusalem. Nechushta married Josiah's son and became the last queen mother of Judea. She went into exile with her son Jehoiachin, grandson of Josiah (2 Kings 24:8,12,15). Nechushta, whose name means "brass" or "snake" or "guesswork," was the most prominent woman in Judea to see the exile. I like to think that Huldah and Nechushta had the necessary wisdom to guide them through the First Exile, which was ultimately one of the most formative epochs in Jewish history. It was exile, after all, that produced midrash.

✑ Bibliography

Adelman, Penina. *Miriam's Well: Rituals for Jewish Women Around the Year*. Fresh Meadows, NY: Biblio Press, 1986.

Adler, Rachel. *Engendering Judaism*. Philadelphia: Jewish Publication Society, 1998.

Agnon, S. Y. *Present at Sinai*. Trans. Michael Swirsky. Philadelphia: Jewish Publication Society, 1994.

Amichai, Yehuda. *Open Closed Open*. Trans. Chana Bloch and Chana Kronfeld. New York: Harcourt, Inc., 2000.

Bialik, Hayim Nachman and Yehoshua Hana, Ravnitzky. *The Book of Legends*. Trans. William G. Braude. New York: Schocken Books, 1992.

Broner, E. M. *Her Mothers*. Bloomington: Indiana University Press, 1975.

Christ, Carol P. and Judith Plaskow, eds. *Womanspirit Rising: A Feminist Reader in Religion*. San Francisco: Harper & Row, 1979.

Curzon, David, ed. *Modern Poems on the Bible: An Anthology*. Philadelphia: Jewish Publication Society, 1994.

Dame, Enid, Lilly Rivlin, and Henny Wenkart, eds. *Which Lilith?* Northvale, NJ: Jason Aronson, 1998.

Encyclopaedia Judaica. Jerusalem: Keter Publishing House, 1972.

Epstein, I., ed. *The Hebrew Edition of the Babylonian Talmud*. Trans. Maurice Simon. London: Soncino Press, 1990.

Frankel, Ellen. *The Five Books of Miriam: A Women's Commentary on the Torah*. New York: J. P. Putnam, 1996.

Friedlander, Gerald, ed. *Pirkei de-Rabbi Eliezer*. New York: Hermon Press, 1965.

Ginzberg, Louis. *Legends of the Jews*. Philadelphia: Jewish Publication Society, 1938.

Gottlieb, Lynn. *She Who Dwells Within*. San Francisco: Harper San Francisco, 1995.

Hammer, Jill. "Eve and Lilith," in *Response*, spring/summer 1995, p. 49.

Hyman, Naomi, ed. *Biblical Women in the Midrash: A Sourcebook*. Northvale, NJ: Jason Aronson, 1997.

Mandelbaum, Allen. *Chelmaxioms*. Boston: David R. Godine, 1977.

Ostriker, Alicia. *The Nakedness of the Fathers: Biblical Visions and Revisions*. New Brunswick, NJ: Rutgers University Press, 1994.

———. *The Crack in Everything*. Pittsburgh, PA: University of Pittsburgh Press, 1996.

Pirke Avot. In *Siddur Sim Shalom*. New York: The Rabbinical Assembly and the United Synagogue of Conservative Judaism, 1997, p. 257–80.

Pitzele, Peter. *Our Fathers' Wells: A Personal Encounter with the Myths of Genesis*. San Francisco: Harper San Francisco, 1995.

Plaskow, Judith. *Standing Again at Sinai*. San Francisco: Harper San Francisco, 1990.

Rosen, Norma. *Biblical Women Unbound*. Philadelphia: Jewish Publication Society, 1996.

Rukeyser, Muriel. *The Speed of Darkness*. New York: Random House, 1968.

Sasson, Solomon. *Moshav Zekenim*. London: Letchworth, 1959.

Scholem, Gershom. *Major Trends in Jewish Mysticism*. New York: Schocken Books, 1941.

Schwartz, Howard, ed. *Gates to the New City: A Treasury of Modern Jewish Tales*. New York: Avon, 1983.

Schwartz, Howard. *Gabriel's Palace: Jewish Mystical Tales*. New York: Oxford University Press, 1993.

Schwartz, Rebecca, ed. *All the Women Followed Her*. Mountain View, CA: Rikudei Miriam Press, 2001.

Simon, M. and H. Freedman, eds. *Midrash Rabbah*. London: Soncino Press, 1939.

Sparks, H. F. D., ed. *The Apocryphal Old Testament*. Trans. R. H. Charles, rev. C. Rabin. Oxford, UK: Clarendon Press, 1984.

Tanakh: The Holy Scriptures. Philadelphia: Jewish Publication Society, 1985.

Teubal, Savina. *Sarah the Priestess: The First Matriarch of Genesis*. Athens, OH: Swallow Press, 1984.

Townsend, J. T., ed. *Midrash Tanhuma*. Hoboken, NJ: Ktav Publishing House, 1989.

Umansky, Ellen M. and Dianne Ashton, eds. *Four Centuries of Jewish Women's Spirituality: A Sourcebook*. Boston: Beacon Press, 1992.

Windle, Susan. "The Lost Coin," in *Living Text*, 5, 1999, p. 21.

Zisquit, Linda. *Ritual Bath*. Seattle: Broken Moon Press, 1993.

The Zohar. Trans. Harry S. M. Simon. New York: Soncino Press, 1984.

Zornberg, Avivah. *Genesis: The Beginning of Desire*. Philadelphia: Jewish Publication Society, 1995.

Index of People and Places